François Mitterrand

A study in political leadership

Second edition

Alistair Cole

London and New York

First published 1994
by Routledge
11 New Fetter Lane, London EC4P 4EE

Simultaneously published in the USA and Canada
by Routledge
29 West 35th Street, New York, NY 10001

Second edition 1997

© 1994, 1997 Alistair Cole

Typeset in Garamond by
Ponting–Green Publishing Services, Chesham, Bucks
Printed and bound in Great Britain by
Biddles Ltd, Guildford and King's Lynn

British Library Cataloguing in Publication Data
A catalogue record for this book is available from the British
Library

Library of Congress Cataloguing in Publication Data
Cole, Alistair, 1959–
    François Mitterrand : a study in political leadership / Alistair
Cole.
    p.   cm.
    Includes bibliographical references and index.
    1. Mitterrand, François, 1916–96–Political and social views.
2. France – Politics and government – 1981–   3. Presidents–
France–Biography.   4. Socialism–France–History–20th
century.   5. Political leadership–France–History–20th
century.   I.Title.
DC423.C63 1994
944.083'8'092–dc20
[B]   93–28183

ISBN 0–415–16336–6

Contents

Tables

Abbreviations

CDS	Centre des démocrates Sociaux
CDU	German Christian Democratic Union
CERES	Centre d'Etudes et de recherches socialistes
CFDT	Confédération française démocratique du travail
CGT	Confédération générale du travail
CIR	Convention des institutions républicaines
CSCE	Conference on Security and Cooperation in Europe
DOM-TOM	Départements d'outre-mer/ Territoires d'outre mer (Overseas departments and territories).
EC	European Community
EFTA	European Free Trade Association
EMS	European Monetary System
ENA	Ecole National d'Administration
EPU	European Political Union
ERM	Exchange Rate Mechanism
ESPRIT	European Strategic Programme for Research and Development in Information Technology
EUREKA	European Programme for High Technology Research and Development
EUT	European Union Treaty
FGDS	Fédération de la Gauche démocratique et socialiste
FN	Front national
FRG	Federal Republic of Germany
GATT	General Agreement on Trades and Tariffs
GNP	Gross National Product
IGC	Intergovernmental Conference
LCR	Ligue pour le combat républicain
MRP	Mouvement républicain populaire
NATO	North Atlantic Treaty Organisation
PSA	Parti socialiste autonome
PSU	Parti socialiste unifié
PCF	Parti communiste français

PS	Parti socialiste
RDA	Rassemblement démocratique africain
RPF	Rassemblement du peuple français
RPR	Rassemblement pour la République
SFIO	Section française de l'internationale ouvrière
SGE	Secrétariat générale de l'Elysée
SGDN	Secrétariat générale de la défense nationale
SGCI	Secrétariat générale du Comité interministérielle
SPD	German Social-democratic Party
UCRG	Union des clubs pour le renouveau de la gauche
UDC	Union du centre
UDF	Union pour la démocratie française
UDSR	Union démocratique et socialiste de la résistance
UGCS	Union de la Gauche des clubs socialistes
UN	United Nations
UNR	Union pour la nouvelle République
WEU	West European Union

Preface to the second edition

The first edition of *François Mitterrand: a Study in Political Leadership* was published in March 1994. There is little in the first edition that I feel compelled to change here. Although the experience of Mitterrand's final years and the publication of numerous new works lead me to adopt a rather more nuanced view of Mitterrand in certain respects, this new edition contains only minor alterations to the initial ten chapters. I have revised Chapter 11 and written a new Chapter 12.

The benefit of hindsight has been eschewed for maintaining the coherence of the original work. I should like to thank the numerous people who have encouraged me to publish a slightly revised edition of the book in paperback. They know who they are! I should also like to thank past and present staff at Routledge for the excellent job they have done in producing this book.

PREFACE TO THE FIRST EDITION

As the order in the title suggests, this book is intended first and foremost as a study of François Mitterrand, with special (but not exclusive) reference to the Mitterrand presidency. It is also aimed to contribute towards the study of political leadership. Through evaluating Mitterrand's political persona, and his activities as a politician spanning the entire postwar period, I hope to be able to draw wider conclusions pertaining to the French polity. Quite apart from being an object of individual fascination, Mitterrand is treated as a vehicle for examining various aspects of the French political system. These include: types and styles of political leadership, the party system, the organisation of the French executive, byzantine governing methods, the role of networks and patronage, continuity and change in French foreign and European policy, etc.

This portrayal of Mitterrand attempts to combine a chronological outline with extensive thematic analysis. Various objections can be levelled against adopting primarily a chronological approach. We run the risk of presenting the subject's career as a neat, uninterrupted progression of interlocking episodes, following logically one from another. This idea of linear progression underpins most biographical life-stories. The key danger here is that of retrospection: through dividing the subject's life into a series of compact episodes, the author invariably places too great a cohesion upon his or her activity. It is far from certain that the subject actually lived those episodes with the cohesion usually accredited to him or her by the author.

An obvious alternative to the episode-based study is one which concentrates upon the varying roles performed by an individual within the political system: the party leader, the head of government, the European statesman and so on. This approach has the advantage of portraying political activity as multifaceted, but itself suffers from several disadvantages, especially if it implies too strict a demarcation between the various roles performed by a political leader. Indeed, the methodological objections to a chronological treatment are less pervasive, but not absent from a more thematic-based approach: the writer continues to exercise his own judgement in deciding which themes are primordial, and in attributing an element of cohesion where none may originally have existed.

The selection of events themselves is to some extent a subjective exercise; why is one event, theme or policy brought to the attention of the reader, and not another? It is probably inevitable that, for certain readers, insufficient attention will have been paid to important events and themes which figure prominently in other works as major staging-posts of Mitterrand's career. I decided, for example, that the constraints of space, and the existence of various policy-based studies of the Mitterrand presidency precluded a more detailed analysis of the policy record of the 1981–93 governments. Other omissions might appear less defensible: little attention is paid to Mitterrand's media personality, for instance, in spite of the obvious importance of mass media in projecting political images and reinforcing the personalisation of the Fifth Republican political system. Detailed consideration of this subject has been sacrificed to word-limit constraints, and the fact that it has been treated elsewhere. As a general point, the themes dealt with in this book re-emerge throughout Mitterrand's long political career. They are intended to highlight the consistencies which underpin the career of a remarkable survivor. The dangers of the selectivity exercise are real, but this should not preclude the enterprise altogether.

I would like to thank those French politicians and civil servants who took time out of their busy schedules to agree to an interview. I offer my understanding and condolences to the legion of Socialist politicians who were too busy fighting for their own political survival to agree to my request for an interview. Among the many French and British sources of inspiration and assistance, I should particularly like to thank Martin Harrison and Peter Morris, both of whom read the manuscript with a keen critical sense and whose comments were welcomed. Finally, I am grateful to the Nuffield Foundation for their generous financial assistance, and to Keele University: without their combined financial and logistical support, this book would have been far more difficult to write.

Chapter 1

The origins of a political leader, 1916–58

François Mitterrand's youthful background left little to presage that he would be elected as the first left-wing president of the Fifth Republic. He was born in 1916 in west central France in the small village of Jarnac, near Cognac in the Charente *département*. This region of France was in many senses representative of the country as a whole during the early twentieth century: rural, Catholic, bourgeois and conservative. He grew up in a family of eight children within which his mother, a devout Catholic, reputedly exercised a powerful influence. Little concrete can be drawn from what we know of Mitterrand's childhood and youthful experience: Mitterrand was an average provincial adolescent from a bourgeois family. Those who knew him during this period assert that he was pious, of above average intelligence, romantic, with a consuming passion for literature.[1]

It would have been surprising if Mitterrand had not been deeply influenced by the Catholic culture within which he grew up: from the earliest age, he was encouraged to participate fully in the rituals of the Catholic Church. His early religious socialisation was strengthened by a Catholic education at the hands of *les pères maristes* at a boarding school in Angoulême. According to one interpretation, this instilled in Mitterrand in later years a dislike for organised Catholic rituals and the hierarchical ethos of the Catholic Church.[2] The Catholic reference point remained with Mitterrand in later years, articulated by references to a distaste for materialist concerns (see Chapter 5). In his autobiography, Mitterrand condemned money as 'the enemy, the corrupter', the antithesis of 'fundamental values such as the nation, religion, freedom and dignity'.[3] In the case of the Mitterrand family, the professed hatred for money appeared typical of those Catholic, provincial bourgeois families who were adequately endowed to afford such sentiments.

In 1934, at the age of 18, François Mitterrand cast aside his provincial background and left for university in Paris to study law at the *École Libre des Sciences Politiques*. His educational background thus distinguished Mitterrand somewhat from that typical of the Fifth Republican political elite. He was too old to have attended the *École Nationale d'Administration* (ENA, created in 1945), but, unlike brother Robert, François did not attempt the examination for the highly prestigious schools, *Polytechniques* or the *École Normale Supérieure*. Mitterrand entered into a Paris dominated by conflict between the left-wing parties (themselves divided) and the extra-parliamentary leagues of the extreme-right, the most important being the *Croix de feu*. According to one of his biographers (Catherine Nay), Mitterrand's political convictions during this period were 'openly those of the *Croix de feu*'.[4] Péan's 1994 book *Une Jeunesse française* provided some support for Mitterrand's *Croix de feu* sympathies, but rejected speculation that he had sympathised with the *Cagoule*, a violent organisation of the extreme-right, or with *Action française*, the standard-bearer of the counter-revolutionary Right.[5] The young Mitterrand adopted a variety of different stances.[6] Despite his later claim to be the inheritor of Léon Blum, there is no evidence that Mitterrand displayed any real enthusiasm for the Popular Front, the first Socialist-led government in France's history. Nor was he mobilised by the Republican cause during the Spanish Civil War, the other great rallying cry of the European Left in 1936–37. What evidence there is suggests that Mitterrand was an average bourgeois student from the provinces, marked by his rather conservative upbringing.

WARTIME AND RESISTANCE

Mitterrand was 22 when the Second World War broke out in September 1939, engaged in his compulsory military service. If we consider his wartime record, three salient themes emerge: courage, captivity and ambiguity.

Courage   Even his enemies have paid tribute to the mental and physical courage of Mitterrand, awarded the *Croix de guerre* after the war for his personal bravery. When the German attack on France began in May 1940, Mitterrand's unit found itself faced with the advancing German armies. In the course of an ordered retreat, Sergeant Mitterrand was wounded on 14 June 1940, hit in the right shoulder by a stray bullet. Taken prisoner by the Germans, he eventually managed to escape – on his third attempt and at great personal risk – into unoccupied Vichy France in December 1941. Mitterrand's courage later as a resistance leader was illustrated subsequently on a number of occasions. The most celebrated of these was on the evening of 10 July 1943, when he openly heckled members of the Vichy elite at a public meeting, at considerable personal risk. In the months leading up to the liberation of France, Mitterrand experienced a number of narrow escapes from the Gestapo and collaborationist police. He personally played a highly symbolic role in the liberation of the capital, by leading an armed assault on the *Commissariat des prisonniers*.

Captivity   Mitterrand later claimed that captivity was one of the most important formative experiences in shaping his political outlook. The notion that captivity forces men to re-evaluate previously held beliefs, and that the experience of wartime crystallises and accentuates movements which might otherwise not have occurred, appears plausible. In his major autobiography, *Ma part de vérité*, Mitterrand claimed that it was while a prisoner in Germany that he first discovered the 'social contract': faced with common adversity, men grouped together and cooperated in their mutual interest.[7] Whatever credibility we accord this, there is no doubt that Mitterrand's eventual escape tells us a great deal about his solitary courage, faced with considerable personal danger.

Ambiguity   Upon returning to France, Mitterrand obtained employment in March 1942 working for the Prisoners' Commissariat (*Commissariat général aux prisonniers de guerre*), a bureaucratic agency of the Vichy government officially responsible for maintaining relations with French prisoners of war in German camps. Many former prisoners worked in the Commissariat, anxious above all to provide material and emotional help to those Frenchmen still being held in captivity.

That he accepted employment for the Vichy state was later used against him by his critics, especially Gaullist ones; the argument runs that other resistance figures would have refused such an eventuality, whatever the justification. But in fact many resistance fighters followed very similar paths to that of Mitterrand, who later justified his participation in the Vichy regime because 'neither Vichy nor the internal resistance were unified entities'.[8] Various types of resistance activity originated within the Vichy regime itself.[9] Mitterrand did not deny some sympathy for the personality of Marshall Pétain, with whom he shared provincial bourgeois origins, a strong dose of patriotism and a sense of shame at the collapse of France in 1940. Indeed, until it became openly collaborationist in 1943, the Vichy regime appeared to many French people as a patriotic, anti-German regime, with Pétain and de Gaulle symbolising in their different ways French resistance to German conquest. On the other hand, Mitterrand refuted the charge that he was sympathetic to the objectives of Pétain's National Revolution.[10] Mitterrand also pleaded ignorance of the anti-Jewish actions of the Vichy regime, due to his captivity in Germany. He insisted that he broke with Vichy in 1943, when the regime's anti-Jewish activities had become more manifest.

Even with a charitable interpretation, the ambiguities of Mitterrand's behaviour during the war were real enough. Péan's *Une Jeunesse française* revealed that Mitterrand had remained in service of the Vichy regime longer than had originally been thought (until late 1943), though it did not refute the argument that the Vichy regime contained numerous genuine resistants and French patriots serving alongside extreme-right elements. Péan depicts Mitterrand successively as prisoner, Pétainiste, Giraudiste and resistant. These 'revelations' in relation to Vichy, which caused such a furore in late 1994, were scarcely new: Mitterrand's service as a minor agent of the Vichy regime had been a regular subject of polemic since the 1965 presidential election campaign, as had his acceptance of the *francisque*.[11] The intensity of the debate over Mitterrand's wartime experience revealed France as a nation still to come to terms with its Vichy past.

Mitterrand's resistance activity developed within the confines of the Vichy regime itself. This pattern was not unusual. Mitterrand's first clandestine activity was to falsify documents and to plan escape routes to help prisoners in German camps. Along with several others Mitterrand resigned from the Prisoners' Commissariat in January 1943, after former chief Maurice Pinot was replaced with an official more compliant to Premier Laval. Although Mitterrand's resistance activities began in earnest in early 1943, he retained some contacts with the Vichy regime until late 1943.[12] In his capacity as resistant, Mitterrand (who adopted the pseudonym Captain Morland) and Pinot helped to create an effective resistance network, the *Mouvement national des prisonniers et déportés de guerre*. This gave him access to the highest reaches of the French resistance leadership, and brought him into contact with the external resistance for the first time. By 1944, a man of 26, Mitterrand had met personally with Marshall Pétain, General Giraud and General de Gaulle, the three most significant figures in France's wartime history.[13]

The detail of Mitterrand's wartime experience which for long caused the most controversy was that of the *francisque*. As a former official of the Vichy regime, Mitterrand was awarded the *francisque* in November 1943, an honour conferred by Marshall Pétain personally on civil servants. Interpretations differ as to his motivations. Catherine Nay takes the *francisque* as proof that Mitterrand sympathised with the objectives of the Vichy regime, and appreciated the personality of Marshall Pétain. Charles Moulin, by contrast, pleads that Mitterrand accepted the *francisque* because 'he considered it to be an excellent cover for his clandestine activities', a path of action recommended by the London-based resistance.[14] Although bestowed routinely, critics contend that Mitterrand did not have to allow his name to go forward for the honour; indeed, his proposers were themselves personalities closely connected with Vichy.[15] Mitterrand's *francisque* must be placed in context. All other leading members of the Prisoners' Commissariat were also conferred awards by Pétain, who appreciated the practical assistance offered to French prisoners in German camps. Finally, once offered, it would have been dangerous not to accept the award.

For years after suspicions lingered that Mitterrand was somehow dealing with both sides, that his integrity was less than complete. Mitterrand was awarded the *francisque* in absentia in November 1943, while attempting to establish contact with the leadership of the external resistance first in London and then in Algiers. By November 1943, de Gaulle had imposed himself as the main leader of the external resistance at the expense of General Giraud. The young Mitterrand was determined that the General should consecrate his leadership of the ex-prisoners resistance movements against the claims of rivals. Mitterrand met de Gaulle briefly, in a short meeting in Algiers, variously described as 'acrimonious', 'rude' and 'polite but frosty'. In the course of this meeting, de Gaulle criticised Mitterrand for not having agreed to fight with the Free French forces in London, and insisted that three rival prisoners' movements be fused, and placed under the command of Michel Caillau, de Gaulle's nephew. Mitterrand resisted this decision, arguing that the internal resistance had its own rules, and that it could not be controlled in an arbitrary manner from outside. De Gaulle angrily concluded the meeting after 30 minutes. In his account in *Ma part de verité*, it was clear that Mitterrand could not accept the manner in which he had been treated by de Gaulle, and carried away a painful memory of the meeting.[16] Most biographies of Mitterrand have selected this episode to conjecture what might have happened to the subsequent course of French history had Mitterrand and de Gaulle entertained warmer personal relations with each other. Such speculation is ultimately fruitless in terms of assessing what actually did happen, but it does explain Mitterrand's anti-Gaullism.

Poor relations between de Gaulle and the young Mitterrand reflected the mutual distrust prevailing between the internal and the external resistance movements. From de Gaulle's perspective, the internal resistance lacked a sense of realism, of what it was possible for the French resistance to achieve by itself, and of the need to collaborate with the allies. Behind all of this lay the fact that the internal resistance was dominated by the Communists, who were portrayed by de Gaulle as fighting an ideology (Nazism) rather than a country (Germany), leaving the external resistance fighters as the only true patriots. It was scarcely surprising that a young turk such as Mitterrand should have met with a frosty reception from the Gaullist administrators in London, and then from de Gaulle himself in Algiers. At the Liberation, all other things being equal, Mitterrand might have expected to have become one of de Gaulle's (junior) associates in the post-war provisional government. De Gaulle and Mitterrand had a great deal in common: they both came from provincial, Catholic backgrounds, had a developed sense of honour, and a proven patriotism. But personal antagonism and mutual political mistrust decreed that this was not to be the case. It was also during the resistance that Mitterrand came to respect, and distrust, the power and organisational discipline of the French Communists.

Mitterrand's contribution to the resistance was recognised by his nomination as General Secretary for prisoners of war in the provisional government formed awaiting de Gaulle's return, a position he held for two weeks. At the age of 27, Mitterrand had already made his mark. But his early contact with power was to be extremely short-lived. Mitterrand's services were not retained by de Gaulle in the 1944 provisional government. Mitterrand's behaviour during the years 1942–44 was certainly not devoid of ambiguity. On balance, however, retrospective appraisals have tended unnecessarily to minimise Mitterrand's status as a resistant, for which he was decorated after the war. They have also distorted the prevailing perception of the Vichy regime amongst many French patriots until November 1942: as a patriotic, anti-German regime within which it was possible to serve the nation without any suspicion of collaborationism with the enemy.[17]

FRANÇOIS MITTERRAND AND THE FOURTH REPUBLIC

François Mitterrand earned his political spurs as a non-Socialist, neo-Radical minister during the Fourth Republic. From 1947 to 1958, he served in a total of 11 governments, occupying the most important Ministries of State: the Interior Ministry under Mendès-France from 1954–55, and the Justice Ministry during the Socialist administration of Guy Mollet from 1956–57. Mitterrand was being tipped by certain commentators as a future prime minister when the regime collapsed in 1958. He was also the youngest minister this century (aged 30) when named to serve in Ramadier's government in January 1947 (see Table 1.1).

Table 1.1 Mitterrand's ministries, 1947–58

Year	Ministry	Government
Jan.–Nov. 1947	Ex-Servicemen	Ramadier (Socialist)
July 1948–Oct. 1949	Information	Marie (Radical)
June 1950–March 1951	Overseas Territories	Pleven (UDSR)
Jan. 1952–Feb. 1952	Minister without Portfolio	Faure (Radical)
June 1953	Council of Europe	Laniel (centre-right)
June 1954–Feb. 1955	Interior	Mendès-France (Radical)
Jan. 1956–May 1957	Justice	Mollet (Socialist)

Source: *Année Politique*, 1947–1958
Note: Premiers mentioned are those at the time of Mitterrand's nomination.

For a politician who exploited the institutions of the Fifth Republic with such tenacity, it is easy to forget that Mitterrand first made his reputation as a centrist parliamentarian in the Fourth Republic. His Fourth Republican career was built outside the main political parties (see section on UDSR, p. 13). It would be inaccurate at this stage to label Mitterrand as a Socialist. He oscillated between political positions associated with centre-right and centre-left during the course of the Fourth Republic, the former by opposition to the

Communist party; the latter in defence of the Republic. The events which shaped the young Mitterrand's political experience were the expulsion of the Communists from government in May 1947 and the onset of the cold war. His political beliefs during this period were permeated by anti-Communism. But this hardly set Mitterrand apart from most of his non-Communist contemporaries: indeed, for all of his Marxist rhetoric, the Socialist Party (SFIO) leader Guy Mollet was even more starkly anti-Communist than Mitterrand.

Following his brief tenure in the provisional government from August to September 1944, there followed a period of oscillation in Mitterrand's career, when he was tempted alternatively by pursuing a career in the legal profession and in journalism, before finally opting to contest the second postwar election of June 1946. His antipathy for organised political parties considerably complicated his task. Mitterrand rejected both the SFIO and the Christian-democratic MRP, standing instead as a member of an independent list in the Seine *département* which ran a poor fifth. He was finally elected as a deputy in Nièvre in the November 1946 election as an independent, standing as representative of another heteroclite list hostile to the governing parties of the tripartite alliance (PCF, SFIO and MRP). Mitterrand retained his seat in Nièvre until his election as President of the Fifth Republic in 1981, with the exception of a short spell from 1958–62. Mitterrand owed his good fortune to the moderate Radical politician (and future premier) Henri Queuille who proposed that he represent the anti-tripartite forces in the Nièvre *département* in central France.[18]

Mitterrand was elected in November 1946 on a strongly anti-Communist, anti-collectivist platform. And yet he first obtained ministerial office, in January 1947, as a member of Paul Ramadier's Socialist-led government, which included five Communist ministers. Mitterrand's best defence against the charge of opportunism was that Ramadier's government – the first of the Fourth Republic proper – contained representatives of virtually all parties in the Chamber, not just the tripartite formations (PCF, SFIO and MRP). The UDSR was a new party with few established notables and Mitterrand was one of its most energetic deputies. It was natural for an ambitious young politician of thirty to accept the opportunity for ministerial office. At this early stage of his career, Mitterrand's beliefs remained fluid, besides reference to the political programme of the resistance, to anti-Communism, and to the imperative of defence against all threats to the Republic (see Chapter 5).

His firm Republican sentiment explained Mitterrand's opposition both to the PCF, and to de Gaulle's RPF, created in April 1947. Mitterrand's opposition to the PCF was hardly remarkable: the entire political class joined forces in isolating the Communists in opposition to the regime at the onset of the cold war. As a young minister, Mitterrand's responsibilities in the anti-Communist campaign were negligible, but his speeches at that period reveal that his opposition to the PCF's 'totalitarian' designs was uncompromising.

His actions were consistent with his words: Mitterrand purged his first two ministries – ex-Servicemen and Information – of agents infiltrated by former Communist ministers. His experience of the Communists during the resistance was certainly not foreign to his sentiment. Mitterrand's commitment to a Third Republican style of parliamentary regime also explained why, from 1947 onwards, he firmly opposed de Gaulle's RPF. At the 1949 UDSR congress, Mitterrand declared that the defence of 'Republican institutions' against 'Communism' and 'Fascism' dictated his opposition to the PCF and the RPF.[19] His opposition to the RPF was in contrast with a majority of UDSR deputies, who rallied to de Gaulle. For the Gaullists, the UDSR had no justification for continuing its existence once the General had founded the RPF as the force of the resistance. Mitterrand's defence of Republican values coincided with a distrust of de Gaulle to prevent him from acceding to the sirens of the RPF. This stance predated his more assertive opposition to de Gaulle after the creation of the Fifth Republic in 1958. Mitterrand's defence of Republican legality should be signalled already as one enduring source of continuity throughout his political career.

It lies beyond the parameters of this chapter to consider in detail Mitterrand's activities as a Fourth Republican minister. Only four of his ministerial portfolios lasted for a period exceeding nine months: Information, Overseas Territories, Interior, Justice. It was within the sphere of foreign affairs and colonial policy that Mitterrand built his ministerial reputation in the Fourth Republic, primarily as a colonial reformer.

MITTERRAND AS COLONIAL REFORMER, 1950–54

Mitterrand's liberal colonialism represented the key vantage point of his political activity during the Fourth Republic. His philosophy was colonial, because he did not envisage a general decolonisation and firmly believed in the benefits of French rule; liberal, because he sought to humanize this rule, to undertake far-reaching socio-economic reform, and to introduce an element of colonial self-government. As early as 1947, Mitterrand had ranged himself on the side of colonial reformers, supporting E. Depreux's proposed Algerian statute, which was in practice discarded under pressure from the French Algerian colons (settlers). His tenure as Minister for Overseas Territories (DOM-TOM) in the governments headed by Pleven and Queuille (1950–51) firmly established his reputation as a liberal colonial reformer.[20] By the standards of the age, Mitterrand adopted a radical stance towards colonial policy, albeit one which fell far short of independence.

His interest in colonial affairs was initially concentrated in Black Africa. As a Christian, Mitterrand was shocked by the French colons' treatment of native Blacks, which recalled parallels with apartheid regimes elsewhere. As a fervent supporter of the French Empire, he was politically intelligent enough to link its future with the need for colonial reform. And as an adept of the French

State, Mitterrand was determined that central laws should be implemented in the French colonies.

Mitterrand's tenure of the Overseas Ministry propelled him into the political forefront. This was due more to the audacious manner with which Mitterrand approached his task than to the inherent importance of the ministry itself. Mitterrand immediately stamped his originality upon his office. Previous Overseas ministers had been unwilling to interfere too closely in the administration of French colonies; the writ of central government was usually ignored. This changed abruptly under Mitterrand. His insistence that laws enacted in Paris be enforced in France's African colonies earned him the lasting enmity of colonial administrators, who were used to acting with impunity. Mitterrand did not recoil from sacking colonial administrators who refused to implement laws passed by the central government.[21] His advocacy of reform to enhance political rights in the colonies, and the devolution of certain powers to colonial Assemblies further aggravated Mitterrand's reputation with diehard supporters of French colonialism. His reformist impetus encountered distrust from the establishment institutions in mainland France: the army, the church, and from within several political parties. The degree of hostility to Mitterrand should not be underestimated. It testified to his reformist purpose, and to his courage.

Mitterrand's cultivation of radical African leaders during his period as Overseas Minister deserves closer attention. Upon arriving in office, Mitterrand was presented with reports of riots on the Ivory Coast, apparently encouraged by the *Rassemblement démocratique Africain* (RDA). The RDA had been created by the African nationalist leader Felix Houphouët-Boigny, to provide for more effective cooperation within the metropolitan parliament between Black deputies from different colonies. French settlers in the overseas territories concerned considered the RDA to be a dangerous subversive threat to the established colonial order. The RDA, which had aligned itself with the PCF group in the National Assembly, was suspected of pro-Communist sympathies: the movement was temporarily banned in 1950.

When he summoned Houphouët-Boigny to Paris, and invited him to prove that there had been no RDA involvement in anti-French rioting, Mitterrand created an uproar which continued to reverberate long after he left the ministry. In his meeting with Houphouët-Boigny, Mitterrand and the African leader agreed to publish a text in which each outlined their views on the future of the French Union and Black Africa. For his part, the RDA leader publicly accepted the need to work within the framework provided by the French Union. In return, Mitterrand stressed the importance of social, economic and political reforms in order to avoid a dramatic degeneration of the situation in French Black Africa. Aside from his genuine reformist desire, Mitterrand's concern was that the RDA must not fall under the lasting influence of the Communist Party, and that prominent colonialists (such Bidault of the MRP, and Mayer of the Radicals) should not be able to frustrate all movement to colonial reform. In Mitterrand's design, reform was an alternative to independence.

The RDA episode was an early testament to Mitterrand's political skills. Not only did Houphouet-Boigny agrée to use his influence to stem anti-colonial riots, but his group of RDA deputies joined Mitterrand's UDSR group within the National Assembly, thereby considerably enhancing Mitterrand's prestige and political standing. Mitterrand's attempt to preserve Black Africa within the French Union might be judged ultimately as a failure. By 1960, all sub-Saharan states involved had achieved national independence, with the former RDA deputies now heading a cluster of African states, and Houpouët-Boigny himself President of the Ivory Coast. And yet, this is a rather shallow assessment. It might be contended that Mitterrand's action in 'coopting' Black African leaders facilitated the eventual (inevitable) process of independence, and preserved close relations between France and its former African colonies. His actions transformed a whole generation of revolutionary independence leaders of the 1950s into conservative representatives of francophone African states in the 1960s, faithful to a neo-colonial model of relations with metropolitan France perfected under de Gaulle. To this extent, Mitterrand's 'turning' of 1951 was of fundamental importance in terms of future relations between France and its African colonies. Thus, a romantic attachment to colonial reform, and a determination to ensure that the writ of central government extended to France's colonies gave a real meaning to Mitterrand's activity during the Fourth Republic.

MITTERRAND, MENDÈS-FRANCE AND MOLLET, 1954–58

Apart from his republican opposition to the PCF and RPF, and his commitment to colonial reform, Mitterrand's political activity during the Fourth Republic was characterised by his relationship with Pierre Mendès-France from 1953 onwards. The attractions exercised by Mendès-France on the young Mitterrand were undeniable: Mendès-France represented modernist, postwar republicanism turned to the future. In turn, Mendès-France valued Mitterrand's sense of tactical genius, which had allowed him to capture control of the UDSR in 1953 (see section on UDSR, pp. 13–15). Mitterrand was manifestly not a *mendèsiste* of the first hour; his participation in the centre-right government of Laniel in 1953, for instance, was criticised by those close to Mendès. He never formed a part of the *mendèsiste* inner circle.

His infatuation with Mendès-France was relatively short-lived. Mitterrand's insistent demand for the Interior ministry in the 1954–55 Mendès-France government invoked suspicion among Mendès' entourage, who suspected his motivations.[22] As Interior Minister in the Mendès-France government, Mitterrand had to deal with the Algerian uprising which broke out on 1 November 1954. On colonial affairs, Mitterrand was a man of his age. He could not begin to conceive of Algerian independence, believing the benefits of enlightened French rule to be overwhelming. His public attitude was that: 'There is no French-Algeria, because Algeria is France.' Moreover, his function as Minister of the Interior meant that Mitterrand was obliged to consider the Algerian uprising first as a problem of public order, and only then to propose ameliorative reforms. Finally, Mitterrand knew that the survival of the Mendès-France ministry depended upon the continuing compliance of the Algerian deputies, and the pro-colonial lobby. This constraint severely limited the government's margins of manoeuvre. In spite of this, it might be contended that Mitterrand over-reacted to the outbreak of violence. His response was to insist on a massive French military presence that exacerbated an already tense situation. In a speech to the National Assembly in January 1955, Mitterrand drew satisfaction from the fact that, under his stewardship, troops in Algeria had increased from 49,700 to 80,300.[23]

Mitterrand's reaction to the Algerian uprising was consistent with his earlier declarations on Black Africa. His proposed remedies combined the threat of force to suppress the uprising, with the promise of socio-economic and political reform within Algeria itself. This dual approach, which had worked in relation to sub-Saharan Africa, proved elusive in Algeria, where the stakes were far higher, and where the parliamentary room for manoeuvre was limited. The Mendès-France government was finally brought down in February 1955, by the dedicated opposition of the Algerian lobby. The fall of the Mendès-France ministry removed from office what transpired to be the most reformist government of the Fourth Republic. And yet even Mendès-France, the colonial liberator in Tunisia and Morocco, refused to condemn repression against the Algerian nationalists first undertaken during his premiership.

Apart from the Algerian uprising, Mitterrand's participation in the Mendès-France government was notable for the so-called Leaks Affair. This was a crude attempt to discredit the reformist government of Mendès-France. It referred to the purported leaking of defence secrets from the confidential Defence Committee, first to the press in 1953, and then to the PCF in 1954. Only a top-ranking civil servant or a minister could have leaked the documents; Mitterrand had been present at Defence Committee meetings on both occasions. Mitterrand was secretly accused of the leaks by the Paris Chief of Police, Jean Dides. Mendès-France instigated a secret enquiry into the activities of leading members of his government, including those of his Interior Minister Mitterrand. The sensitivity of the leaks was heightened by the fact that they concerned the Indochinese war, which Mendès-France was intent on concluding and to which Mitterrand had declared his public opposition. Mitterrand was not informed by Mendès-France that an enquiry into his behaviour had been instigated. The main legacy of the Leaks Affair was to engender distrust between Mitterrand and Mendès-France, a mutual suspicion which survived until the latter's death in 1982. Mitterrand resented the fact that Mendès-France had failed to inform him of the leaks before the affair broke out into the public limelight, and, indeed, that he had instigated an enquiry without informing him.

The official truth in relation to the Leaks Affair was established in a court judgement, followed by a parliamentary enquiry in 1956: the press leaks had emanated from police informants, the PCF had never obtained the minutes of the committee, and Mitterrand was fully cleared of any misdemeanour, as were his fellow ministers. Preceding this date, however, a number of doubts remained and Mitterrand was subjected to much personal abuse. His subsequent belief that the leaks had been the work of Gaullists determined to discredit the political class of the Fourth Republic reputedly accentuated his anti-Gaullism.

Public disquiet over the Leaks Affair was short-lived. After the 1956 election, Mitterrand returned to government as Justice Minister in Guy Mollet's administration in February 1956. Unlike Alain Savary, or Mendès-France, he steadfastly refused to resign from Mollet's government because of the repressive drift of its Algerian policy. His decision to remain within Mollet's government while others quit was easy to criticise, with or without the benefit of hindsight. Mitterrand argued that he had already resigned once on a matter of principle (over Indochina, from Laniel's government in 1953), and that, along with Gaston Defferre, he supported a liberal policy towards Algeria. It is also possible that, having occupied the Interior and Justice ministries, he genuinely believed in his chances of becoming prime minister in the near future, in accordance with the ethos of the Fourth Republic. Mitterrand's anxiety for self-promotion did not endear him to left-wing critics of the Mollet government and aggravated his relationship with Mendès-France. The conduct of the Algerian war (1954–62) caused a serious fracture within the French Left, with a vocal opposition condemning the inaction (or worse) of politicians such as Mollet and Mitterrand in relation to the Algerian uprising. For these people, there was a deeply ingrained belief after 1958 that Mitterrand was a rather cynical opportunist unworthy of carrying the colours of the Left.

As Minister of Justice, Mitterrand did not have direct control of Algeria (devolved to R. Lacoste, the resident minister), but did participate in several contentious decisions: for example, he co-signed a decree dated 17 March 1956 which laid down rules for exceptional military justice, notably by creating special tribunals to deal with acts of 'terrorism'.[24] This led to allegations against Mitterrand of condoning the torture of Algerian nationalist fighters. Although this judgement was rather harsh, there is little doubt that Mitterrand's decision to remain within the Mollet government compromised his previously progressive reputation as a colonial liberal. Other ministers were less hesitant: Alain Savary resigned from the Mollet government over the Ben Bella affair; Pierre Mendès-France followed shortly after. Years later, Mitterrand pleaded his self-defence against the accusation of opportunism:

Gaston Defferre and I defended within Cabinet ideas which were not adopted. I finally understood that our ideas had little chance of being accepted, and so I refused to remain within the government, when Guy Mollet's successor, Mr Bourgès-Maunory, asked me to stay at the Justice ministry. It was on the issue of Algeria, therefore, that I quit the government.[25]

This occurred a little late, all the same, for his critics on the anti-colonialist left. Before drawing together the various aspects of Mitterrand's political activity during the Fourth Republic, we shall first briefly consider the political formation with which Mitterrand was associated from 1946–58.

MITTERRAND AND THE UDSR

Throughout the Fourth Republic, Mitterrand eschewed the constraint of belonging to a disciplined party. His chosen formation, the *Union Démocratique des Socialistes de la Résistance* (UDSR), was little more than a loosely organised cadre party, not really existing as a cohesive organisation outside of the National Assembly. His refusal to consider joining any of the three tightly organised postwar parties (PCF, SFIO, MRP) and his rejection of the old formations of the Third Republic meant that Mitterrand probably had little choice but to associate himself with a formation such as the UDSR. By its early opposition to tripartism, the UDSR could be loosely classified as lying on the centre–right of the postwar political spectrum, yet it retained a wide diversity of political beliefs within its ranks. Within the UDSR, Mitterrand gradually came to be associated with anti-Gaullism, with a new postwar political generation, with a modern political style and with a political position located on the left of the party.

At its origins, the UDSR was a genuine party of the French resistance. The first postwar elections of October 1945, which witnessed the emergence of three powerful parties (PCF, SFIO, MRP), effectively killed off the idea of a single unified resistance party. This vision of a single movement incorporating the various non-Communist currents of the French resistance, such as Socialists, Catholics, Gaullists and progressives, had been cherished by several resistance leaders, but vanished once it became clear that neither de Gaulle nor the Socialists were willing to sanction such an exercise. The UDSR was created in 1945 as a party for those who refused to allow the resistance legacy to disappear, and who anyway rejected all existing parties. It was the only party specifically to claim the legacy of the French resistance in its title. Such an organisation suited Mitterrand's fierce spirit of independence, his belief in the resistance legacy, as well as his uncertainty in relation to traditional classifications along lines of left and right. He preferred the UDSR to either the Christian Democratic MRP (the logical organisation to join, given his Catholic background and resistance past) or the SFIO (the other non-Communist resistance movement). Unlike most fellow UDSR deputies, Mitterrand stead-fastly refused to join de Gaulle's RPF, created in 1947 (see p. 7–8).

From its origins, the ideological diversity of the UDSR proved that there was no single heritage of the French resistance.[26] It was initially composed of a varied assortment of Gaullists, non-Marxist Socialists, Liberals, moderate Conservatives and Independents. The rationale for the UDSR was called into question in 1947, when General de Gaulle created the RPF as a rally intended to incorporate the Gaullist resistance legacy. With the departure of a majority of UDSR deputies to the new Gaullist formation in 1949, the UDSR became less of an organisation marked by the resistance legacy, at least in its Gaullist incarnation.[27] This suited Mitterrand's purposes. Although the departure of Gaullists in 1949 weakened the UDSR, it greatly strengthened Mitterrand's position within it. The young minister became one of a triumvirate of prominent UDSR politicians (the others being R. Pleven, and E. Claudius Petit). By far the most dynamic of the three, Mitterrand eventually took over the leadership of the formation in 1953.

Philip Williams characterised the UDSR as too small to be feared, yet too important to be ignored.[28] The fact that the UDSR occupied a pivotal position within the political spectrum of the Fourth Republic afforded its deputies a degree of influence disproportionate to their influence within the country. His agile manoeuvres as Minister for Overseas Affairs (1950–51) greatly increased Mitterrand's prestige within the UDSR. The rallying of fourteen reformist African (RDA) deputies in 1951 to the UDSR parliamentary group (at the expense of the PCF) bore ample testament to Mitterrand's political skills. Given that the UDSR had hitherto counted only nine metropolitan deputies, this gave Mitterrand a majority among the UDSR delegation.[29] In June 1951, Mitterrand was unanimously elected as president of the new UDSR parlia-mentary group. He became president of the UDSR proper on 24 November 1953 at the movement's annual congress.

In 1952, the UDSR proclaimed itself to be 'the party for those with an independent spirit'.[30] The UDSR was simultaneously a collection of independent-minded deputies in the Radical tradition of the old Third Republic and an organisation which – deriving its legitimacy from the French resistance – could not be tainted with the failures of the Third Republic. In some senses, though, it was unquestionably representative of a Third Republic political style, more especially that of the Radical party. The weakness of party discipline, for example, recalled that of the old pre-1940 Radicals and, likewise, the fact that electoral alliances at the grass-roots level bore only a weak relationship with political alliances at the national level. The ideological fluidity itself within the UDSR was similar to that of the pre-1940 Radicals. The greatest difference from the Radicals (apart from the Resistance legacy) lay in the fact that the UDSR was bereft of established notables, which allowed ambitious young politicians such as Mitterrand to make their mark earlier than might otherwise have been the case.

In short, despite its creation as a resistance party, the UDSR came increasingly to resemble the old Radical party. Indeed, electoral and political cooperation was commonplace between the UDSR and the Radicals. The UDSR gave resistance respectibility to the Radicals, while the Radicals disposed of electoral clienteles in various regions that could be harnessed by the UDSR. The emergence of Mendès-France and *mendèsisme* within the Radical party in the early 1950s lent an element of ideological cohesion to this alliance.

The UDSR prefigured the later political formations associated with Mitterrand (see Chapter 5) in one important sense: it contained men with varying political views, anxious to participate in power, but not naturally at home in any of the existing parties. Under Mitterrand's leadership after 1953, the UDSR became somewhat more of a cohesive centre-left organisation, although it never lost its heteroclite character. Throughout its existence, the UDSR was riven by divisions on policy (Europe, the European Army, Africa), over personality (Mitterrand versus Pleven) and over institutional remedies for the chronic problems of governmental instability in the Fourth Republic. The fall of the Fourth Republic in 1958 signalled the imminent demise of the formation. The UDSR executive's decision to campaign for a No vote in the constitutional referendum of September 1958 caused a formal split, with the minority based around Pleven deciding to break away from the movement.[31] The UDSR episode revealed above all how Mitterrand fundamentally distrusted the discipline and collective responsibility implied by belonging to a traditional party of the old SFIO variety. A first Fourth Republican generation of *mitterrandistes*, comprised of close political associates from the UDSR, was clearly recognisable from this period onwards, comprising men such as G. Dayan, G. Beauchamps, and R. Dumas. Mitterrand displayed great loyalty to these men, who reciprocated the sentiment.

CONCLUSION: MITTERRAND AS REPRESENTATIVE OF THE FOURTH REPUBLIC?

In certain important respects, Mitterrand might be regarded as a representative *par excellence* of the Fourth Republic. He fully exploited his control of the UDSR after 1953 to build himself an important power base, vital in the unstable, coalition-dominated Fourth Republic. In a tradition as reminiscent of the Third Republic as the Fourth, moreover, there was a clear discordance between the nature of Mitterrand's local political base in the Nièvre *département* and his national strategy. He was consistently elected by a centre-right electorate in Nièvre, although he came to represent the 'centre-left' tendency within the UDSR, symbolised by his participation in the Mendès-France government of 1954–55, and the Republican Front of 1956–57. While Mitterrand became a leading spokesman for the merits of parliamentary alliance between the UDSR and the SFIO, in Nièvre he consistently fought against the

SFIO, including in the 1956 election, when nationally the UDSR and SFIO formed a part of the same Republican Front alliance.

The portrayal of Mitterrand as an opportunistic manoeuvrer during the Fourth Republic is a superficially attractive one. There was no lack of occasions when he appeared to promote his own self interest above anything else. His participation in Laniel's centre–right government of 1953 was one example; the decision to remain within the Mollet government provided another case in point. Moreover, this perception was shared by many of Mitterrand's contemporaries. And yet, there was some evidence of principled political activity as well, notably in relation to liberal colonial reform, even if little in terms of policy achievement could be directly attributed to Mitterrand. That this was the case was indicative of the shortcomings of the Fourth Republic, within which governmental and ministerial tenures were incessantly interrupted, as much as it was of Mitterrand's qualities.

The idea that Mitterrand epitomised the Fourth Republic is perhaps unfair. We should recall that, notwithstanding his participation in eleven governments, Mitterrand was not in the first-rank of Fourth Republic statesmen. He was neither Mendès-France, nor Schuman, nor Pinay. In fact, several lesser statesmen acceded to the post of Prime Minister, such as Laniel, Pflimlin, or Bourgès-Maunoury. If anything, he was too much of a loner ever to be completely at ease as an insider. He had voted against the constitution of October 1946, and on numerous occasions had criticised the manner in which the regime functioned. In each of the ministries he had occupied, Mitterrand could boast a moderate reformist record. The essential point to note relates to the Fourth Republic itself: the political system transformed honourable men seeking solutions to difficult questions into apparent political manoeuvrers obsessed with the machinations of the regime. This was the price of their own political survival. Only those who stood outside of the regime altogether, such as de Gaulle, derived any political credit from its collapse.

Chapter 2

From Republican opponent to President of the French, 1958–81

The collapse of the Fourth Republic proved to be a watershed in François Mitterrand's political career. From being intimately connected with the regime, Mitterrand became an isolated outsider, rejected by old and new alike. Far more than any other event, Mitterrand's political career was shaped by his confrontation with de Gaulle in 1958. Opposition to de Gaulle enabled Mitterrand to project a new political identity (as a man of high Republican principle), refine a new political strategy (the union of the Left) and gradually evolve a new personal philosophy (the proclaimed commitment to socialism). His Republican resistance in May–June 1958 set Mitterrand apart from most Fourth Republic politicians, who rallied to de Gaulle, believing erroneously that they could later control the General once the immediate crisis had passed. Mitterrand's stance in opposing de Gaulle demanded undoubted political courage. He was joined by the PCF, by a minority of Socialist deputies, and by a minority of progressive *mendèsiste* Radicals in his opposition to de Gaulle's investiture as premier on 1 June 1958.

Mitterrand justified his opposition to de Gaulle by reference to Republican legality and the refusal of personal rule. In a courageous manner, he declined to accept the creation of a regime he considered to contravene French republicanism. He expressed this sentiment in a passionate speech to the National Asssembly on 1 June 1958, the day of de Gaulle's investiture as Prime Minister:

> When General de Gaulle spoke to the Constitutive Assembly in September 1944, after the struggles of the Resistance, his two companions were Honour and the Nation. His companions today, whom he has not chosen, but who have followed him until now, are called Force and Sedition.[1]

Behind Mitterrand's fine rhetoric lay a particular type of French Republicanism. He was a Republican in the old Radical tradition. The events of May–June 1958 were a tremendous shock to those with a genuine republican conscience. Mitterrand was appalled by the conditions surrounding de Gaulle's return to power: the suspension of parliament, the menacing role played by the armed forces, the lingering threat of force, the appeal to the providential leader and the acquiescence of the old parties (and President Coty) to de Gaulle. Mitterrand was also from a strongly juridical background: his professional practice as a lawyer was not foreign to his opposition to de Gaulle on legal constitutional grounds. For a man with such a refined sense of history, moreover, Mitterrand feared that the French tradition of the providential ruler subverting Republican institutions would be repeated.[2] Superimposed upon Mitterrand's genuine sense of republican outrage, there was no doubt that personal relations between the two men were difficult. Whereas Mendès-France had facilitated Mitterrand's accession to high office (despite the latter's jealously of the former), de Gaulle immediately proved an obstacle to Mitterrand's ambitions and provoked an intense personal dislike as well.[3]

Mitterrand suspected that, whatever his personal qualities, de Gaulle would be unable to control the forces which propelled him to power: the army, the colonial administrations, and the extreme-right. The fact that history disproved Mitterrand should not detract us from the force of his initial sentiment. His insurgence against the 'coup d'état' of 13 May 1958 was that of a classic Republican in another sense: Mitterrand lamented the fact that de Gaulle had been carried to power by an undisciplined army. At key moments of French history, the army, along with the church, had been historically associated with the defence of an anti-Republican brand of right-wing politics, which Mitterrand diagnosed as underpinning de Gaulle's return.[4]

Thus, Mitterrand's opposition to de Gaulle in May–June 1958 was a principled act. It was one which condemned him to almost certain opposition for the foreseeable future, after having been intimately connected with the Fourth Republic as a minister on eleven occasions. For a man of Mitterrand's reputation, the opportunistic course of action would have been to follow the example of the Socialist leader, Mollet, who colluded in de Gaulle's return to power, helped to draw up the 1958 constitution, and split his party in the process.

Mitterrand's early condemnation of the Fifth Republic was most eloquently expressed in his influential book *Le coup d'état permanent*, published in 1964 as a verdict on five years of extra-constitutional government.[5] Mitterrand accused de Gaulle of repeated constitutional violations. Having been created by a *coup d'état* in 1958, de Gaulle's Fifth Republic maintained its power through its permanent recourse to arbitrary rule. This was qualified by Mitterrand as *le coup d'état de tous les jours*. He lamented the exceptional powers, the executive courts, the special police, the omnipotent executive and the absence of habeas corpus. Whatever de Gaulle's qualities, Mitterrand urged that there were inherent dangers with his form of personal rule, which might be used to subvert democracy. By these repeated attacks, Mitterrand gradually established himself as one of several leaders of a burgeoning left-wing opposition to Gaullism.

In November 1958, Mitterrand lost his Nièvre seat to an independent Gaullist, despite benefiting from the withdrawal of the Communist candidate in his favour at the second ballot.[6] Having lost his parliamentary seat, there followed a renewed period of crossing of the desert, during which Mitterrand temporarily returned to his professional practice as a lawyer, and concentrated upon restoring his position as the favourite son of the Nièvre *département*. In the municipal elections of March 1959, he was elected mayor of the small commune of Château-Chinon (3,000 inhabitants).[7] This represented an inverse *cursus honorum* to that of most other national politicians, at least at the beginning of the Fifth Republic: he had become a national political figure before acquiring a local base. One month later, Mitterrand was returned as senator for the Nièvre, re-establishing a close relationship with his adopted *département*. His political resurrection was rudely interrupted by the Observatory Affair.

The Observatory Affair   This was, in essence, another attempt by his right-wing enemies to discredit Mitterrand. On 16 October 1959, the press announced that the senator François Mitterrand had escaped an attempted murder. His car had been followed by a vehicle containing a group of assassins; ascertaining that he was being followed, Mitterrand had veered sharply rightwards, and jumped out of his car, to the temporary safety of a hedge in the *Jardins de Luxembourg*. Mitterrand's car was then hit in seven places, before his pursuers fled. This was the version of the episode that Mitterrand recounted to the police immediately afterwards. It led to an instant wave of public sympathy.

What Mitterrand had not informed the police was that he had previously been warned by R. Pesquet, a right-wing deputy, that he was on the hit-list of a group of pro-Algérie Française gunmen. Several days after the attack, when public sympathy was at its height, Pesquet claimed that Mitterrand had all along planned a fake attempt on his life in order to gain public sympathy, and that he had collaborated in this venture. This charge was vigorously denied by Mitterrand, but he admitted later to the police that there had been contact between the two men before the attempted attack, a fact he had originally concealed. According to Mitterrand, Pesquet had approached him a short time before with the news that a commando had received instructions to assassinate him; Pesquet had himself been instructed to execute the act, but recoiled and forewarned Mitterrand. Mitterrand stoutly rejected the idea of his having framed an artificial attack to restore some political glory.

Mitterrand's account of events was that he had genuinely believed he was on a hit-list, that he was misled by Pesquet, and that his initial failure to mention the meetings with Pesquet was in order to safeguard the latter from terrorist reprisals for failing to carry out the attack. Although we are inclined to accept Mitterrand's version of events, he has been criticised for a lack of political judgement, for accepting as truth the fantastic plot of a known political opponent, and for failing to inform the police that he had been warned by Pesquet of the danger to his life. And yet these criticisms underestimate the climate of fear which reigned among many of the old politicians of the Fourth Republic faced with acts of violence committed in the name of Algérie-Française.

On a personal level, the Observatory Affair undoubtedly tested Mitterrand's capacities of political endurance to the full. At one stage, Mitterrand's parliamentary immunity was lifted so that he could stand trial. That the case was never brought to court, and that Pesquet fled the country shortly afterwards tended to back Mitterrand's version of events. It is plausible to contend that Mitterrand's character as a solitary and secretive figure, unwilling to trust even those closest to him, was reinforced by the Observatory Affair. As with the earlier furore over the *francisque*, the Observatory Affair revealed an important aspect of Mitterrand's character. His determination not to respond to the provocations of adversaries was arguably an admirable feature; nonetheless, it projected an image of ambiguity, duplicity and untrustworthiness which was hard to dissipate. And there remained the uneasy question of why Mitterrand was targeted as an object of scandal by adversaries. That this should be the case ought to be imputed to certain consequences of his political style and persona, notably his secretive nature, and his unwillingness to address agendas defined by others. The Observatory Affair certainly revealed an element of naivety and political miscalculation on Mitterrand's part. But it also confirmed the extent to which he was detested by the extreme-right, which might ultimately have reinforced the image he was attempting to project as a man of principle. His opponents were so obviously unprincipled.

MITTERRAND AND THE EVOLUTION OF THE FIFTH REPUBLIC, 1962–71

Once his initial sense of outrage had passed (and once the Observatory Affair had died down) Mitterrand came to appreciate the political possibilities opened by de Gaulle's accession. In the appreciation of one observer, Mitterrand's 'stroke of genius' was to recognise that whoever imposed himself in the eyes of public (and international) opinion as de Gaulle's principal opponent would have his political future mapped out for him. That Mitterrand would become this privileged opponent was at first sight rather improbable.

There could be no doubt about Mitterrand's deeply rooted belief in Republican legality, or that this coexisted within Mitterrand with an unquestionable sense of political pragmatism. This was typified in relation to his attitude towards the direct election of the French president, introduced by de Gaulle's constitutional referendum of October 1962. The essence of Mitterrand's case against de Gaulle had been to safeguard against the abuse of personal rule. Consistent with this stance, Mitterrand campaigned for a No vote in the October 1962 referendum. And yet, he was one of the first politicians to recognise the importance of the direct presidential election as a means of coordinating anti-Gaullist political activity. The creation of Convention in 1964 illustrated this (see Chapter 5). Mitterrand's pragmatic stance in relation to presidentialism (condemning it in principle, but accepting the new political challenge) is typical of his mixture of idealism and opportunity. Against the odds, he succeeded in his ambition of positioning himself as de Gaulle's principal opponent. The unwillingness displayed by Mendès-France to affront the General was perhaps the chief explanation for this, followed by the failure of Defferre's presidential candidacy. But the political skill exercised by Mitterrand must not be underestimated either, especially in the 1965 presidential election.

After the split within the UDSR in 1958, Mitterrand was without a party worthy of the name. From 1959 onwards, he became involved with the burgeoning political club movement that had arisen as a new opposition to Gaullism outside of the existing parties of the Left.[8] In 1959, he founded the *Ligue pour le Combat Républicain*, a minuscule political club dedicated to combating the Gaullist Republic. The Ligue was primarily of interest in that it provided a refuge for Mitterrand's most faithful lieutenants and manifested his continuing political existence. It was one of the forty or so groupuscules at the origin of the *Convention des Institutions Républicaines* in 1964 (CIR), Mitterrand's main political vehicle in the early years of the Fifth Republic (see Chapter 5 for further detail).[9] From its first meeting in 1964, the CIR attracted the loyalties of a small number of dedicated activists: they were fiercely anti-Gaullist, but alienated by the existing parties of the left, the PCF, the SFIO and the Radicals. The genealogy of most of the clubs within the CIR could be traced either to *mendèsisme* or to left-wing radicalism, the title of the Convention itself being a direct reference to the French revolution and to the imperatives of Republican defence. The CIR became a kind of mini-party whose major short-term objective was to promote Mitterrand, its most prominent member, as a candidate for the 1965 presidential election, with a longer-term view of building a new dynamic party to supersede the old SFIO.

The 1965 presidential election was a fundamental landmark both in the history of the Fifth Republic and in the evolution of Mitterrand's career. In ordinary circumstances, Mitterrand would not have been the most obvious choice to lead a revived left-wing opposition to Gaullism. He was a member of neither the SFIO nor the PCF, the main left-wing parties. His left-wing credentials were seriously contested by some of the most dynamic elements of the 'second left'. The obvious figure was Mendès-France, the most inspirational premier of the Fourth Republic. And yet, if Mendès-France was as outspoken as Mitterrand in his condemnation of the Fifth Republic, he refused even to participate in what he considered an illegitimate regime.[10] This ruled out Mendès. The next pretender to be de Gaulle's main challenger was Gaston Defferre. An SFIO moderniser, Defferre was the first Socialist personality to attempt to harness the new presidential election to a realignment and modernisation of the French party system. Defferre declared his intention of standing as a candidate against de Gaulle in September 1963 after pressure from the journal *L'Express*, which had named a Mr X (which it soon transpired was Defferre) as the ideal candidate to run against the General in 1965. Defferre's bid failed for two principal reasons. First, he made his presidential candidacy conditional on the creation of a large federation composed of the SFIO, the Christian-Democratic MRP, the Radical party and the political clubs. This ambitious catch-all initiative was almost certainly premature: it sparked the animosity not just of the Communist party (against whom it was principally aimed), but also of the SFIO leader Mollet, threatened by the creation of a new confederation outside his control. On a formal level, talks between the parties foundered on whether the word Socialist should appear in the title of the Federation and on the issue of reform of the church schools, upon which the SFIO could not agree with the MRP. Second, both Mollet and the PCF leader Waldeck-Rochet were determined to sabotage Defferre's centre–left initiative, which clearly threatened both established party leaderships. Realising the insuperable obstacles he faced, Defferre withdrew his candidacy in September 1965.[11]

Mitterrand became de Gaulle's principal challenger almost by default. After the failure of Defferre's bid the idea of Mitterrand's candidacy was accepted with some relief by the main parties of the Left, the PCF and the SFIO. These parties supported Mitterrand partly because they were afraid to put up candidates themselves, for fear that their score in the presidential contest against the legendary de Gaulle would be inferior to that which they could expect to obtain in parliamentary elections (where they could rely on well-tested organisations and deputies with proven grass-roots support). And yet the Left had to have a candidate. That Mitterrand was acceptable to both Communists and Socialists reflected his position as a political outsider, a member of neither of the main left-wing parties. In fact, neither the PCF nor the SFIO leadership considered that Mitterrand could possibly represent a threat to their position. The idea that an isolated individual such as Mitterrand could take over as the effective leader of the Left, when his political base was limited to a motley gathering of political clubs, was absurd. And yet this was essentially what happened. It was a testament to the impact of the new presidential institutions on the party system, and the advanced state of decay of several of the old parties.

Mitterrand based his candidacy upon the fact that he represented a symbol of Republican opposition to the Gaullist regime, a symbol around which all progressive Republicans could unite. Mitterrand's 1965 programme was couched in terms of Democratic and Republican principles, rather than the Socialist message characteristic of certain later appeals. Republican opposition to Gaullism compelled the cooperation of the parties of the Left. There could be no centrist or conservative alternative to de Gaulle, of the type Gaston Defferre had attempted to promote. The centrepiece of Mitterrand's 1965 campaign strategy was the support of the PCF. Mitterrand's cultivation of

Communist support represented an astute political move after the setback of Defferre's centre–left alternative. For Mitterrand, the only feasible opposition to de Gaulle was one which included the Communists, who were anxious to reinsert themselves into the political mainstream after two decades of cold war isolation. It was a measure of Mitterrand's political skill that he recognised this. The 1965 presidential election helped associate him in the public mind with the pursuit of a definite political strategy (the union of the Left), to which Mitterrand remained faithful until his election as president. Mitterrand's 45 per cent in the second round against de Gaulle was an honourable performance, which exceeded most media predictions.

On a personal level, Mitterrand's decision to stand as a presidential candidate in 1965 was a courageous one, which could have disastrously backfired. It is, perhaps, pertinent to consider what the alternative scenario might have been for Mitterrand had he not been a candidate in 1965. His career would almost certainly have stagnated, although someone else probably would have emerged eventually to perform a similar role (i.e. uniting the dispersed forces of the Left behind a common presidential candidate). By the same reasoning, the fact that he did stand as the united left's first presidential candidate, and that he performed credibly probably ensured his political future, especially after the alternative centre–left strategy advocated by Defferre had been tried and failed in 1969. From 1965 onwards Mitterrand was able, convincingly for the most part, to present himself as the only plausible presidential alternative to the right-wing coalition, and as the natural exponent of the united left strategy.

Mitterrand built upon the presidential stature he acquired during the 1965 campaign to impose his political leadership upon the Left. His 1965 presidential candidacy was the stimulus for an important step towards a realignment of the party system. The major forces of the non-Communist left (CIR, SFIO, Radicals, and various other political clubs) joined together in September 1965 to form the Federation of the Democratic and Socialist Left (FGDS), the 'small federation' that backed Mitterrand's candidacy.[12] The FGDS was the precursor to the new PS created in 1971. Shortly after the 1965 election, the implications of presidentialism as a new organising principle became clearer: Mitterrand, the presidential leader of the Left, dominated the FGDS throughout its existence (1965–68), rather than Mollet, the leader of the SFIO, which was the most powerful organisation within the federation when measured by its deputies and party members.

There was an underlying consistency in Mitterrand's approach after 1962. It involved a dual objective. The first was to unify the disparate forces of the non-Communist left within a single organisation under his leadership. Second, Mitterrand sought to tie the PCF into a binding alliance in order to diminish its influence. The FGDS represented the first serious attempt to unify the centrifugal forces of the non-Communist Left within a single organisation. As President of the Federation, Mitterrand displayed considerable political skill, called upon to perform a delicate balancing act between parties, and intra-party factions with opposed political standpoints. These ranged from the anti-Communist, anti-Fifth Republican elements surrounding Mollet,the SFIO leader, through to the strongly pro-*unitaire* and pro-Mitterrand clubs within the CIR and, most difficult of all to classify, to the embryonic 'second left'. The 'second left' was still at this stage embodied by Pierre Mendès-France, but was later to become associated with Michel Rocard. The rivalry between Mitterrand and Mendès-France was such that the latter consistently refused to join the Federation, believing the FGDS to be above all a crude exercise in electoralism.[13] Ultimately the FGDSproved too fragile to survive the strain of its internecine pressures, broughtto a head by the events of May 1968, and the crisis of confidence in Mitterrand's leadership that ensued.

The second facet of Mitterrand's control of the FGDS stemmed from his status as de facto leader of the united left after 1965: Mitterrand took the decision to negotiate a formal electoral alliance with the PCF. This took the form of a nationwide electoral pact for the 1967 legislative elections, and the publication of a Common platform in February 1968. The function of this platform was to outline common points of agreement and discord, rather than to accept a tightly binding legislative programme, the price demanded by the Communists for a lasting alliance.[14] The consistency with which Mitterrand pursued the strategy of closer electoral cooperation with the Communists belies some portrayals of him as narrowly opportunistic: rather, there was a tenacity to stick to a defined strategy, a trait which marked Mitterrand apart, for instance, from Mollet.

May 1968 If the impressive gains made by the FGDS in the 1967 legislative election consolidated Mitterrand's leadership, the events of May–June 1968 very nearly ruined his political career. During the month of May 1968, France engaged in one of its periodic bouts of revolutionary nostalgia, when students and workers celebrated a decade of Gaullism by bringing the country to a standstill and threatening the future survival of the political regime itself. The demands articulated by the students went far beyond those of the traditional left-wing parties such as the FGDS, and PCF. The FGDS in particular performed a minor role during the May movement, with its leaders appearing irrelevant and archaic in the eyes of the student leaders. According to Daniel Cohn-Bendit, 'M. Mitterrand is not an ally, although he might possibly be useful for us'.[15]

There were profound reasons for Mitterrand's mistrust of the student movement. As a longstanding parliamentarian, Mitterrand instinctively distrusted 'autonomous' popular movements such as those of May 1968, which he feared open to manipulation by extremists. His reaction to May 1968 was indicative of a certain style of political action, centred on capturing the state through winning elections, rather than encouraging popular movements. This was the real politics that Mitterrand understood. Since 1958, Mitterrand had elevated himself into de Gaulle's principal adversary, by adopting a strategy squarely centred upon conquest of the central state. For this reason, he formed an integral part of the 'system' abhorred by the students. The political programme espoused by Mitterrand was that of the traditional statist Left. Yet the authority of the state, upon which Mitterrand placed such importance, was arguably the antithesis of the May movement.

Mitterrand was also a provincial notable, conscious of the likely negative reaction in the provinces to any durable outbreak of Parisian disorder. His speeches throughout May 1968 were centred around the theme of a lack of government authority and the vacuum of power, rather than the demands articulated by the students. As an old-style Republican himself (and a former interior minister), he viewed with genuine dismay the outbreak of mass disorder, especially when control of the movement escaped the parties of the traditional Left. The only established politician to enjoy any credit among the students was Mendès-France, who, unlike Mitterrand, had stubbornly refused to have anything to do with the Gaullist Republic.[16] Mitterrand's old sentiment of jealousy towards Mendès emerged again to cloud further his political judgement.

When Mitterrand did eventually intervene, it was probably already too late. On 24 May, de Gaulle strove to reassert his authority by proposing a referendum on 'participation', a theme close to the General's heart, but risible for the students. This unwise manoeuvre was immediately denounced as a plebiscite by Mendès-France, Mitterrand and the leaders of the student movement. De Gaulle's action apparently opened a window of opportunity for Mitterrand: the referendum could be portrayed as a classic electoral battle between Left and Right. Mitterrand's crucial intervention came on 28 May. On that day, he held a press conference at which he called for the government to resign after its inevitable defeat in the proposed referendum and to be replaced by a ten-man caretaker administration, presided over by Mendès-France. This government would prepare new legislative and presidential elections. He proposed himself as a future presidential candidate, and Mendès-France as his Prime Minister.[17] Mitterrand's press conference represented an attempt to recover the initiative for the traditional forces of the Left. And yet it satisfied nobody. It was portrayed by the *gauchistes* as pure opportunism. It was eagerly latched upon by the Gaullists to portray Mitterrand as a subverter of the Republic, precisely the charge he had laid against the General ten years earlier. It appeared as a flagrant attempt on Mitterrand's part to exploit the prestige enjoyed by Mendès-France among the students for his own benefit. Mitterrand's ill-fated initiative provided the excuse de Gaulle needed to recover control of the situation. On 30 May, the General confirmed Pompidou in his post as Premier, and dissolved the National Assembly. This was immediately followed by a vast pro-Gaullist demonstration on the Champs Elysées, and an overwhelming Gaullist victory in the legislative election of June 1968.

Mitterrand's intervention has been judged harshly in almost all accounts. There is little doubt that he did not understand the youth culture motivating the demands of the students. And yet, the type of leadership required by the political situation was extremely delicate. In truth, it surpassed Mitterrand's normal experience. As a responsible leader of the opposition, Mitterrand had little alternative except to distance himself from the violence surrounding the students' activities. He also had a duty to oppose the Gaullist regime. This delicate balance led him to adopt the course he did. There did seem to be a real vacuum of power. As the leader of the opposition, he had to do something. Mitterrand was anxious to restore the authority of the state, and to resume with politics as normal. Of course, when the opportunity presented itself, he relished the prospect of revenge upon de Gaulle, the objective of his past ten years of political action. Paradoxically, the effect of Mitterrand's actions was the reverse of his desired objective: in spite of his repeated calls for a restoration of state authority throughout the crisis, he appeared to many as an apprentice dictator urging a *coup d'état* against the legitimate government. Mitterrand was to become a scapegoat for the Left's failure in May–June 1968, and in the opinion of many former colleagues he had only himself to blame.

The failure of Mitterrand's call for a provisional government led to fierce recriminations within the FGDS. The Federation remained intact for the legislative elections of June 1968, fought in a desperate damage limitation alliance with the Communists; but it fell apart shortly afterwards, the *coup de grâce* being provided by the Soviet invasion of Czechoslovakia in August 1968, following which the Radicals withdrew. In spite of continuing loyalty from the *conventionnels*, Mitterrand resigned as President of the Federation in November 1968. Mollet's SFIO, in conjunction with several small political clubs, then set about transforming what remained of the FGDS into a new political party.[18]

May 1968–June 1971   There followed a second Fifth Republican period of crossing the desert. The widespread distrust of Mitterrand touched Mollet, Defferre and Mendès-France in equal measure.[19] This distrust of Mitterrand by former colleagues suggests that one aspect of Mitterrand's political persona was an inability to divest himself of the image of the perennial manoeuvrer, an image always ready to resurface in difficult situations. His ability to recover from seemingly hopeless situations was all the more remarkable for this. The image of the perennial manoeuvrer is certainly insufficient to understand Mitterrand, but it is inescapable, and might explain why even close colleagues reserved their trust. This enigmatic quality of Mitterrand was compounded by his secrecy, by his mistrust of others and by his aloofness (see Chapter 5). Those within the CIR (and elsewhere) who remained loyal to Mitterrand during this period would later be rewarded by positions of authority within the Socialist Party after 1971 and the Socialist governments after 1981.

The delayed reaction of the French nation to the demand for political change expressed in May 1968 occurred one year later, when a majority of French electors (53 per cent) had the audacity to vote No in de Gaulle's final referendum of April 1969, prompting the General's swift resignation and a precipitate presidential election. In early May, Mollet moved swiftly to prevent any recurrence of a Mitterrand candidacy by pledging the SFIO's support for Defferre, standing as a centre-left candidate without Communist support. The credibility of this 'third force' option in 1969 was diminished by the fact that Alain Poher, the popular centrist President of the Senate (and acting President of the Republic) had already announced his candidacy, and appeared better placed to appeal to non-Gaullist opinion than Defferre. Mollet swung the SFIO behind Defferre in order to bury any prospect of Mitterrand presenting his candidacy as a *fait accompli*.

In retrospect, Mitterrand's inability to repeat his united left candidacy of 1965 was a blessing in disguise. Had Mitterrand stood in 1969, he would almost certainly have been defeated, and, faced with a strong centrist challenge, he would not even have been certain of winning through to the second round. This would have proved a fatal setback to his political career. In the event, Mitterrand carefully avoided intervening in the 1969 presidential campaign, once he had made known his decision not to stand. Defferre's piteous performance discredited not only the 'third' force strategy upon which his candidacy was based, but also everybody who had been associated with it, not least Mendès-France (Defferre's running mate) and Mollet. Mitterrand was left as the only plausible presidential leader, and alliance with the PCF as the only realistic strategy.

The poor performance enregistered by Defferre in the 1969 election discredited the rebaptised *Parti Socialiste*, created without Mitterrand in May 1969 as a fusion of the SFIO and several small political clubs.[20] During the period from 1969 to 1971, Mitterand fell back upon the personal bastion represented by the *Convention des Institutions Républicanes*, while awaiting the eventual unification of the PS and CIR into a single organisation. Mitterrand himself launched the process leading to the creation of the new party by calling for the unity of all Socialists in November 1970, an offer which the existing PS leadership of Alain Savary could scarcely refuse. Mitterrand's uncommon capacity for recovery was confirmed in June 1971, when, after extensive manoeuvring, he captured control of the new party at the head of an audacious alliance.

MITTERRAND AS FIRST SECRETARY OF THE SOCIALIST PARTY, 1971–81

Mitterrand finally captured control of the Socialist Party (*Parti Socialiste*) at the Congress of Epinay in June 1971, a momentous event which reflected his status as de facto leader of the Left since the presidential election of 1965, and his gradual rehabilitation after the events of May–June 1968. Mitterrand captured the leadership of the PS at the head of a heteroclite alliance, which spanned the ideological spectrum of the new party: Mitterrand's CIR (Mermaz–Pontillon motion) allied itself with the modernising anti-Mollet wing of the old SFIO (Mauroy–Defferre), and the young turks of the left-wing CERES faction led by J-P. Chevenèment. Mitterrand obtained the narrowest of victories, placing in its proper perspective the notion forwarded by some commentators that the party rallied enthusiastically to Mitterrand as the obvious presidential candidate.[21] Mitterrand's tenure as First Secretary of the Socialist Party will be considered from several interrelated angles: factionalism, relations with the Communists, and the effects of presidentialism.[22] Other features of the PS revival in the 1970s are considered in Chapter 6.

The resurrection of the PS during the 1970s was linked to its accommodation of a variety of pre-existing political groups who fused into a single party: SFIO, CIR, UGCS, UCRG, PSU. The party was thus created as the result of a process of *fusion*; as with other such parties, the existence of factions reflected in part the continuing reference point provided by separate historical origins.[23] More generally, promotion within the party hierarchy was dependent upon support for one of the party's factions. Indeed, this was arguably encouraged by PS statutes adopted at the Epinay congress, which introduced a system of proportional representation for election to the party's governing organs. It has been contended that this provided a stimulus for competing factions to present texts (*motions*) to Socialist congresses.

During the decade of renewal (1971–81), the Socialist Party was composed of four main intra-party groupings, as well as numerous smaller currents. Mitterrand's supporters were by far the most ideologically heteroclite group within the party, ranging from the neo-Marxists such as P. Joxe, to social-Christians such as J. Delors, and the whole range of party positions in between. Association with Mitterrand proved to be a fruitful course for aspiring politicians, since as party leader Mitterrand disposed of more patronage than any other PS politician. His promotion during the 1970s of a new party elite specifically beholden to *his* leadership helped to forge the PS into a party which was more than the sum of its component parts. It also enhanced Mitterrand's control over the party. This new elite controlled the party after the Metz congress in 1979, and provided the core of Mitterrand's most dedicated supporters during the 1980s. Apart from the *mitterrandistes*, the PS contained three other recognisable groups. The CERES group, led by Chevènement, most closely approximated to a tightly organised and highly ideological left-wing faction. The group led by Rocard, who joined the PS in 1974, represented a curious synthesis of May 1968-inspired new-left ideals and *mendèsiste* economic prudence. Finally, the group led by Pierre Mauroy represented the political and organisational interests of the old SFIO within the new party.

From its inception, Mitterrand was able to occupy the centre of gravity of the new Socialist Party. As party leader, he laid a claim to represent the *juste milieu*, the party's natural governing equilibrium, threatened alternatively by the irresponsibility of the party's left (the CERES faction), or the ideological 'revisionism' of the party's modernist right (Michel Rocard). In 1975, Mitterrand allied with Rocard, as an excuse to expel the left-wing CERES faction from the leadership. Four years later, in 1979, a reverse process occurred, with Mitterrand turning to CERES in order to eject Rocard from the leadership. This carefully cultivated pivotal position made it extremely difficult for party rivals to challenge Mitterrand's suzerainty over the PS. Michel Rocard discovered this to his cost in 1978–80 (see p. 31). The skill with which Mitterrand played off PS factions against each other during the 1971–81 period was undoubtedly a condition of his own political survival. It enabled him to consolidate his initially fragile control over the party, and to promote a new PS elite, which looked to Mitterrand as the fount of all legitimacy. But it also built up considerable resentment among wounded party rivals (such as Rocard, Chevènement, Savary and many others). These would not be forgotten.

Under Mitterrand's leadership, the Socialist Party declared its commitment to the Union of the Left (alliance with the Communists), consecrated by the signing of the common programme of government with the PCF in June 1972. The common programme was the culmination of Mitterrand's strategy of alliance with the Communists, consistently advocated since the 1965 presidential election. It committed the PS to far more wide-ranging reforms than it had ever previously envisaged, including wide-scale nationalisations, important structural reforms, redistributive economic and fiscal measures (such as the wealth tax) and increases in welfare benefits and the minimum wage. Undoubtedly, for reasons of political strategy, Mitterrand accepted a far more detailed, radical programme of reform than he would ideally have liked. His goal in signing the common programme was expressed in a speech to the Socialist International only days after the programme had been signed:

> Our fundamental objective is to rebuild a great Socialist Party on the ground occupied by the PCF itself. We intend to demonstrate that, of five million Communist voters, three million will feel themselves able to vote Socialist.[24]

Mitterrand calculated that once the parties of the Left presented a coherent alternative, they would recover support within the electorate; moreover, electors would prefer the image-conscious, more moderate Socialists to the archaic *ouvriériste* Communists. The strengthening of the Socialists was thereby a condition for the victory of the Left as a whole. For as long as the PCF remained the dominant left-wing party, a status it enjoyed from 1945 to c. 1974, the Left would be condemned to permanent opposition.

If commentators questioned Mitterrand's philosophical sincerity, few cast any doubts upon his strategic choice in favour of the alliance with the PCF. He remained faithful to this strategy of left-wing unity at least until 1981, when he invited four Communist ministers to join Pierre Mauroy's second government. And yet, from 1972 onwards, Mitterrand treated the common programme more as a presidential platform, open to perpetual reinterpretation, than as a binding manifesto. He probably always judged that as a future left-wing presidential candidate he would be able to free himself from too many programmatic constraints. This occurred in the 1974 presidential election, when he was once again the United Left's candidate. Mitterrand's anodyne presidential platform watered down the radical commitments of the common programme and replaced them with a series of vague policy preferences. He argued that as the common programme was a parliamentary manifesto, it did not concern a candidate in a presidential election. In addition, Mitterrand's 1974 campaign largely bypassed the official PS and PCF party organisations, with the candidate relying instead on a network of presidential support committees.[25] The presidential logic of the Fifth Republic's political system, which forced serious candidates to stand 'above' party in order to develop a broad appeal for the second ballot, thus prevailed. Mitterrand eventually ran a close second to Valéry Giscard d'Estaing on the second ballot of the 1974 presidential election (49.3 per cent against 50.7 per cent). The impetus provided by the presidential election, by the idea that a united left dominated by the Socialists offered a coherent alternative, and by far-reaching changes in French society consolidated PS leadership of the Left after 1974 at the PCF's expense.

The PCF immediately realised the inherent dangers in Mitterrand's 1974 performance: it threatened to alter the internal balance of power within the left-wing coalition in favour of the Socialists. After a series of manoeuvres from 1974 to 1977 aimed at weakening the PS, the Communist Party finally broke off the alliance with the PS in September 1977, on the pretext that the Socialists were unwilling to agree to proposed PCF 'improvements' of the programme. Mitterrand refused to give way to the PCF's maximalist demands (including an unprecedented increase in nationalisations), which would have ensured that the Left lost the next election anyway. The disunited left was duly defeated in the legislative election of March 1978, enhancing Mitterrand's reputation as a loser. In fact, this was a further blessing in disguise for Mitterrand, although it challenged the strategy of alliance with the PCF with which he had been associated since becoming PS leader in 1971. It seems clear that a disunited, economically incompetent left-wing government elected in 1978 would have ruined Mitterrand's chances of victory in the 1981 presidential election. When finally elected as President on his third attempt in 1981, Mitterrand owed his election at least in part to the fact that the Left was disunited, and that PCF leader Georges Marchais was himself a candidate. This made Mitterrand a more acceptable candidate to non-Socialist voters, since he had clearly illustrated his independence from the PCF.

Mitterrand's recovery from the setback of 1978 illustrated once again his extraordinary resilience in the face of adversity, as in 1958 or 1968. His skill in internal party politics was revealed during the period 1978–79 in particular, when he was faced with a strong challenge for the PS 1981 presidential nomination from Rocard, whom the opinion polls portrayed as the party's best candidate. Faced with Rocard's unwelcome challenge, Mitterrand moved swiftly and skilfully to portray his rival as being foreign to French Socialist traditions, the product of a 'Christian' conspiracy intent on taking over the PS (see Chapter 5). At the party's Metz congress in April 1979, Mitterrand defeated Rocard in a contest which determined who would obtain the 1981 PS nomination. Whereas, in 1975, Mitterrand had promoted Rocard as an alternative to CERES, in 1979 CERES was delighted to return the favour by allying with Mitterrand and relegating Rocard into the minority.

That he fended off a powerful challenge from Rocard was due, ultimately, to the belief among PS activists that, more than anyone else, Mitterrand had restored the fortunes of the Socialist Party and that he incarnated the past, present and future of French Socialism. His victorious election on 10 May 1981 as the first Socialist president in the Fifth Republic earned Mitterrand a prominent place in contemporary French history. In spite of his political origins in the Fourth Republic, Mitterrand situated his election in 1981 in a line of historical continuity with the great past Socialist heroes.

Chapter 3

François Mitterrand and the Left in power, 1981–93: an overview

By his own admission, François Mitterrand – a man of letters and philosophical reflection – was very much an economic novice prior to his election as president. His discomfort with economic issues had become apparent during the 1974 presidential election campaign, when the candidate of the united left appeared in an unfavourable light in a televised confrontation with Giscard d'Estaing. The more experienced candidate of 1981 (expertly advised) avoided earlier pitfalls by concentrating upon the economic record of Raymond Barre's governments. But he remained somewhat ill-at-ease in relation to economic dossiers, especially when they were presented as a limitation on political priorities. Mitterrand did not conceal his distrust for those such as Rocard who repeatedly stressed the economic constraints a left-wing government would inevitably face.[1]

Elected in 1981 when committed to a 'break with capitalism', Mitterrand was re-elected in 1988 preaching the imperatives of national unity and social consensus. In the intervening years French Socialism moved away from being the European exception into the mainstream of the European social-democratic tradition. President Mitterrand presided over more governments than any of his Fifth Republican predecessors. Swept to power in May 1981, almost certainly as a reaction against the incumbent, President Giscard d'Estaing, Mitterrand supported a radical programme of social and economic change presided over by his first Prime Minister, Pierre Mauroy, who headed a Socialist-led government with Communist ministers for the first time since 1947. Mauroy was replaced by Laurent Fabius in July 1984, at the head of an homogeneous Socialist government which the PCF refused to join. After the victory of the RPR–UDF coalition in the legislative election of March 1986, Jacques Chirac became Mitterrand's third Prime Minister, the first the President had been constrained to appoint. Re-elected for a second presidential term in May 1988, Mitterrand named his old Socialist Party rival Rocard to head a minority Socialist-led government. Rocard was replaced after three years in office by Edith Cresson in May 1991, France's first woman Prime Minister; Cresson survived for barely 11 months, to be replaced in turn by Pierre Bérégovoy in April 1992. Mitterrand's seventh and final Prime

Minister was Edouard Balladur, RPR premier during the second *cohabitation* from March 1993 to April 1995 (see Chapter 12).

In the present chapter we shall attempt to combine analysis of distinct chronological periods within the Mitterrand presidency with broad thematic undercurrents. It is hoped thereby to give an impression of the extent to which Mitterrand was forced to react to crucial core policy choices, especially during his first *septennat*, rather than being fully master of events. If there is a danger in underplaying elements of continuity, a periodisation does reveal the extraordinary adaptibility shown by Mitterrand, an adaptability which facilitated a progressive learning process, and which enabled his re-election in May 1988.

THE STATE OF GRACE, 1981–82

During the 1981 presidential election campaign, Mitterrand repeated that, with sufficient willpower, the Left would be able to carry out its radical programme and overcome the obstacles to reform represented by the economic constraints of the existing capitalist system. Mitterrand's position was contested vigorously by his great rival Rocard, who adopted a *mendèsiste* attitude that social change must be compatible with sound management of the economy. The former approach figured in Mitterrand's presidential platform, the *110 Propositions*. During the 'state of grace' (May 1981–June 1982), the reforms carried out by the Left stemmed directly from Mitterrand's *110 Propositions*. Mitterrand shared the belief, previously imposed upon Léon Blum in 1936, that after such a long absence from power it would have been politically impossible for the Left not to have gone ahead with an ambitious social and economic reform programme.

The measures enacted during the 'state of grace' comprised a classic left-wing programme, conceived predominantly in the mainstream centralising tradition of the French left: large sections of French industry and the entire banking system were nationalised; new powers were decentralised to the regions and local government; labour relations were reformed; important redistributive social and fiscal reforms were enacted (notably through increased welfare benefits, and the introduction of a wealth tax), and significant progress was effected in the field of civil rights. In fact, this was a model of socialism which – apart from the decentralisation legislation – reflected the enormous faith placed in the state as an agent of social transformation.[2]

The 1982 Nationalisation Act, the centre-piece of the Socialists' reform programme, proved a case in point. The 1982 law took into public ownership all large private banks, several of France's largest industrial groups, and a number of smaller concerns. The groups nationalised comprised Thomson, Compagnie Générale de l'Electricité, Rhône-Poulenc, Péchiney, Saint-Gobain, Usinor and Sacilor.[3] In the defence sector, the state took 51 per cent holdings in Matra and Dassault. The telecommunications firm CGCT was also nationalised. In all, thirty-six banks were taken into public ownership, as well as the financial companies Suez and Paribas. The result was that the public sector increased from about 8 per cent to about a quarter of French industrial capacity and 50 per cent of industrial investment, while the national-isation of the main banks left the state in control of virtually all credit.[4] This was *dirigisme* with a vengeance.[5] It has been contended that Mitterrand's faith in nationalisations was motivated by a curious synthesis of Marxism, republica-nism and catholicism, which equated the rule of money with alienation and exploitation.[6] Only the state could serve the general interest, which could not be entrusted to individual entrepreneurs, as postulated by the tenets of economic liberalism. The Mauroy government undertook the nationalisations exactly according to stated intentions: 100 per cent of the capital of all targeted companies and banks was nationalised by the state, including certain merchant banks within which the state already had a majority shareholding.[7] Mitterrand personally insisted on the need to acquire 100 per cent of capital, whereas 51 per cent would have been sufficient to assure control: this was the only means for Mitterrand of ensuring that private capital (with its infinite capacity for manoeuvre) did not recover control of the nationalised industries after a short interval. Mitterrand's insistence on 100 per cent also made the whole pro-gramme far more expensive and thus ensured that the scope for nationalisation was more limited than it needed to have been.

It was evident that nationalisation took place for moral and political as much as for economic criteria. This was illustrated with spectacular effect in relation to massively increased investment in the newly nationalised steel industry (a bastion of left-wing support), despite the fact that everywhere else in Europe investment was being reduced in this sector. Nationalisation was in part a means of keeping the Communists within the government. It was in addition vaunted for its *autogestionnaire* impact, including the introduction of labour representatives (one third of the total) on the boards of the nationalised industries. Most important, it was to be the tool for the Left's industrial policy: the idea prevailed that, with sufficient investment, no policy sector was unviable; that the Malthusian private sector was incapable of making long-term strategic investments, and that the new nationalised industries would spearhead industrial innovation. These justifications were somewhat confused and contradictory; arguments based on moral rectitude, economic efficiency, social equity and political necessity were interchanged with alarming facility. The idea of an interventionist industrial policy, which ultimately lay behind these reforms, required a massive injection of public expenditure before any positive results could be expected. The result was that this programme was enormously expensive and contributed to the severe financial crisis which faced the government after one year in office. A further reason why the programme was so expensive was the ruling of the Constitutional Council that the financial compensation initially proposed was inadequate.

It was clear that, upon achieving office, Mitterrand did not have a well-thought-out economic policy: the primacy of ideological and political considerations had ensured that the economy was largely overlooked. Once in government, the Left relied upon Keynesian-style reflationary policies based on increased popular consumption as the key to growth and for fighting unemployment. This reflationary economic policy contrasted starkly with the macroeconomic policies being pursued by France's principal trading partners. The Socialists' decision to reflate the French economy failed unambiguously. This was in part because the French Socialists decided upon a relaunch at a time when the world economy was moving into recession; worse, the hoped-for international upturn did not materialise. The economic relaunch had virtually no effect on unemployment (on an underlying upward curve), but had extremely damaging and negative effects in relation to a whole range of other economic indicators: especially inflation, the trade balance, and the budget deficit.[8] There *was* a substantial increase in short-term consumer spending, concentrated among the poorer sections of society whose incomes increased exponentially (boosted by social security reforms, and a raising of the minimum wage by 25 per cent). The Socialists had believed this would signal a new era of prosperity for French industry, but in fact it mainly boosted the economies of France's chief industrial rivals, especially that of West Germany. The trade and budget deficits exacerbated by these policies forced the Socialists into an embarrassing economic U-turn. By mid-1982, it had become clear that Socialist economic policies had failed: the old taunts that the Left was synonymous with economic profligacy reappeared.

There is little reason to doubt Mitterrand's personal commitment to the model of change outlined in the *110 Propositions*. The attempt at economic reflation and thoroughgoing social reform illustrated Mitterrand's belief in the ascendancy of the political over the economic, a belief strongly maintained until France was constrained to change course in 1982–83. Once elected President in 1981, all the evidence suggests that Mitterrand, with an imbued sense of history, was conscious of the fact that he symbolised the hopes of the left-wing electorate, and that he was unwilling to relinquish this mantle. Thus Mitterrand was initially reluctant to accept the need for a 'pause' in the reform programme, as demanded by his Finance Minister, Jacques Delors, since the notion of a 'pause' was redolent of the history of the Popular Front. Mitterrand was more insistent in this respect than Mauroy, a politician with a more convincing claim to the mantle of Léon Blum, but also with a more pertinent sense of economic realism.

THE U-TURN

Mitterrand initially resisted the introduction of a tighter, anti-inflationary economic policy, urged with increasing insistence by Jacques Delors, and later by Pierre Mauroy. Such a course of action became increasingly less tenable after the June 1982 G7 summit in Versailles, at which the Americans refused to lower interest rates in order to stimulate western economies. The Left's economic U-turn took place in two stages, in June 1982 and in March 1983, despite Mitterrand's early reservations. In June 1982, President Mitterrand finally succumbed to the pressure exerted by Mauroy and Delors and agreed to a temporary wage and price freeze, accompanied by a second devaluation of the franc (after an initial devaluation in October 1981 had failed to produce its desired effects). At this stage, neither Mitterrand nor Mauroy was willing to admit publicly that the Left had changed course. The crucial turning point in Mitterrand's first *septennat* occurred in March 1983, when the President was called upon to arbitrate between two opposing economic policies in a move which set the course for the rest of his presidency.[9] The choice lay between whether to remain within the European Monetary System (EMS), devalue the franc for the third time and accept a deflationary economic package (the choice adopted); or else to withdraw from the EMS, adopt protectionist measures for French industry and continue on the reflationary path traced since May 1981. After much hesitation and various indications to the contrary, Mitterrand chose the former course of action. He confirmed thereby that France could neither isolate itself through protectionism, nor indefinitely pursue radically different economic policies from those of its main trading partners, especially those within the EEC (and in particular the FRG, France's closest trading partner). The great paradox of the Socialist administration of 1981–86 was that, once they had failed to make what they perceived to be Socialist policies work, Mitterrand's governments proved reasonably competent at administering capitalism.[10] The economic record of the 1988–93 governments was even more laudable, especially viewed from a British perspective (see pp. 43–52). This was of great significance, since the Socialists gained considerably in terms of economic credibility: by the time they left office in 1986, Socialist ministers had become competent experienced administrators, respectable personalities to be entrusted with the burden of governing the country at some future date.

The hesitations surrounding Mitterrand's March 1983 decision were particularly indicative of his governing style (see Chapter 7). The crucial decision on economic policy was rendered more complicated because the President had simultaneously to decide whether a change of government and prime minister were needed, and, if so, what economic policy the government would be required to enact. It has been strongly argued that Mitterrand had decided against withdrawal from the EMS after three days, but that this decision was kept secret in order to pressurise the Germans into negotiating a favourable devaluation in order to keep France within the European Monetary System.[11] However tactically astute it might have appeared in retrospect, at the time Mitterrand's hesitations gave the impression that there existed a vacuum of power at the head of the French state. That Pierre Mauroy was re-confirmed as Mitterrand's prime minister on 25 March 1983, after ten days of an apparent interregnum, only served to confuse the issue further.

BETWEEN SOCIALISM AND LIBERALISM (MARCH 1983–MARCH 1986)

With a measure of hyperbole, Catherine Nay argues that, having abandoned the Left's mission of legislating a break with capitalism, Mitterrand became the new apostle of economic liberalism, imported from Reagan's America and from Thatcher's Britain.[12] Nay points to Mitterrand's personal crusade to lower taxes in 1984, to his belief that artificial financial aid for lame-duck industries should cease, to the new presidential discourse endorsing profit and success, and to a belief in the superior efficiency of the private sector to provide the evidence for this comparison. It is certainly worth retaining the fact that Mitterrand's commitment to lower taxes by 1 per cent of GNP in 1984, in conjunction with tough guidelines on reining in public expenditure, had a highly constraining effect on the economic freedom of manoeuvre of the government led by Pierre Mauroy.

But the comparison with Ronald Reagan owes more to flights of journalistic fantasy than to anything else. Despite certain superficial similarities there were limits to Mitterrand's liberalism, most notably in relation to the role of the state in economic policy. It is interesting, for example, that the state, in the form of the nationalised industries, played the lead role in the process of modernising the French economy under the premiership of Laurent Fabius. Rather than becoming the apostle of economic liberalism, Mitterrand attempted to refine his political philosophy as being based on the 'mixed economy', of the type the genuine economic liberals were attempting to dismantle in the USA and in the UK (see Chapter 5). But there was clearly a qualitative change in Mitterrand's presidential discourse after March 1983 as the new economic direction was consolidated. Initially rather hesitant, Mitterrand fully legitimised the new economic cause by repeated expressions of support in 1983–84.

His public speeches and actions from around late 1983 onwards would suggest that this transformation away from old-style socialism towards 'modernisation' was condoned by Mitterrand. In February 1984 the Council of Ministers announced a draconian 'industrial restructuring' plan, involving huge job losses in the nationalised steel, coal and automobile industries, and in the shipyards; this testified that the drive to modernisation preceded the advent of Fabius as prime minister, and lay firmly rooted in a presidential decision.[13] For as long as Mauroy was prime minister, however, the public had the impression that the Léon Blum variety of reformist socialism remained on the agenda. This was symbolised dramatically in 1983–84 by the church schools' crisis, which revived old anti-clerical/catholic tensions that many considered belonged to another age. The withdrawal of the Savary bill by Mitterrand in July 1984, after an unprecedented mobilisation of public opposition, appeared to signify the death knell of classical Socialist anti-clericalism, a political U-turn to complement the economic abandoning of

Keynesianism two years earlier.[14] It also led to the resignation of Savary, followed abruptly by that of Mauroy.

In July 1984, the old-style Socialist Pierre Mauroy was replaced with Laurent Fabius, at thirty-seven the youngest prime minister this century, a man carefully nurtured by Mitterrand since the early 1970s. Laurent Fabius was an undisputed *mitterrandiste* protégé: this repeated a pattern established under previous Presidents whereby the first prime minister was imposed by the political circumstances of the presidential election, whereas the second reflected a personal presidential preference. He was also regarded as a technocrat, a product of the elitist *École Nationale d'Administration*. Fabius headed an homogeneous Socialist government bereft of Communist ministers. Analysis of the Fabius government between 1984 and 1986 reveals that the key theme underpinning the administration was that of 'modernisation', which was interpreted by some as a euphemism for the Left abandoning its left-oriented reformist programme of 1981–82. Once Fabius had become prime minister, his full-scale modernisation programme certainly consolidated the transformation away from old-style socialism in France. In a whole range of policy areas, the Left's sacred cows were quietly called into question in the name of economic efficiency: this occurred notably in relation to economic planning, welfare policy, employment policy, attitude towards the private sector, fiscal policy, and industrial policy.[15] Illustrations of the spirit of modernisation were legion during the period 1983–86. Examples included: the refusal to provide state financial assistance for 'lame-duck' industries; a determination to modernise outdated industrial capacity (notably in the steel, mining, automobile and shipbuilding industries); the rehabilitation of the notion of profit, symbolised by the reform of the Paris Bourse and tax cuts; and the weakening of already feeble corporatist demand management techniques.[16] Above all, Finance Ministers Delors and Bérégovoy were determined to pursue a tough anti-inflationary policy, and, if necessary, to allow unemployment to rise to unprecedented levels (as it did, from 8 per cent in 1981 to 11 per cent in 1986). These moves often started under Mauroy, but they culminated during the Fabius premiership, who unflinchingly claimed the credit for them. They were often overdue measures which demanded undoubted political courage.

This conversion to the ambiguous notion of modernisation was un-ambiguously revealed in the case of the nationalised industries. During the period 1983–86 the Socialists introduced the policy known as the *respiration du secteur publique*, the dilution of state control over the industries national-ised two years earlier, in a bid to make them as efficient as possible. The loosening of state control took two forms: the sale of wholly-owned sub-sidiairies to the private sector (usually to foreign multinationals); and the opening of up to 25 per cent of the capital of various nationalised firms to the private sector in the form of non-voting shares *(titres participatifs)*. Both measures were justified by the need for these firms to raise finance, in the light of new budgetary strictures imposed upon them; they could be portrayed as elements of partial privatisation. One of the leitmotifs of nationalisation had been the defence of the national patrimony; it is somewhat ironic, then, that nationalised firms such as Péchiney were able to sell off subsidiaries, when a similar course of action had been vetoed by the Barre government when these companies were in the private sector.[17] From 1983–84 onwards, the nationalised industries were given orders that economic criteria were henceforth the only ones that counted. As a counterpart, government ministers were entreated not to interfere too closely with the administration of the nationalised industries, but to allow their management sufficient autonomy to achieve strict financial targets.[18] Nationalisation led, paradoxically, to a degree of ruthless industrial restructuring in sectors such as coal or steel, which would have been unlikely if these industries had been in the private sector. The notion of a coordinated industrial policy was quietly abandoned, although certain vestiges remained (notably in relation to dynamic sectors such as telecommunications and defence-related industries). The financial success of the new direction was confirmed by a Senate Finance Commission report of 1986, which affirmed that: 'four out of seven industries nationalised in 1982 are in a state of financial equilibrium, whereas only one (the CGE) had been in 1982'.[19] Nationalisation enabled French industry to modernise and restructure in a blunt, indeed brutal manner. The success of the 1982 nationalisation programme was confirmed by the popularity of these firms when privatised by the 1986–88 government of Jacques Chirac.

During this period, Mitterrand was frequently to be heard justifying the policy-options of his ambitious young prime minister. The disagreements that did occur between Mitterrand and Fabius were over the latter's over-arching ambition, caustically dampened by Mitterrand, rather than over the content of government policy. Mitterrand allowed Fabius to proceed with his programme of modernisation, and to prepare the PS for the 1986 legislative election. While retaining his capacity to intervene in any sphere of governmental activity if necessary, during the Fabius administration Mitterrand's attention was increasingly preoccupied by foreign policy and (especially) European affairs. The French President was one of the uncontested architects of the Single European Act, agreed at the Luxembourg summit of December 1985 (see Chapter 8). In fact, in the aftermath of March 1983, Mitterrand turned to the construction of Europe as a surrogate sphere of presidential activism. By turning to external affairs after internal politics had proved distasteful, Mitterrand was engaging in a practice widespread among presidents and prime ministers everwhere.

Relations between Mitterrand and Fabius were soured by the *Rainbow Warrior* affair of 1985. The sinking of a Greenpeace vessel in Wellington harbour by French secret service agents caused an international diplomatic uproar, and a domestic political storm. The chief politician held responsible was the Defence Minister, Charles Hernu, one of Mitterrand's closest political allies since the early Fifth Republic. Under pressure from Fabius, Hernu was eventually forced to resign. As Commander-in-Chief of the armed forces, and as guarantor of the reserved presidential sector, however, Mitterrand was not exempt from public criticism. The President was accused either of sacrificing his defence minister in an act of *realpolitik*; or else of being unaware of, or unable to control the activities of the secret services. The furore gradually died down once the New Zealand government had charged three French agents with acts of sabotage, only to re-emerge during the Chirac premiership. As with the other affairs surveyed, the secretive nature of executive power in France, and the weak means at the disposal of official enquiries meant that the truth was probably impenetrable. The issues raised were, however, of paramount importance. They involved first the impunity of the French secret services, and the loss of effective political control over their activities, and second the blurred lines of political responsibility within the Fifth Republican executive: government critics could legitimately accuse the Defence Minister (the minister directly responsible), the Prime Minister (officially charged with coordinating government policy) and the President (the ultimate power-broker in the sphere of defence policy). Whatever Hernu's responsibility, Mitterrand resented having to sacrifice his trusted Defence Minister, and blamed Fabius for a lack of effective coordination of government policy.

The Rainbow Warrior affair weakened Mitterrand in several respects. The President lost his Defence Minister, Hernu. The record of his second premier Fabius was damaged, something from which he never really recovered. The affair also complicated French relations with the countries of the South Pacific region. Mitterrand's refusal personally to intervene in the Greenpeace affair stemmed in part from his status as head of state: somewhat like the Queen of England, the French President considered himself above having to respond to accusations made by the mass media. The presidency had at all costs to be protected, even at the expense of diminishing the prestige of the Prime Minister and the defence minister. Mitterrand thus revealed himself to be consistent with the constitutional practice of the Fifth Republic, whereby the safeguard of the presidency had to prevail over all other considerations.

Through the evolution of his political attitudes and discourse from 1981–86, François Mitterrand symbolised the transformation away from a curious Gallic model of socialism, to a cautious social reformism bent on modernising the French economy and society. As the chief executive, Mitterrand must take the credit (or blame) for reconciling the Left with the economy, and the Socialist Party with its reformist fate. Whether this transformation was consciously willed by Mitterrand or not is another matter. The above analysis would suggest that Mitterrand reacted to events, rather than foreseeing them clearly in advance, but then legitimised new directions by explicit endorsement. His key political virtue was that of adaptability, rather than that of unbending conviction. Given the intense pressures faced by his governments, this quality of adaptability served him well. His ability to comprehend the nature of the constraints facing his governments involved the Left sacrificing various of its sacred cows, but it also ensured that the Socialist Party gained governmental respectability and the credibility essential to play a key political role in the future. It facilitated Mitterrand's survival after March 1986 and his ultimate re-election in May 1988.

THE ARBITER-PRESIDENT OF *COHABITATION*, 1986–88

In the legislative elections of March 1986, the PS, the presidential party, was defeated at the hands of the right-wing RPR–UDF coalition. This inaugurated a constitutionally unprecedented period of *cohabitation* between a Socialist President and a right-wing parliamentary majority in the National Assembly. At one stroke, the political basis for the executive presidency – the existence of a parliamentary majority to back the President – was removed. The experience of *cohabitation* proved that presidential power in the Fifth Republic had owed at least as much to the cumulative practices of French Presidents, and to the legitimacy conferred by direct election, as it had to any strict reading of the 1958 constitution. By nominating Jacques Chirac, the head of the majority coalition in the National Assembly, as prime minister, Mitterrand appeared to create a new constitutional precedent in French politics: that the leader of the majority party or coalition had a right to be called upon to form a government.[20] This indispensable principle of most parliamentary regimes had never previously been applied as a matter of course in France's semi-presidential system. It provided an alternative prime ministerial model of executive leadership to that which had prevailed until 1986, when the premier's main source of legitimacy had stemmed from the fact that he had been named by the President, and could be sacked by him.

Although no one could deny Mitterrand's right to remain as president until the end of his seven-year mandate in 1988 (and he could not be forced to resign) the fact that the nation had voted unambiguously for the Right could not be ignored. By naming Chirac as prime minister (rather than experimenting with a non-partisan technocratic government) Mitterrand respected the eminently democratic logic that control of the government must be confided to the victors of the latest election.

From being the source of executive authority from 1981 to 1986, Mitterrand now declared himself to be an arbiter, the constitutional justification for which lay in Article 5 of the 1958 Constitution. He did not challenge the government's right to govern according to the 1958 Constitution, but attempted to redefine the presidential function to his advantage. Prime Minister Chirac's will prevailed largely unchallenged in most major areas of policy, except in the traditional presidential sector of foreign policy, defence and European affairs, where there was a struggle for influence (see Chapter 8). Although initially frustrated by his limited ability to influence government policy, Mitterrand was sufficiently astute politically to realise that any partisan interference in government policy would be counterproductive. Moreover, with the 1958 Constitution for once being applied to the letter, it was accepted by most commentators that Mitterrand did not possess the constitutional prerogatives to frustrate the course of governmental policy. This was illustrated in relation to the Chirac government's privatisation programme: on 14 July 1986, Mitterrand refused to countersign the decrees issued by Chirac inaugurating the government's privatisation programme; in so doing, the President was well within his constitutional powers. The government responded by reintroducing the bill into the National Assembly, and using the restrictive article 49, clause 3 of the 1958 Constitution to ensure its speedy passage through parliament. Once it had been formally enacted as a parliamentary Act (rather than a government decree), Mitterrand was powerless to prevent its implementation. A similar pattern was repeated across a range of policies which, in his role as presidential arbiter, Mitterrand declared to be unworthy for the nation.

From the outset, Mitterrand positioned himself as *Président de tous les Français*, the arbiter-president above the political fray, and he claimed to speak in the name of the French people when he condemned particular policies as being against the national interest. His primary objective in stressing his role as president of all the French was to promote consensus across the left–right boundary, in an attempt to efface the electorate's memory of the Left's unpopularity from 1982–86, and to promote a new image for himself as a wise, just and kindly but firm president, a figure above the humdrum of daily politics. The successful exploitation of this new image was a precondition for Mitterrand to be able to rehabilitate himself in public opinion. It was a task he performed with consummate skill. Indeed, Mitterrand was careful to intervene only in those areas in which he could attract the support of a majority of the population: this occurred either by refusing to sign government decrees (for example, on privatisations, employment policy, or electoral reform); or by making public his reservations about government policies (the Nationality Act, or the abortive Devaquet university reforms, which sparked off the mass student demonstrations of November–December 1986). When Mitterrand criticised government policies, he was careful not to refer to the divisive idea of socialism, but to consensual notions such as national independence, the Republic and pluralism.

To some extent, Mitterrand's attempt to portray a new ecumenical image as president of all the French could be reduced to political manoeuvring (the attempt to attract centre–right voters alienated by Chirac's confrontational style). But it appeared also to reflect a personal conclusion reached after the Left's years in power, that the great problems facing France could not merely be reduced to the perennial combat between Left and Right. Part of his restored popular credibility throughout the course of 1987–88 came from the centre–right, which conferred a new source of legitimacy onto the presidency as a bipartisan institution representing the superior interests of the French nation and people, above those of particular factions, parties or even governments. The dispersion of such a positive political image was of considerable benefit to the incumbent President.

As the 1988 presidential campaign approached, the image of the arbiter-president was supplemented by that of *Tonton Mitterrand* (Uncle Mitterrand), in whose hands France was secure. In reality, *Tonton* was a misnomer; the real image was that of the father of the nation whose primary objective was to promote national consensus and reconciliation. A number of precedents in twentieth-century French history (Clemenceau, Pétain, de Gaulle) suggested that the father-figure met with success when a generalised feeling of powerlessness, insecurity and antipathy towards politicians prevailed among a significant proportion of French people. Although the comparison with his forebears must not be exaggerated, it was striking how the development of Mitterrand's personality cult in 1986–88 took place in the context of an increasing distrust of politicians, and a high degree of pessimism in relation to the future of the nation. Mitterrand's convincing second-ballot victory against Chirac (54/46) confirmed the remarkable transformation in his political fortunes brought about by *cohabitation* and illustrated once again his capacity to bounce back from seemingly irretrievable situations.[21]

MITTERRAND'S SECOND TERM, 1988–93

Despite having fought the 1988 presidential campaign upon the theme of an 'opening to the centre', Mitterrand dissolved the Assembly elected in 1986 some five days after his re-election (as he had done in 1981) and called upon the voters to return a Socialist majority. [22] Mitterrand thereby reaffirmed, to all extents and purposes, the presidential practice of the Fifth Republic, temporarily suspended during the 1986–88 *cohabitation*. Dissolution of the National Assembly and the call for a pro-presidential majority were hardly designed to reassure the centre-right CDS, whom premier Rocard had tried unsuccessfully to rally to support the government. The public impression, at least, was that Mitterrand had reneged upon his campaign commitments to open up his majority to centrist participation; the familiar charge of duplicity was again widely levelled at the President. In the 1988 legislative elections, the PS emerged as the largest party, but without an overall majority. Mitterrand's triumvirate of prime ministers (Rocard, Cresson, and Bérégovoy), succeeding each other from 1988–93, headed minority Socialist-led governments, with the symbolic participation of several non-Socialist centrists and assorted 'personalities'.[23] These governments survived largely thanks to the difficulties of overthrowing governments in the Fifth Republican constitution of 1958: the 1988–93 experience illustrated that even minority governments could govern without undue parliamentary interference, in the absence of a committed parliamentary majority determined to overturn the government.[24]

Michel Rocard: the politics of consensus

Once Mitterrand was re-elected in May 1988, he named his old rival Rocard as premier; this choice was to some extent constrained, in that Mitterrand had fought the presidential campaign on the theme of a united France and ideological consensus, and that Rocard had consistently been the most popular Socialist politician, including among the non-Socialist electorate. Some commentators likened the Rocard premiership to that of a second *cohabitation*; the President was constrained to cohabit with a prime minister imposed upon him by political circumstances, and Rocard governed in a more autonomous manner than any other of Mitterrand's prime ministers apart from Chirac. In the light of their past divergences, the genuine surprise was that the Mitterrand–Rocard pair formed a generally efficient partnership for three years. In the 18 months following Mitterrand's re-election, the executive couple could point to high levels of popularity. Even after three years in office, Michel Rocard enjoyed respectable levels of public support: the real haemorrhage of support for Mitterrand followed upon his nomination of Mme Cresson as prime minister in May 1991. Rocard was one of the rare French politicians who left Matignon with his public reputation more or less intact.[25]

Rocard's premiership was conducted in a similar modernising vein to that of Fabius. This could best be characterised as unspectacular, cautious reformism, accompanied by a rigorous economic policy, with the latter taking increasing precedence over the former. Despite its cautious, rather conservative approach, Rocard's government had several major reforms to its credit when he left office in May 1991, as well as an honourable record in relation to management of the economy. The main reforms enacted during the Rocard government (May 1988–May 1991) included the reintroduction of a moderated wealth tax (suppressed by the 1986–88 government), the introduction of a guaranteed minimum income, the elaboration of a new statute for New Caledonia, a major investment in education, a reform of the legal profession, a move to a more egalitarian method of financing the social security system, and the modernisation of the public sector.[26] The net effect of these important but unspectacular measures was a reformist record second only to that of the Mauroy government.

In many respects, Rocard proved to be the President's tactical equal: he consistently referred to Mitterrand's 1988 *Letter to the French People* as a justification for governmental policy, and took extreme caution not to criticise Mitterrand. Indeed, in order not to contradict the President, Rocard 'made the absence of political theory or doctrine into a method of governing'.[27] Rocard's anxiety not to offend the President was intended to weaken the basis for presidential undermining of the prime minister, but this proved impossible. In addition to their difficult personal relations, the two rivals retained differing conceptions of political activity and of the desirable social agenda, to some extent reminiscent of the deeply embedded mistrust between the two cultures of the French left.[28] There was little doubt that Mitterrand resented criticisms that social inequalities had increased during his decade in power. Periodically, the President attempted to maintain an equilibrium between the claims of the government's natural supporters, and the disciplines imposed by the need for sound economic management.[29] This was in part a continuation of the presidential arbiter role, with the President standing above the fray of domestic politics, intervening only to recall the imperatives of social justice. But it was also in part a manoeuvre used by Mitterrand to ensure that governmental unpopularity reflected on Premier Rocard, rather than on himself. The manner in which Mitterrand sought to undermine the record of the Rocard government, notably by calling for a *nouvel élan* in 1990 and 1991, reflected poorly on his qualities of statesmanship, as well as undermining his own bases of political legitimacy, since public opinion tended to regard the Mitterrand–Rocard pair as a couple whose fortunes were linked.[30] And while Mitterrand and Rocard were old political sparring partners, there was no evidence that Rocard was anything other than loyal to Mitterrand while prime minister.

Quite apart from its reformist effort, Rocard's government could boast an honourable economic record. On most economic indicators, the Socialist governments led by Rocard, Cresson and Bérégovoy compared favourably with most others in Europe: throughout the period 1988–93, France had one of the lowest inflation rates in the European Community, combined (until the 1991–92 downturn) with steady growth, rising productivity, a strong exchange rate, a moderate budget deficit and a balance of trade surplus by 1992.[31] Only unemployment continued to be regarded as a clear policy failure. In the aftermath of the economic U-turn of March 1983, the German economy became the all-important benchmark against which French governments judged their performance. It was indicative of the economic conversion of the Socialists that Mitterrand was the prime mover behind the drive to a single currency at the Maastricht Summit (see Chapter 10); this indicated, among other factors, that the Socialists were confident that the French economy could meet the tough criteria for economic convergence before a single currency could be introduced.

As prime minister, Rocard adopted an overtly consensual style, consistent with his own pragmatic approach towards the resolution of conflicts. This style worked with dramatic results early on, notably with the apparent resolution of the conflict in New Caledonia. The Rocard government was capable of imaginative compromise in its search for government by consensus; major concessions were on occasion made to the opposition parties (especially the centrist UDC) in return for their support for government legislation.[32] More than a mere political necessity (given the government's lack of a majority), such compromise formed a part of Rocard's governing style, a permanent search for an elusive consensus. But it was, arguably, a style ill-adapted to the resolution of harsh disputes and hard political choices. In spite of its early successes, the three years of the Rocard government were marked by increasingly bitter disputes within French society: the government had to deal with an ongoing series of industrial disputes, concentrated largely among the government's own supporters, such as nurses, students, teachers and industrial workers, as well as predictable opposition from more traditional sources (notably farmers and the liberal professions). The undisputed success of Socialist economic policies created an expectation that economic rewards be redistributed among the government's natural constituency, yet the government was unwilling (or unable) to engage in clientelist politics of the 1981–82 variety. This led to the disaffection of many of the government's natural supporters, especially those likely to be affected by rising unemployment.

In spite of its creditable economic and international performance, Rocard's government was accused by critics of a crisis of confidence in its mission, leading many observers to question whether any coherent philosophy guided its actions. For left-wing critics (especially but not only within the Communist Party) the economic perspective appeared so dominant under Rocard that the Socialist government had lost its *raison d'être* and had become indistinguishable from those of the centre–right. Rocard's advisers effortlessly constructed a defence: the cautious reformism of Rocard's term in office was consistent with Mitterrand's *Letter to the French People*, which had invited a new compromise between Left and Right after a decade of ideological turbulence; criticisms of lacking an overriding purpose should be addressed to the President. Moreover, after a decade of heightened ideological divisions, French society needed an ideological pause which Rocard's government was admirably suited to deliver. This modest attitude towards the role of government was appreciated by public opinion: Rocard left office the most popular of Mitterrand's six prime ministers.

With the benefit of hindsight, the Péchiney scandal of 1989 must be considered as a milestone in Mitterrand's progressive discredit in public opinion. The details of this affair were obscure and murky. In late 1988, the state-run aluminium firm Péchiney launched a takeover bid for the US company American Can. Key figures close to the President and to the Finance Minister, Bérégovoy, were alleged to have profited from insider information of an imminent bid for the American firm, to have taken part in illicit share-dealing before knowledge of Péchiney's planned takeover was made public. The key figures incriminated included Alain Boulbil, formerly Mitterrand's industrial adviser at the Elysée, and then a key adviser to the Finance minister, Bérégovoy; as well as two close friends of the President, Patrice Pélat and Maurice Théret. All were accused of using insider information to obtain shares in American Can before knowledge of the bid was made public, shares which greatly appreciated in value once Péchiney had declared its intentions. Mitterrand's behaviour was not personally called into question, but there reigned the suspicion that men close to the President were abusing their positions of authority. The key themes involved were familiar: the apparent abuse of executive power; the implication of Socialist politicians in financial scandal, the irresponsibility of politicians close to the core of the executive, and the President's inability or unwillingness to control the activities of close advisers. Mitterrand's style of leadership, which placed great trust in personal relations maintained by the President with key personalities, was directly called into question. The Péchiney scandal was the first in a series of financial affairs during Mitterrand's second term that gravely compromised the Socialists' reputation for moral rectitude.

It was noticeable how, during the three years of Rocard's premiership, the public image portrayed by Mitterrand was that of an international and European statesman, preferring to occupy himself with the traditional presidential domain of European affairs, foreign policy and defence, rather than with the minutiae of domestic policy (see Chapter 9).[33] The height of Mitterrand's embodiment of French foreign policy occurred during the Gulf War, from which Rocard was largely excluded from influence. The extent to which Mitterrand concentrated on foreign affairs during his second mandate led to accusations that he had shown a total lack of interest in domestic politics (somewhat like George Bush in the US); it was in part to reassert his control over domestic policy that Mitterrand named Cresson as premier in May 1991.

Edith Cresson: the Iron Lady

The nomination of Edith Cresson as prime minister in May 1991 was portrayed by *Le Monde* journalist J-M. Colombani as Mitterrand's 'present to himself as a celebration of ten years of rule'; this observation gives some measure of the surprise which accompanied Cresson's nomination in political circles. There remains some uncertainty as to why Mitterrand replaced Rocard with Cresson. The most common explanation was that the nomination of a woman was a clever hand of political poker, destined to regenerate the flagging fortunes of the Socialist administration. More machiavellian interpretations have been propounded. In the opinion of one disabused Socialist deputy, not only did Mitterrand fulfil his desire to rid himself of a premier whom he personally disliked, but, by choosing Cresson, the President nominated someone who was Rocard's opposite, with the express intention of minimising the record of the 1988–91 government, and frustrating Rocard's future career. If such were indeed the motivation, Mitterrand's act revealed a liking for personal *règlements de comptes* which clouded his normally sound political judgement.[34] It has also been suggested that Mitterrand felt a touch of nostalgia for the early reformist period of his presidency, and aspired to recover the spirit (if not the substance) of the 'state of grace' by naming an interventionist premier.[35] Finally, it is plausible that Mitterrand aspired once again to intervene in the domestic political arena, by placing a faithful lieutenant at the helm of the French state (in contrast to Rocard). For these and other more unfathomable reasons (the personal whim theory), Mitterrand counted upon his fifth prime minister to restore Socialist fortunes prior to the 1993 National Assembly elections. In fact, the nomination of Cresson respected the model established in the first term, whereby the initial presidential choice of prime minister (Mauroy, Rocard) took into account the political circumstances surrounding the presidential election; whereas the second and fifth prime ministers (Fabius, Cresson) responded more openly to Mitterrand's personal preference.

Whatever Mitterrand's motivations were in nominating Cresson, it soon proved to be a serious misjudgement. The collapse of public support for the Prime Minister in the course of 1991 was dramatic: as measured by SOFRES, those who expressed their 'confidence' in Mme Cresson as premier diminished by minus 23 percentage points in the six months following her nomination. This beat all records of the Fifth Republic, including those established by Barre and Mauroy. By the time she left office in April 1992, the proportion expressing 'confidence' (SOFRES) with Cresson as prime minister had declined from 49 per cent to 22 per cent; while those expressing their 'satisfaction' with Cresson's performance (IFOP) had diminished from 25 per cent in June 1991 to 19 per cent.[36]

The fall from grace of Mme Cresson cast aspersions on Mitterrand's political judgement. Cresson had no experience of this level of office; indeed, she brought to the premiership a harsh streetfighter image hardly propitious for appealing to non-Socialist opinion in the run-up to the 1993 general election. There was little logic in Mitterrand's declaration that he had chosen Cresson 'in order to prepare France for the single European market of 1993', when the new premier was known for her firm views on industrial policy, which were arguably incompatible with the objectives of the single market. Moreover, the new premier was deprived of the means of influencing European policy, as well as the central thrust of economic and fiscal policy. By nature a state interventionist, Cresson was ill at ease with the neo-liberal economic orthodoxy strictly adhered to since 1983. Mitterrand made it clear that she was not to be allowed to get her way on industrial matters, and that the fiscal conservatism of Finance Minister Pierre Bérégovoy was to hold sway. Furthermore, Cresson had little control over the composition of her own government; she had to collaborate with heavyweights left over from the Rocard era, especially Bérégovoy whom she cordially detested. The overriding impression was that Cresson had been nominated by Mitterrand as a political gimmick, to provide convenient window dressing for closer presidential interventionism in domestic policy. This political ruse backfired badly, not least because Cresson was unwilling to be reduced to such a role. At the same time, Mme Cresson's inadequacies meant that Mitterrand had to take a more prominent role than he would probably have wished in defending both the policies being pursued, and the personal qualities of his Prime Minister.

Mme Cresson perhaps had an unfair press; she was, in fact, a highly activist prime minister who attempted to do her best with limited political resources. In selected areas of policy initiative – such as training policy, or aid to small businesses – the Cresson method (simple measures rapidly implemented, and explained in a direct manner) revealed itself to be efficient. There were, however, few concrete signs of policy success, owing to the short duration of her premiership. But from the moment of her nomination she gave proof of an abrasive style in stark contrast with the consensual approach of Michel Rocard, and without the popular mandate of Mrs Thatcher, with whom she was often compared. In addition, a series of unfortunate comments made at an early stage in her premiership probably did her irreparable damage. Within the space of three months, Mme Cresson likened the Japanese to a nation of ants (causing serious diplomatic and commercial damage to Franco-Japanese relations); proclaimed that half of all Anglo-Saxons were homosexuals, and advocated the use of charter flights to return illegal immigrants and failed asylum seekers to their countries of origin. Cresson's comments on immigration caused outrage among French anti-racist organisations, such as *SOS Racisme*, traditionally close to the Socialist government; they were so offensive precisely because they closely echoed the discourse on immigration employed by J-M. Le Pen, the leader of the *Front National*.[37]

Such ill-considered comments revealed a depth of political inexperience. The public perception of Cresson as intimately associated with the President's own political choices obviously reflected in a negative fashion upon Mitterrand himself: Mitterrand's popularity ratings descended from the Gulf War apogee of January 1991 to an unprecedented low twelve months later. The fact that Cresson was so associated with Mitterrand in the eyes of public opinion marked a contrast with the previous premiership of Michel Rocard: paradoxically, Rocard's high profile had shielded Mitterrand from unpopularity, since the President was less associated than the Prime Minister with fundamental domestic policy choices and continued to cultivate the image of an arbitral President. And yet it was impossible for Mitterrand to escape from the consequences of Cresson's unpopularity because the President was so obviously behind the change of government in the first place. The regional elections of March 1992 witnessed government unpopularity sink to unprecedented new depths, the Socialists being reduced to 18.3 per cent, barely ahead of the Ecologists or the *Front National*. The regional election result was an unambiguous public rebuttal of the Socialists, of Mitterrand, and of Edith Cresson, whose position proved untenable: in spite of her manifold displeasure, she was replaced by Mitterrand's sixth prime minister, Pierre Bérégovoy, on 2 April 1992.

Pierre Bérégovoy, or Antoine Pinay revisited

As with the Cresson administration, the short duration of the Bérégovoy premiership (11 months) rendered difficult any attempt to measure its impact. The key objectives outlined in Bérégovoy's inaugural speech on 8 April 1992 remained largely without effect in March 1993.[38] The politically hazardous commitment to reduce unemployment (especially the number of long-term unemployed) was negated by the announcement of three million unemployed only days after he left office in March 1993. The priority commitment to combat political corruption produced an innovative anti-corruption law, but appeared sadly incongruous with the Premier's own involvement in questionable financial operations. The pledge to combat insecurity lacked credibility for a government with an assured lifespan of less than twelve months. By contrast, the priority commitment to Europe respected the logic of Mitterrand's leading role in European affairs since the early 1980s. This objective was scrupulously pursued, although the key responsibility in this sphere was that of the President, rather than the Prime Minister. The personal involvement of President Mitterrand in the crucial policy choices in European policy was reaffirmed by the President's decision to call a referendum on ratification of the Maastricht treaty in September 1992 (see Chapter 10). The campaign for the Maastricht referendum witnessed a combative Mitterrand fighting a final political battle upon political ground he had himself selected: premier Bérégovoy was constrained to play a supporting role, but there existed virtually no difference between the two men in respect to European policy. The insistence with which premier Bérégovoy insisted on defending the franc against speculative attack in the run-up to the referendum had a clear European dimension, since defence of the ERM was an indispensable prelude to moves towards a single European currency envisaged in the Maastricht treaty.

The real significance of Pierre Bérégovoy was as a symbol for the evolution of the governmental Left since 1981. No one was more representative than Bérégovoy of the Left's transformation in government. As General Secretary of the Elysée staff in 1981–82, Bérégovoy symbolised the arrival of a new elite at the command of the state; the importance of the Socialist Party in the new institutional machinery, and the support for the Left's expansionist economic policy and ambitious nationalisation programme of 1981–82. His replacement as General Secretary of the Elysée by J-L. Bianco in 1982 signalled a return to a more classical conception of the Elysée staff (see Chapter 6). In March 1983, Bérégovoy was one of the leading upholders of *l'autre politique*, the call for France to withdraw from the EMS and to continue on the reflationary path traced since 1981. Yet it was as finance minister from 1984–86 and 1988–92 that Bérégovoy's legacy was the most pertinent.

As Finance Minister, Bérégovoy symbolised of the policy of the *Franc fort*, the determination to lead a tough monetary policy based on maintaining the existing franc–mark parity and refusing further devaluation, whatever the short-term cost in terms of social or economic consequences. This policy became known as one of competitive disinflation: through productivity gains and a historically low inflation rate, France would gain market share against her European neighbours with less productive records and higher levels of inflation. The complete prevalence of the economic, indeed monetarist, perspective under Bérégovoy made the Finance Minister far more popular in international financial circles than among PS deputies.[39] Bérégovoy's conversion to the cause of fiscal conservatism lends support to a bureaucratic power thesis: the Finance Minister was re-educated by monetarist civil servants in the Finance ministry to espouse the cause of sound money as the fundamental justification of governmental activity. The prolongation of these policies once Bérégovoy had become premier was a logical evolution: it was indicative in this respect that Premier Bérégovoy moderated his attacks on the opposition parties during the 1993 election campaign for fear of destabilising the franc.

Bérégovoy was also representative of the new relationship with industry, as well as the fascination exercised by leading industrialists upon Socialist ministers. The dynamism of captains of industry appealed to Bérégovoy. On a positive level, Bérégovoy's neo-liberal policy as Finance minister liberalised important aspects of the hitherto-protected French economy, and progressively reduced costs faced by industry.[40] This occurred especially in the context of the measures required to implement the single European Act (notably the ending of price and exchange controls). The reform of the Paris stock exchange offered another example of an audacious financial reform which helped to modernise French capitalism. Bérégovoy was symbolic of the Left in government in another sense. Reputed to be a man of scrupulous moral reputation, the credibility of the Premier was fatally undermined by the revelation of the Pélat affair weeks before the first round of the 1993 National Assembly election: it was revealed that Bérégovoy had accepted an interest-free loan of one million francs in 1986 to purchase his Parisian appartment. While in no sense illegal, this revelation undermined Bérégovoy's claim to moral rectitude upon which he had staked his political reputation. This disclosure forced Bérégovoy to perform a minor role during the 1993 election campaign when he had been preparing to act as its leading tenor.

Premier Bérégovoy left office with no audacious social reform attached to his name. Mitterrand's sixth prime minister was symbolic of the Left's timidity in relation to social reform; although appreciating his managerial competence, disabused PS deputies were critical of Bérégovoy's lack of reformist audacity.[41] And, however unjust, it was undeniable that Bérégovoy, a Man of the People, came to be associated with the defence of a technocratic and business elite removed from the concerns of routine daily existence. No one symbolised more completely than Bérégovoy the prevalence of an economic perspective which excluded bold political or social reforms, and which was impotent faced with the rise in unemployment. To this extent, Bérégovoy embodied, as much as anyone else, the Socialists' historic defeat in the 1993 National Assembly election (see Chapter 5). The tragic aftermath of Bérégovoy's suicide in May 1993 closed the final chapter on the Left in power in an atmosphere of recrimination, melancholy and finality.

Mitterrand's achievements as president were rather curious ones. To some extent his achievements are in the eye of the beholder and in relation to the original standpoint adopted. There is a strong case to be made that the achievements were not necessarily in accordance with the original goals. In fact, the most significant achievements were either against the spirit of the *110 propositions* (economic policy), or else had little to do with the original platform (Europe).

The above overview of the evolution of presidential policy during Mitterrand's presidency would suggest that his leadership was mainly of a reactive variety: in most spheres, Mitterrand reacted to events he did not control and could not have foreseen. His reactive, adaptable style facilitated his legitimisation of new policy directions throughout the course of his presidency. This was notably the case in relation to economic policy. The most paradoxical role performed by Mitterrand stemmed from his function as legitimator; through his commitment to European integration, Mitterrand came to symbolise the modernisation and liberalisation of capitalism, despite his firm belief in the virtues of central state action. The key architect of the technical details of this policy was Pierre Bérégovoy, but the ultimate impulsion came from Mitterrand himself, especially by the critical economic arbitrations made during the period 1982–84, and by the role performed by Mitterrand as an artisan of closer European union. These themes are developed further in Chapter 12.

Chapter 4

The enigma of François Mitterrand

Biographies of François Mitterrand proliferated throughout the course of his presidency. These ranged from intellectually reputable journalism, to the totally scurrilous tract. They have been of variable quality.[1] Each work forwarded a somewhat different portrayal of François Mitterrand, but most despaired of reconciling his apparent contradictions as a political leader. In this chapter, we shall attempt to unravel Mitterrand's complex political persona, to explain the evolution of his beliefs and to situate him within the context of French Republican culture and of European social-democracy.

PORTRAYALS OF MITTERRAND'S POLITICAL LEADERSHIP

After such a colourful career, peppered with so many incidents and apparent inconsistencies, the prevailing assumption is that Mitterrand is a tough political operator and a survivor, rather than a man of high principle. Biographers have frequently used bestial imagery to depict Mitterrand as a political animal adept at cunning, deviousness and an unerring instinct for survival. The characterisation of Mitterrand as an old fox perfectly embodies this tendency.[2] Closely related is the portrayal of Mitterrand as a sphinx-like figure (Catherine Nay), mysterious, obscure and ancient. Most biographers converge to discern in Mitterrand a machiavellian prince. Underpinning this image is the notion of Mitterrand as an unprincipled political leader, ready to compromise beliefs in the interests of self-promotion: in short, a political opportunist and a skilled political manoeuvrer. What have been described as Mitterrand's machiavellian qualities might alternatively be con-sidered as prerequisites for survival in a ruthless political environment. They do not in themselves inform us about the sincerity and cohesion of his beliefs. The portrayal of Mitterrand as the machiavellian Prince is probably necessary, but certainly insufficient.

Various portrayals of Mitterrand have concentrated upon his presumed character traits, either as a matter of general interest, or else to judge his capacity for effective statesmanship. We should exercise considerable caution before imputing any direct relationship between character traits (which, almost by definition, are difficult to verify) and the exercise of political leadership. Even in anecdotal form, however, appreciations of Mitterrand's character traits can be suggestive of aspects of his political personality. The most common personality traits attributed to Mitterrand include intense secrecy, loneliness, vanity, distrust of others; but also a formidible power of seduction, an ability to attract loyal followers, a marked loyalty towards these followers and a personal resilience and capacity for endurance.[3] The interaction between these personality traits and Mitterrand's style of political leadership is considered further in Chapter 11.

At a more speculative level again (and with the same reservations), we might deduce Mitterrand's attitudes from aspects of his past experience. Certain examples can illustrate the point. The fact that Mitterrand did not follow the educational path common to the Fifth Republic political elite might explain his initial suspicion of *énarques* such as Rocard or Giscard d'Estaing, whom he accused of apolitical technocracy.[4] The fact that Mitterrand encountered a lack of sympathy on behalf of a certain type of French intellectual during the Fourth Republic might explain his disdain for a certain type of intellectual thereafter. Mitterrand's interest in culture (and in self-projection) most certainly explained his ardent desire to leave several monuments to his presidency at various key locations in Paris. And it is no coincidence that, as an aesthete with minor literary pretensions, Mitterrand should cultivate men of letters.[5]

These insights into Mitterrand's character are valuable, insofar as they help us to build an impression of a man who invariably appears to his chroniclers as an enigma.

THE ENIGMA OF FRANÇOIS MITTERRAND

In the light of Mitterrand's status as the most successful Socialist leader in the Fifth Republic, his personal background and aspects of his political philosophy have surprised many observers. According to one biographer, 'the peculiarity with François Mitterrand is that he expresses many values usually associated with the Right'.[6] A pervasive sense of patriotism, combined with a valorisation of his rural origins, underpins Mitterrand's published works. This is expressed with themes such as French identity being rooted in the eternal nation, the commitment to the origins and the continuity of the French people, the timeless characteristics of rural Catholic France, and the romantic attachment to the land.[7] It is instructive that the three *départements* most associated with Mitterrand were all representative of a rural, bucolic France: the Charente, the Nièvre and the Landes. Images of the pine forests of the Landes recur with remarkable frequency in Mitterrand's works, as if bestowed with a spiritual quality. Mitterrand's writings are replete with references to a bygone age. As Mitterrand himself observed in 1969: 'I lived my childhood in another century; it took an enormous effort to leap into the present one'.[8] To this extent, Mitterrand often appears as a man of the past.

As we surveyed Mitterrand's career in Chapter 1, there is no doubt that his familial and social background was that of conservative provincial France. Aspects of his conservative upbringing remained with Mitterrand throughout his career. The most obvious legacy in this respect was that of French catholicism, an almost obligatory framework of reference for a man of Mitterrand's background and generation. The influence of residual catholicism was best expressed in relation to Mitterrand's repeated condemnations of the evils of money.[9] This reference remained with him throughout his career, however difficult it appeared on occasion to reconcile with the financial manoeuvrings of several of his closest advisers.[10] And yet a provincial Catholic background in no sense predetermined future political orientations. During the Fourth Republic, Mitterrand adopted a moderately anti-clerical outlook which was shared by many Catholics of his generation, suspicious of their own origins, and hostile both to Christian democracy and to the conservative right.[11] This was expressed in his opposition to the *Loi Barangé* of 1951, his distrust of the MRP and his dislike of the Catholic hierarchy.[12]

What really characterised Mitterrand's background was the importance of provincialism and its associated belief-patterns. These included a sense of tradition, a belief in the centrality of family, an instinctive belief in the virtues of the land, a fascination with history, and an obligatory reference to catholicism. One well-placed source contends that relations between Mitterrand and Helmut Kohl were facilitated by the fact that both were provincial Catholics, genuinely committed to the European ideal.[13] These provincial values adhered to by Mitterrand were, broadly speaking, conservationist values, more usually associated with the political Right than with the Left, but not predetermined in this direction. His opponents frequently sought to tarnish Mitterrand on account of his family background. For his left-wing critics, any proclaimed commitment made by Mitterrand to Socialist values was bound to be opportunistic and to conceal cynical political designs: the man was, after all, a bourgeois Catholic renegade. In the words of Guy Mollet, the Socialist Party leader from 1946–69: 'Mitterrand has not become a Socialist, he has learnt how to speak in a Socialist manner. This is not the same thing.'[14]

This traditionalist aspect to Mitterrand's political persona led critics to label him as being essentially a conservative traditional figure. In fact, it is striking how he relied upon images of a peaceful, rural, bygone France for purposes of election campaigning. This was epitomised by the portrayal of Mitterrand as the Quiet Force *(Force tranquille)* in the 1981 campaign, with election posters placing the candidate against the backdrop of a small church, symbolic of a bucolic, ancestral France. For critics, the imagery employed in this poster campaign recalled that of Marshall Pétain. And despite his mastery of political tactics, Mitterrand as President appeared initially as a provincial outsider, rather ill-at-ease with the cosmopolitian values of the Parisian establishment, and distrustful of the existing politico-administrative elite. This confluence of these older traditionalist values with those more commonly associated with the Left reinforced the perception held by most of his biographers of the paradoxical nature of Mitterrand's beliefs. Rather than taking refuge in the easy charge of opportunism, however, an attempt will be made to understand the complexity of Mitterrand's political persona by retracing the main steps of his philosophical evolution.

Mitterrand's ideological odyssey

It is, in fact, possible to chart the evolution of Mitterrand's beliefs with a measure of coherence which should qualify any portrayal of him as an unprincipled opportunist, and which gives a sense to his political activity. We can delineate a number of stages which reveal a certain logic to the progression of Mitterrand's professed ideas. In Mitterrand's own assessment, the experience of the French resistance had a critical importance in his evolution away from being an apolitical student to becoming a young politician marked by the legacy of the resistance.[15] This path was followed by a whole generation of Frenchmen from a similar background, for whom the experience of the resistance had a profound impact. In Mitterrand's case, it marked the first major political evolution, probably the most significant because it called into question much of his family socialisation.[16]

The second phase in Mitterrand's political evolution was as a young, ambitious politician in the early Fourth Republic, whose activity was situated squarely within the programme of the French resistance. The political formation chosen by Mitterrand, the UDSR, was the only party specifically to reclaim the heritage of the resistance in its title. And yet, the legacy of the resistance led to no unified political stance within the UDSR: the movement split between Gaullists (who later joined de Gaulle's RPF), and non-Gaullists. But the wartime resistance remained a fundamental reference point for Mitterrand.

One key aspect of the resistance programme was the development of the French Community, an aphorism for metropolitan France and its overseas colonies. The strengthening of the French Community was an essential patriotic reference during the early postwar period, a means whereby France could restore its rightful place among leading nations. The formative charter of the UDSR in 1945, for instance, proclaimed its belief in the need 'to raise the cultural level of the indigenous populations', and 'strengthen the links' which bound France to its colonies.[17] Mitterrand's key political activity during the early Fourth Republic was his involvement with sub-Saharan Africa. In his capacity as Overseas Minister from 1950–51, he was determined to reform the French empire as a means of rebuilding France's status as a major world player. Mitterrand's colonialism suited the spirit of the age; it was a means of reaffirming the national identity and pride of France after the terrible period of wartime occupation.

A third stage in Mitterrand's philosophical evolution was the devotion to Pierre Mendès-France, the radical premier of 1954–55, who was probably the most inspirational figure of the Fourth Republic. The attractions exercised by Mendès-France on the young Mitterrand were undeniable: Mendès represented modernist, postwar republicanism turned to the future.[18] In turn, Mendès-France valued Mitterrand's sense of tactical genius, which had allowed him to capture control of the UDSR in 1953. Mitterrand never formed a part of Mendès-France's inner circle, and was subjected to a measure of derision from the intellectuals around *L'Express*, the unofficial *mendèsiste* mouthpiece. The infatuation with Mendès-France was relatively short-lived. Mitterrand came to distrust Mendès-France's tone of moral superiority, and the overt intellectualism of those surrounding him. The disillusionment with Mendès-France thus stemmed both from personal antagonism and divergences of appreciation over the correct political strategy.

A fourth recognisable stage in Mitterrand's philosophical evolution was that of anti-Gaullism, already apparent in genesis during the Fourth Republic. Mitterrand's political career in the Fourth Republic had been conducted as a neo-radical with a strong sense of republican legality. The events of May–June 1958 were an immense shock to those with a genuine republican conscience (see Chapter 2). Mitterrand's Republican identity guided his opposition to de Gaulle, given its most elaborate expression in *Le coup d'état permanent* of 1964. Mitterrand's anti-Gaullism was a gut political instinct. He was unable to forget de Gaulle's treatment of him in the past and he never really succumbed to the fascination exercised by de Gaulle upon other republican opponents such as Mendès-France.

The brutal break with the Fourth Republic also brought Mitterrand into closer contact with the PCF. Mitterrand was fascinated by the PCF as representative of millions of ordinary French people, and as the only organisation able effectively to combat Gaullism. It is clear that Mitterrand's fascination with the PCF stemmed first from preoccupations of political strategy; his stroke of genius was to recognise that no opposition to de Gaulle was feasible without the cooperation of the Communist Party. At the same time, the gradual birth of a new political strategy (the alliance with the PCF) brought Mitterrand increasingly into contact with a political ideology and movement with which he was not naturally acquainted, but which intrigued him, and which influenced his political beliefs.

The fifth recognisable stage in Mitterrand's political evolution was the proclaimed commitment to socialism. Although his status as a centre–left Republican was firmly established during the Fourth Republic, his conversion to socialism in the 1960s smacked of hypocrisy for many observers. According to this interpretation, Mitterrand's 'conversion' stemmed from a purely tactical use of ideology, whereby ideas were marshalled to suit specific political purposes and then discarded. The accusation deserves attention.

In 1978, Mitterrand proclaimed: 'My objective is to attempt to bring socialism to France, and France to socialism.'[19] And yet, as outlined in Chapter 1, Mitterrand did not generally claim to espouse the cause of socialism during the Fourth Republic, although he occupied a political position commonly associated with the centre–left. His evolution towards an overtly Socialist political discourse was a progressive one.

References to socialism were scarce until after the 1965 presidential election, during which Mitterrand represented the formations of the 'united left' (Socialists, Communists and left-wing clubs). As the leading politician associated with the Left union strategy thereafter, Mitterrand was to be heard claiming the mantle of socialism with greater regularity. There was an irrefutable functional justification for this. As the example of Guy Mollet (1946–69) illustrated, any French Socialist leader felt constrained to adopt a 'radical' language in order to safeguard the party's left flank from the overbearing presence of the Communist Party, the larger of the left-wing parties until the mid-1970s. It was demonstrated in Chapter 2 how Mitterrand specifically set out to compete with the PCF upon the political ground occupied by that party. Mitterrand's espousal of a radical political doctrine and discourse in the 1970s was an indispensable feature of his effort to break the hold of the PCF over the French left. It worked with exemplary efficiency in 1981. It was a necessary political exercise.

The issue of whether Mitterrand's socialism was genuine or not is a matter of interpretation, with both sides able to draw upon evidence to support their case. There certainly appeared on the surface to be an element of opportunism in Mitterrand's whole-scale embrace of socialism. There undoubtedly was an element, imposed by circumstances and the dictates of political strategy. And yet it is rather unsatisfactory to reduce Mitterrand's movements purely to tactical switches. In the opinion of one commentator: 'François Mitterrand represents better than anybody else the synthesis of the main currents of the French left: religious, moralistic, and centralising.'[20] This is perhaps to accord too great an intellectual cohesion to his philosophy, but we should refrain from dismissing Mitterrand as an unprincipled opportunist motivated uniquely by the conquest of power. Mitterrand's pronounced sense of social justice had been prevalent long before he proclaimed himself to be a socialist, and, similarly, his belief in the virtues of the central state. Insofar as it could be dissociated from his leadership of the PS, Mitterrand's socialism of the 1970s could be understood as the product of a strong sense of morality ultimately derived from catholicism, grafted upon an unshakeable reference to the French republican tradition, and a belief in the central state. Taken at this level, Mitterrand's socialism, however anodyne for some, appeared sincere. It represented the optimistic spirit of the age, as evidenced by the fact that Mitterrand was accompanied in the movement from *mendèsisme* to socialism by a generation of political leaders, notably men such as Hernu, Bérégovoy, and Dumas. The most persuasive evidence in support of Mitterrand's genuine espousal of the cause of socialism lay in his early activities and symbolic actions as President. There is thus a case to be made that Mitterrand's commitment to socialism followed plausibly, if not unproblematically, from his gradual political evolution since the Fourth Republic.

At the level of policy, the evolution from republicanism to socialism was far from being devoid of impact. The commitment to openly socialist objectives and to an alliance with the PCF led Mitterrand to become associated with a range of policy stances which far surpassed those previously encompassed by the French Socialists.

The point might be illustrated by outlining the evolution of Mitterrand's CIR. The Convention had been created in 1964, dedicated to republican opposition to Gaullism; its founding charter contained no explicit reference to socialism. From Radical, neo-*mendèsiste* origins, the CIR gradually evolved into a more recognisably Socialist organisation under the impact of Mitterrand's leadership and its incorporation into the FGDS. By May 1970, with the adoption of its *Contrat socialiste*, the CIR's formal ideological evolution from republicanism to socialism was complete, presaging the Socialist Party's own programme of March 1972, *Changer la vie*. Both documents contained a commitment to replace capitalism with socialism, and outlined detailed reform programmes, predicated upon the nationalisation of key industries, state economic planning and the redistribution of wealth. The detailed reform packages contained in these documents contrasted markedly with Mitterrand's earlier (and later) disinclination to accept constraining programmatic commitments. The culmination of this move occurred with the Common Programme of June 1972, which committed the Socialist–Communist alliance to extensive reforms, prefiguring those actually carried out (albeit in a milder form) during the early reformist period of the Mitterrand presidency.[21]

Whatever interpretations critics made of his philosophical evolution, Mitterrand personally situated his political activity in the traditions of Jaurès and Blum, the two reverential figures of the twentieth-century Socialist movement. His actions as President from 1981–83 suggested that Mitterrand had come to identify strongly with the past Socialist heroes he evoked. For an ostensibly pragmatic, opportunistic politician, Mitterrand's political message had a peculiar intensity at the beginning of his presidential mandate. His perception of 'socialism' clearly guided the actions of his governments until forced to alter course in 1982–83. By the force of portraying himself as a Socialist throughout most of the 1960s and 1970s, Mitterrand had come to believe in the remedies he had been expounding for the previous fifteen years. This was perhaps the real significance of the 1981–82 period. With a fine sense of history, Mitterrand believed that he represented popular aspirations by his electoral victory in 1981 that surpassed his own personality and commanded recognition. The parallel with Leon Blum and the Popular Front was a real one. This placed the President firmly in the camp of the idealists, faced with the pressures for a social and economic slowdown from within the Mauroy government.

MITTERRAND AND THE TWO CULTURES OF THE FRENCH LEFT

François Mitterrand's proclaimed socialism prior to his election in 1981 placed great faith in the transformative capacities of the state, and in the conquest of political power. Within the cultural context of the French left, this set him apart from what became known as the 'second left', embodied first by Mendès-France, and later within the Socialist Party by Michel Rocard.[22] Mitterrand's distrust of the 'second left' had a long pedigree. It stemmed initially from the experience of the Mendès-France premiership from 1954–55 and the difficult personal relations existing between the two men. A series of episodes later confirmed this. In 1959, Mitterrand was refused membership of the *Parti socialiste autonome*, to which Mendès-France was admitted. In 1964, the *Assises de Vichy* set itself up as a rival grouping of political clubs to Mitterrand's Convention. The 'Grenoble colloquium' of March 1966 complicated further already difficult relations. This was a gathering of political clubs, trade unions and assorted left-wing personalities. The organisers of the Grenoble meeting perceived of their initiative as separate from Mitterrand's efforts to unify the Left within the FGDS: they were determined to consider questions of doctrine and programme, rather than political strategy. Mitterrand's name was hissed at the colloquium, at which Mendès-France was the star performer, and Rocard an early protégé.

The themes expressed at the Grenoble colloquium presaged many of those associated later with Rocard within the PS, such as decentralisation, regionalism, and economic realism.[23] The divergence between Mitterrand and Mendès-France could to some extent be understood as a conflict between the conquest of power (a major preoccupation of Mitterrand, notwithstanding the philosophical evolution noted above) and the exercise of power (what the Left would actually do in office, the principal concern of Mendès-France). Mitterrand had always considered himself to have been unjustly treated by this 'second left', who criticised him for his attitude during the Algerian war and his chequered past as a Fourth Republican minister. He became convinced that the 'second left' was an adversary resolutely opposed to the interests he articulated as presidential leader of the Left from 1965 onwards.

One of the major paradoxes concerning the political persona of Mitterrand lies in the complex relationship between religion and politics. His personal catholicism was an important point of reference. Even at the height of his anti-Rocard tirade in 1979, Mitterrand was eager to stress that 'I come from a Catholic background and culture'.[24] And yet, he mistrusted the influence of organised religion in politics. His education at the hands of Catholic brothers reputedly left Mitterrand with a lasting distaste for the Catholic hierarchy.[25] His moderate anti-clericalism was manifested in his denunciation of the Christian-democratic MRP at various stages during the Fourth Republic. It reappeared during the early Fifth Republic, notably directed against what remained of the MRP, and against various confessional groups within the political club movement. Mitterrand also complained bitterly in relation to the treatment he received at the hands of left-Catholic publications such as *Témoignage chrétien*, which cast doubts upon the sincerity of his political engagement.

Within the PS, this sentiment carried over into a particularly virulent criticism of the 'social-christian current' represented, according to Mitterrand, by Rocard, and by outlying organisations such as the CFDT. In the style of a Third Republican Radical politician, Mitterrand interpreted republicanism to be synonomous with a degree of anti-clericalism. As he explained in 1979: 'the Catholic Church has always supported conservative forces. At the beginning, socialism built itself without, or against the Church'.[26]

Mitterrand's personal catholicism thus coexisted alongside strong misgivings about the penetration of religion into the political sphere, especially in the form of Christian-democratic, or left-Catholic political movements. Mitterrand found the propensity of left-Catholics to dispense lessons in morality particularly irritating. But it should also be stressed that Mitterrand wilily exploited the religious issue in an attempt to label his opponents within the Socialist movement as being foreign to the noble traditions of that movement, and therefore in some sense illegitimate. This was most obviously the case in Mitterrand's treatment of Michel Rocard. His opposition to Rocard stemmed from his distaste at the alliance between an austere Protestant, the left-Catholic movement and a clutch of intellectuals, all constituencies he disliked.

In other spheres apart from religion, Mitterrand and Rocard came to represent rather different traditions of the French left. From Mendès-France through to Rocard, the 'second left' stressed the importance of realistic political programmes which fully recognised the social, economic and political constraints that would be faced by an incoming left-wing government. It believed that the need for realistic programmes should take precedence over complicated assessments of political strategy, at which Mitterrand was a past master. On these traditional *mendèsiste* concerns was superimposed an anti-statism inherited from the May 1968 movement, a movement distrusted by Mitterrand as a challenge to established political formations.

In a speech to the 1977 PS congress, Rocard postulated the existence of two cultures of the French left: a centralising Jacobin culture which placed its faith in the transformative capacities of the state; and a decentralising culture, inherently suspicious of excessive state interventionism.[27] This dichotomy between two cultures was rejected by Mitterrand, who concluded that each was necessary, and who stoutly defended his attempted synthesis between the two:

I have been labelled as a centraliser. That makes me smile. I am mayor of a small commune, President of a provincial departmental council, and I have always argued in favour of a thoroughgoing decentralisation, for the suppression of the institution of Prefect, and for increased powers and finance for local authorities. It is true, however, that I do not consider that a break with capitalism can come about by a collection of social experimentations. I firmly believe in the power of state as well.[28]

Mitterrand preferred the historic socialism represented by the conquest of the state to that of the second left, which he considered both utopian and irrelevant. Mitterrand was ill-at-ease with the legacy of May 1968 (which had almost ruined his career) and poured scorn on themes such as social experimentation, and *autogestion*, as alternatives to concerted action by the central state. It is unquestionable that Mitterrand firmly believed in the necessity of conquering the state as a *sine qua non* of any transformation, and that he articulated the sentiment of the mainstream of the French left on this issue. Mitterrand's actions, before and after becoming President, could be located firmly within the centralising tradition of French republican political culture. Even a policy such as decentralisation, strongly supported by Mitterrand, required an initial conquest of the state apparatus to become a reality.

FRANÇOIS MITTERRAND AND THE SOCIAL-DEMOCRATIC TRADITION

To situate François Mitterrand within the European Social-democratic tradition would be a highly contentious exercise. The classical Social-democratic ethos is an ideal laying great importance on state-directed redistribution of wealth, the preservation of a mixed economy, the pursuit of Keynesian economic policies, and the conciliation of opposing interests. From the above discussion, it appears that Mitterrand lay more squarely in the European Social-democratic tradition than his rival Rocard, who contested essential features of the Social-democratic model in the name of anti-statism.[29]

Within the neo-Marxist discursive and ideological culture of the French left, Social-democracy carried negative connotations for a long time. The reasons for this distrust stemmed in part from the history of the French left itself and the division between Socialists and Communists at the Tours congress of 1920. The Socialists had never relinquished their claim to be the legitimate inheritor of the pre-1920 party, a party officially committed to Marxism. They retained the party's name (SFIO) and declared themselves to be a revolutionary party. To admit to being 'reformist' or Social-democratic would have been to legitimise the creation of the PCF at Tours as the only 'revolutionary' party. The political practice of the SFIO under Guy Mollet's leadership in the Fourth Republic bore little relationship to the party's theoretical foundations, but the myth of the revolutionary party remained intact.

Under Mitterrand's leadership after 1971, there was an important strategic reason for the PS to refute being a Social-democratic party. The alliance with the PCF was intended as a means of breaking Communist domination which, in Mitterrand's analysis, condemned the Left to perpetual opposition. To compete effectively with the PCF, the PS had to attract Communist voters, unlikely to succumb to the sirens of social-democracy, but amenable to a more radical political profile. The refusal of social-democracy was thus in part tactical.

The PS genuinely did not consider itself as a Social-democratic party. Quite simply, Social-democracy was alien to the French cultural tradition. In the optimistic climate of the 1970s, the French party regarded itself as qualitatively superior to its European counterparts, capable of advocating a 'third way' between capitalism and Communism. Social-democratic parties were accused of having abandoned any perspective of social transformation. As leader of the PS, Mitterrand fully shared the pervasive distrust towards the concept of social-democracy. In his own words:

> What I criticise is that fact that European Social-democrats have too often ceased to consider Capital as their enemy. I think that they were wrong not to carry out the social appropriation of the means of production.[30]

There were important differences between the French Socialists and the classic Social-democratic model. In organisational terms, there was no institutional link with organised labour, for instance: indeed, the most powerful French trade union (the CGT) provided the backbone of organisational support for the rival Communist Party. Furthermore, as a result of the party's oppositional status throughout the Fifth Republic, there was no established history of involvement in the corporatist-style governmental practices prevalent elsewhere in Europe. The existence of a powerful Communist rival imposed an additional burden on the French party, unfamiliar to most (if not all) European Social-democratic parties.

Its practice in government gave an element of substance to its claim to be distinct from classic European social-democracy. The reforms carried out in the first eighteen months were qualitatively different from the routine economic management characteristic of the contemporaneous German Social-democrats under Helmut Schmidt, or the 1974–79 Wilson/Callaghan administrations in the UK. It might be the case that, once the rhetoric had been brushed aside, the Socialists' reform programme was in the mould of classic expansionary Social-democratic governments of the postwar era; but the truth remained that these governments had abandonned reflationary Keynesianism since the oil crises of the early 1970s, and were everywhere pursuing deflationary anti-inflation policies.

Even after the economic U-turn of 1982–83, which forced the French Socialists back into line with Social-democratic and conservative administrations elsewhere, there remained important differences between the French case and other (North European) Social-democratic experiences. The first of these related to the faith placed in nationalisation as a tool of industrial policy, a notion paid little more than lipservice elsewhere. It has been argued above that the Left's faith in industrial policy was one of the casualties of the modernisation drive after 1983. But the fact remained that the Socialists relied on the state sector as the avant-garde of the modernising drive. Moreover, vestiges of *dirigiste* industrial interventionism remained, notably in the electronics, telecommunications and defence-related industries. In 1991, for instance, the French government protested vigorously after the European Commission had blocked the takeover of the Canadian firm de Havilland by the nationalised Aerospatiale. The second difference related to the weakness of corporatist-style management techniques under the French Socialist administrations, typified by the weakness of the trade unions in particular, and the government's lack of dealings with them: the Fabius administration again marked the culminating point of this trend.[31] The French Socialists in power thus persisted with a deeply ingrained facet of French political tradition: the autonomy of the state, and its superiority to organised sectional interests. In this respect, as in others, the national context proved decisive. Until the mid-1980s, moreover, a belief in the virtues of *dirigiste* state activity in the economic sphere comprised a relatively cross-party view that included powerful aspects of the Gaullist tradition and was not specifically socialist.

Notwithstanding these subtle differences, it is clear that Mitterrand became a political leader in the European Social-democratic tradition, based on incremental reform, preservation of a mixed economy, and sound economic management. The French President attempted to conceptualise his position by developing the concept of the 'mixed economy society', and by referring to republicanism and the Republic to justify his action as president.

The mixed economy society and Republicanism

Throughout the 1981–86 governments, Mitterrand refused to admit that there had been a change in his basic economic philosophy, referring to the concept of a mixed economy as a constant feature of his economic thought, and condemning the anarchy of economic liberalism. It is true that Mitterrand did refer to the 'mixed economy' both before and after the economic transformation of 1982–83, but to most observers the significance of this formula altered radically between these periods. In Socialist programmes throughout the 1970s (and to a lesser extent during the early reformist period, 1981–82) the mixed economy was represented as an economic reality: a left-wing government would not be able to dispense with the private sector, however much it distrusted its Malthusian nature. Even the radical provisions of the 1972 Common Programme envisaged the bulk of economic activity remaining in private hands. But there was a pervasive distrust of the private sector; an equation of private enterprise with 'affairism', and a ritual denunciation of the activities of multinational companies, these 'new lords of modern society'.[32] The nationalisation programme of the Mauroy government revealed a preference for a strong and vibrant public sector as a dynamic pole of the French economy; this programme fully reflected Mitterrand's belief in the virtues of the French state.

In an interview in May 1984, Mitterrand proposed a rather different interpretation of the mixed economy, more in line with the norm elsewhere in Europe: public and private sectors overlapped and should cooperate; ownership was no longer equated in an ideological manner with control, therefore there was no need for the state to retain 100 per cent of the capital of nationalised firms; the state should refrain from direct interference in the management of nationalised firms; the private sector must be encouraged to invest, notably by lessening the fiscal burden on industry.[33] The entrepreneur was rehabilitated by Mitterrand, and the pursuit of private wealth legitimised. The reception afforded by intellectuals to Mitterrand's espousal of the 'mixed economy' was a derisory one; the French President was accused of adopting an outmoded concept at the same time as it was being abandoned everywhere else.

The state remained an important reference point in Mitterrand's formulation of economic and industrial policy. The President remained firmly opposed to wide-scale privatisation of state-run firms, as became clear in his opposition to the Balladur privatisation programme of 1986–87. In his *Letter to the French People* of 1988, Mitterrand pledged that there would be a halt to the Chirac government's privatisation programme, but that no new industries would be taken into public ownership. This was formally modified in 1991, under pressure from Finance Minister Bérégovoy: nationalised companies were again to be allowed to sell off part of their shares to raise capital, but the state would retain a majority shareholding. Mitterrand refused to engage in the full-scale privatisation practised elsewhere in Europe. In essence, there remained in Mitterrand's activity strong elements of continuity with established French traditions of state economic interventionism, although the limits of state interventionism were circumscribed by the economic U-turn of 1982–83; by the provisions of the Single European Act of 1986, and by moves towards greater European economic and political integration behind which Mitterrand himself was a driving force (see Chapter 10).

While reaffirming that socialism comprised his personal philosophy, Mitterrand declared in May 1984: 'I do not speak of socialism very often because it is my duty to speak for the French nation as a whole'.[34] There is a school of thought which contends that the cause of socialism was doomed from the moment Mitterrand entered the Elysée: the Socialist candidate became transformed into the President of All the French and adapted his political message accordingly.[35] This appears excessive: the *peuple de gauche* figured prominently in Mitterrand's early deliberations and activities. But it is unquestionable that references to socialism were rarer after 1983, and sub-scribed to as a 'personal philosophy', rather than as an ideology guiding governmental action. The divisive notion of socialism was replaced with that of Republicanism, more suitable for an ecumenical presidential appeal.[36] This represented the sixth stage in Mitterrand's philosophical evolution, in some sense a return to his political roots. The reversion to republicanism as the cornerstone of Mitterrand's political message fulfilled several functions. It helped to fill the ideological void left by socialism; it acted as a rallying cry against the extreme-right leader Jean-Marie Le Pen; it provided a source of anodyne doctrine upon which all currents within the Socialist Party could agree; it was sufficiently ambiguous to propel a catch-all message beyond the ranks of the traditional left-wing electorate; and it reflected upon the fact that Mitterrand, as incumbent President, was the supreme Republican himself.[37] Thus, in terms of domestic policy, a practice based on social-democratic incrementalism was accompanied by a restored reference to republicanism as the *raison d'être* of Mitterrand's presidency.

CONCLUSION

To some extent, portrayals of Mitterrand depend upon the starting point adopted. At one level, it is easy to portray him as a machiavellian prince. The heightened sense of political strategy, the taste for manoeuvre, the obsession with the *rapports des forces*, the apparently unending shifts in proclaimed beliefs: all of these point to a politician for whom the objective of political activity lay in the activity of politics itself. Politics became reduced to a game of chess. To understand the complexity of Mitterrand, it would be unwise to underplay this aspect of his persona. Indeed, the image of the rather cynical strategist has prevailed in interpretations of Mitterrand, often to the extent of refuting any underlying principled rationale. This is perhaps because the strategist appeared more starkly in Mitterrand than in most other successful political leaders, but we must admit that no successful (or aspiring) political leader can dispense with a strategy for conquering power.

Upon deeper reflection, it is not difficult to forward a more noble interpretation of Mitterrand's political activity. From the above discussion, we might conclude that, in each of the main stages of Mitterrand's career, a relatively small number of core themes and motivations gave a real sense to his political activity. The transitions between the various stages were in their own terms logical, with the fundamental breaks being the influence of the Resistance and the creation of the Fifth Republic. During the Fourth Republic, the obsession with colonial reform, superseded by the flirtation with *mendèsisme* placed Mitterrand firmly within the legacy of the French resistance and forward-looking republicanism. The political space occupied by Mitterrand during the Fourth Republic was, in the context of the period, resolutely located on the moderate reformist left.

The opposition to Gaullism from 1958 was itself predicated upon a principled defence of the Republic that other lesser politicians were prepared to overlook in their perceived short-term political interests. His experience almost as a lone resistant to Gaullism after 1958, his close contact with the PCF, and the ideological climate of the period (what he perceived to be the arbitrary, abusive, and inegalitarian nature of Gaullism) gradually led him to a more explicit endorsement of socialism. Close sources suggest that Mitterrand lived these different phases with sincerity.[38]

There was evidence of principled political activity in a variety of spheres. From 1981–83, an activist President Mitterrand had to be ranged among the idealists, advocating a continuation of the reform programme against more cautious counsels. Mitterrand was also highly motivated by the construction of the European Community, a policy which developed the aura of a mission for the French President. By the end of his second presidential mandate, Mitterrand had reverted to the key themes present throughout his career. These were the defence of republicanism and the advocacy of liberal constitutional reform; European integration; the defence of social reforms enacted under his presidency; pride in national achievements and patriotism, and valorisation of the state. He continued to subscribe to socialism, but 'as a personal philosophy', rather than a leitmotif of presidential action.

If a more principled Mitterrand is portrayed in this chapter, this is in an attempt to counterbalance excessively machiavellian portraits. It is not to deny the contradictions and inconsistencies that surround his political persona. It would indeed be surprising if there were not contradictions, given that Mitterrand's career spanned the entire postwar period in France. The challenges to be faced by politicians during this period were themselves contradictory. The style of Mitterrand's political leadership allowed the French President to assume the consequences of contradictions in a more convincing manner than that of a declared conviction politician such as Margaret Thatcher (see Chapter 12). This was perhaps his real achievement.

Chapter 5

The party leader

As an independent-minded minister throughout the Fourth Republic, and a political outsider for the first decade of the Fifth Republic, François Mitterrand fundamentally distrusted the discipline and collective responsibility implied by belonging to a traditional party. His refusal to join any of the mainstream parties after the Liberation testified to his independence of spirit, as well as his ambiguity in relation to classification in terms of left and right. Mitterrand's relationship with the UDSR in the Fourth Republic has been outlined in Chapter 1. His distrust of classical political parties carried over into the Fifth Republic. To some extent, this was reflected in the style he adopted as the Socialist Party leader after 1971 and as President of the Republic after 1981. In the present chapter, Mitterrand's leadership will be assessed from the perspective of his complex, uneven and ambivalent relation ship with political parties in the Fifth Republic.

MITTERRAND AND THE CONVENTION: THE PROTOTYPE PRESIDENTIAL PARTY

Only cursory attention has been paid to the *Convention des Institutions Républicaines* (CIR), the movement Mitterrand dominated from 1964–71. And yet a study of the CIR exemplifies not only Mitterrand's capacity to attract fierce partisan loyalties, but also the early influence of the presidentialism of the Fifth Republic on political parties, as well as being an important staging post in the evolution of Mitterrand's political beliefs.

It was revealed above how the regeneration of the Left after the calamitious events of 1958–62 occurred outside the established political parties, and especially within the political club movement. The CIR was created in 1964 as a confederation of some forty, partly fictitious political clubs. The Convention sought to preserve the flexible structure permitted by the club format, deemed essential to attract those political activists disillusioned with the established left-wing parties.[1] It was only as a result of Mitterrand's rising political stature after the 1965 presidential campaign that the CIR permitted individual membership (previously members had joined the relevant political club, rather than the CIR itself), and made an effort to organise itself within the *départements*. At its height, the CIR never claimed more than 15,000 members. From its creation in 1964, the CIR was governed by a praesidium composed of nine members, chaired by Mitterrand's confidant Hernu until December 1970. Mitterrand refrained from occupying official leadership functions within the Convention in order to portray himself as leader of the entire Left.[2]

The loose organisational structure of the Convention initially recalled that of the UDSR. A permanent Standing Committee was created in February 1966 to 'assist' the praesidium, initially composed of 55 members (rising to 76 by 1970).[3] The Standing Committee originally had no elective basis, with its members being indirectly coopted by the largest clubs (effectively by Mitterrand and Hernu). This changed slightly in October 1968, but the organisational principle underpinning the CIR was in practice highly elitist, with Mitterrand exercising a preponderant influence throughout its history. The relative weakness of counterbalances to Mitterrand's leadership confirmed the presidential rally aspect of the CIR.

The Convention was typical of the type of organisation preferred by Mitterrand: loose, relatively unstructured, and ideologically flexible (at least at its origins). CIR spokesmen liked to contrast these organisational forms with the more disciplined chain of command present within other political parties. And yet political success constrained the CIR to become rather less a collection of clubs, and more of a political party. After the 1965 presidential election, the Convention set about organising itself in a more systematic way: whereas in early 1966 the CIR still had no regular structures in the *départements*, by 1971 departmental Conventions existed virtually everywhere. In the 1967 legislative election, 16 CIR candidates were elected, a total which ensured the Convention's future influence within the FGDS. CIR candidates, indeed, performed better than either the SFIO or Radicals. Those candidates directly associated with Mitterrand benefited from a personal vote not forthcoming to SFIO or Radical candidates; an inverse effect produced itself in June 1968, when CIR candidates suffered disproportionately from Mitterrand's unpopularity. The zones of regional strength of the Convention closely reflected the implantation of its leading political figures: the CIR was strongest where it had elected deputies in 1967, and where it faced little competition from the SFIO.[4] Local Conventions were more the appendages of provincial notables, in the Radical tradition, than they were imitations of the disciplined local sections of the Socialist Party.

The counterpart to such flexibility was an absence of genuine internal democracy within the Convention. Not only did Mitterrand personally coopt other members of the praesidium and standing committee, but he used his authority to prevent unwelcome votes being taken on critical motions at CIR conferences. Expressions of dissatisfaction with Mitterrand's leadership were occasionally articulated: in March 1968, for instance, the CIR deputy for

Haute-Saône, Jacques Maroselli, resigned from the Convention, arguing that there was an effective lack of any democracy at the summit.[5] In December 1970, at the CIR Assises of Suresnes, no less than eight separate motions were tabled, some critical of Mitterrand's leadership (including rare expressions of dissent from Pierre Joxe and Charles Hernu). But these were exceptions: the strength of the bond linking Mitterrand and the *conventionnels* represented a powerful leader–follower relationship. The loyalty of the *conventionnels* was never in doubt, not even after the height of Mitterrand's unpopularity in May 1968. Experience of the Convention comprised an important future reference point for the genealogy of the *mitterrandiste* elite. This is testified by a roll call of the CIR's Standing Committee in December 1970. Apart from Mitterrand himself, the Committee included several future ministers or prominent parliamentarians such as: L. Mermaz (President of the National Assembly, Agriculture), P. Joxe (Interior and Defence), G. Fillioud (Audiovisuel), R. Dumas (Foreign Affairs), L. Mexandeau (PTT), Y. Roudy (Women's Rights), C. Estier (PS deputy), G. Penne (Mitterrand's African adviser), C. Hernu (Defence), R. Badinter (Justice, President of the Constitutional Council) and a host of lesser known personalities.[6]

FIRST SECRETARY OF THE SOCIALIST PARTY, 1971–81

François Mitterrand's conquest, mastery and subjugation of the French Socialist Party was one the major political feats of the 1970s. Mitterrand's conquest of the Socialist Party (*Parti socialiste*) at the Congress of Epinay in June 1971 was a momentous event which reflected his status as de facto leader of the Left since the presidential election of 1965. His initially tenuous control of the leadership was consolidated partly because of the Party's early successes, partly because he was its only plausible presidential candidate, and partly because of the absence of any serious alternative.

Even the most ardent advocate of the great man theory of history could not pretend that Mitterrand himself created the social movement or the philo-sophical trends he was to articulate as leader of the Socialist Party from 1971–81. The rise of the Socialists during the 1970s was explicable only in relation to a number of closely interconnected spheres, which surpassed the personality of Mitterrand: these included political opportunity, sociological change and ideological evolution. These themes will be considered presently. Mitterrand's political skill was revealed by the fact that he came to symbolise these evolutions, and to associate his leadership with the demand for political change, despite his past as a Fourth Republic minister and his political discredit in 1968. The clear strategic choices adopted by Mitterrand in the 1970s, in favour of alliance with the Communists and programmatic revision, helped to resurrect the PS as a credible alternative party of government (see Chapter 2).

The ambiguity occasionally dispelled by Mitterrand as PS leader was a reflection of the complexity that his leadership tasks demanded. The need for alliance with the PCF had to be reconciled with an attempt to broaden the political bases of the Socialists as a catch-all party. This task necessarily involved a strong element of ambiguity, by which the political message advocated varied according to the audience addressed. Mitterrand crystallised the contradictions implied by these choices within his own personality.

The revival of the PS during the 1970s under Mitterrand's leadership was remarkable, as illustrated by its electoral performance shown in Table 5.1.

Table 5.1 Socialist electoral fortunes since 1958

Year	%	Year	%
1958 (SFIO)	15.4	1978 (PS/MRG)	24.97
1962 (SFIO)	12.5	1981 (PS/MRG)	37.77
1967 (FGDS)	18.7	1986 (PS/MRG)	31.61
1968 (FGDS)	16.5	1988 (PS/Allies)	37.55
1973 (PS/MRG)	20.7	1993 (PS/Allies)	20.27

Note: per cent refers to percentage of the voters who actually turned up to vote, rather than registered voters.

Quite apart from the upturn in its electoral fortunes, the party's new vitality was certified by the number of new party members who flocked into the PS, including many enthusiastic activists influenced by the ideas of May 1968. The infusion of such activists led to a definite transformation away from the rather stagnant SFIO, whose activists were in a minority in most federations by 1975. The rallying of Michel Rocard and a minority of the Unified Socialist Party (PSU) to the PS in 1974 removed the party's most ostentatious rival for the inheritance of May 1968, only to relocate the ideological conflict between the 'two cultures' of the French left within the Socialist Party itself.

During the 1970s Mitterrand's PS was a party well-attuned to the institutional, social and political imperatives of the political regime of the Fifth Republic and the social structures of French society. Unlike the Communist Party (PCF), the PS was a party which, on an *institutional* level, could credibly contend to win the presidency, the supreme political prize of the Fifth Republic. Mitterrand's presidential stature had been of considerable importance in explaining why he, de Gaulle's challenger in 1965, had been able to capture the leadership of the Socialist Party in 1971. He understood that there was no future for a party, such as the old SFIO, which refused to respect the new political rules of the Fifth Republic, centred upon victory in the decisive presidential election. The PS was thus created at least in part as a presidential party. But the PS was always more than just a presidential party: in fact, it was a party with a strong sense of self-sufficiency and party patriotism, a party which resented the effects of presidentialism, while at the same time depending upon its strategic position to hope to win a presidential election. Notwithstanding Mitterrand's gradual domination of the party, the PS found it difficult to feel completely at ease with the presidential rules of the game of the Fifth Republic. This theme will reappear later.

In terms of political strategy in the 1970s, the approach adopted by Mitterrand's PS was a highly complex one. It involved not just attempting to attract non-Socialist centre voters (essential for the election of any left-wing government), but also a concerted effort to break the hold of the PCF over the traditional left-wing electorate. It should be recalled that the PCF remained the larger of the two left-wing parties throughout the period from 1945 until c. 1974. The need to deal with the reality of an overpowering Communist Party explained why Mitterrand signed the PS-PCF common programme of 1972: this was intended to wean PCF voters away from their party to support the PS, presented as a more credible left-wing party. The PS was remarkably successful in this respect: by 1981, one-quarter of 1978 PCF voters had switched over to the PS.[7] But the PS also appealed to centrist-inclined voters, for whom the party represented the only prospect of political change. In the course of the 1970s, the Socialist Party thus attempted simultaneously (and somewhat paradoxically) to attract support beyond the Left as a 'catch-all' party; to appeal to the traditional left-wing electorate attracted by orthodox Marxism (the culture represented by the French Communist Party); and to represent the interests of new social movements, and new social strata within French society as well as to articulate new ideological themes given expression in May 1968. This successful heterogeneous electoral coalition was finally brought together in 1981.

On a *sociological level*, the new French Socialist Party appeared in the 1970s to be a genuinely interclass party, repeating a feat achieved previously only by the Gaullists in the 1960s. This was in marked contrast with the old SFIO in the Fourth and early Fifth Republics: the SFIO had become reduced to being an institutional expression of lower civil servants, and public sector workers, penetrating neither the ranks of the industrial working class, nor the new emerging social groups. Mitterrand's PS, by contrast, attracted support from many of the new social groups produced by postwar socio-economic and demographic change: new tertiary sector workers (especially in the public sector), the new and expanded professions (such as teaching and social work), as well as a high proportion of the *cadres*, the managerial strata whose ranks had increased dramatically in the postwar period.[8] In addition to these dynamic, expanding groups within French society, the party proved remarkably successful in attracting the support of older, more traditionally left-wing constituencies, such as industrial workers, and low status office and shopworkers (*employés*), over whom the Communist Party had traditionally exercised a strong influence.[9] The development of the PS during the 1970s and early 1980s under Mitterrand's leadership thus witnessed the party transformed into being a virtual microcosm of French society as a whole.

In contrast with the 'interclass' basis of the Socialist electorate, various studies into the sociological composition of party activists and office-holders converged in their conclusions: the new Socialist Party was 'a party of intellectuals', peopled predominantly by secondary school teachers, university lecturers and those involved in the intellectual professions.[10] There was an overwhelming shortfall of workers, so much so that one authority concluded that 'in reality, the PS is an exclusion zone for industrial workers'.[11] Moreover, the higher up the party hierarchy one went, the greater preponderance there was of an intellectual elite exercising real power.[12]

Ideological transformation   The progression of the Socialist Party was replete with contradictions, not least that the party proved capable of appealing for the support of the crucial swing groups in the electorate, while at the same time radicalising its political discourse and programme. For Mitterrand, the party's formal radicalism was the necessary price to be paid for realising the objective of alliance with the Communists, an alliance consolidated in the Common programme in June 1972. Moreover, although the formal alliance between the PS and PCF did not last for long (in September 1977 the parties failed to agree on an 'updated' programme), it had become politically impossible, according to Mitterrand, for the PS to abandon the key proposals of the 1972 programme; this would only provide ammunition for the Communists. Subsequently, the party's *Projet socialiste* of 1980, and even Mitterrand's *110 Propositions*, the 1981 presidential platform, reiterated many of the main demands of the 1972 programme. There was, however, a qualitative difference between the *110 Propositions*, drafted by Mitterrand alone with a view to maximising electoral support, and the unreadable and unworkable *Projet socialiste* drawn up by the CERES leader Chevènement in order to frustrate Michel Rocard in his quest for the party's 1981 presidential nomination.

It is interesting to compare the evolution of the French PS with that of other European Socialist and Social-democratic parties. In order to stand a realistic chance of forming a government, or else as a result of their experience in government, European social-democratic parties had generally moderated their political programmes, originally based on Marxism, in the postwar period. This had usually occured *before* obtaining power, with the evolution of the German SPD providing a role model for other parties to imitate.[13] The French Socialists apparently underwent a reverse process: in order to facilitate alliance with the Communists, the party made radical policy commitments on a scale no other European Socialist Party would envisage. The French PS maintained a far more radical language and programme than that of any other European Socialist Party. This was a product of three factors: the constraint represented by the need to take into account the PCF; the fact that it had been absent from power for almost twenty-five years, and the enduring radicalising influence of May 1968, which inspired a whole new generation of PS activists.

Although in 1971 the PS recruited its own providential leader in Mitterrand, it would be misleading to reduce the post-1971 party to being a mere appendix of Mitterrand's presidential ambitions. As illustrated above (see pp. 27–31) the PS was formed after a process of fusion of existing political formations and its component elements only gradually became forged into a coherent political party. Mitterrand's supporters were originally in a minority and Mitterrand was not at liberty to ignore rival factions within the PS. Only after his triumphant defeat in the 1974 presidential election was Mitterrand able to govern the PS in a more presidential manner and pay less attention to internal party constraints. But it became clear during the 1970s that Mitterrand's presidential status had a fundamental impact upon the organisation of the PS. From 1974 onwards, Mitterrand governed the party in a largely presidential manner and created a 'dual circuit of legitimacy' within the party leadership, by appointing hand-picked delegates to parallel the work of the official National Secretariat, the party's main executive organ.[14] These delegates were responsible to Mitterrand alone, and facilitated the leader's task of keeping himself informed on all of the party's main policy areas and activities without having to rely on the official organisation. Their existence recalled that of the presidential advisers at the Elysée palace, whose function is to advise the President on all policy sectors. Indeed, this unofficial leadership elite created by Mitterrand often occupied positions within the presidential *entourage* after 1981.

François Mitterrand's personal contribution to the rejuvenation of the French Socialist Party in the 1970s was undoubtedly considerable. Although it is logically impossible to predict with accuracy an alternative scenario (what might have occurred had Mitterrand *not* taken over the PS), most observers concur that the balance of flexibility and strategic vision offered by Mitterrand served the party well. Ultimately, however, the party's revival stemmed from more immutable structural factors than the personality of its leader, in particular from far-reaching changes in French society and in the ideological climate, which were always likely to favour the PS at the expense of the PCF.

PRESIDENT MITTERRAND AND THE SOCIALISTS, 1981–88

Viewed as a whole, the emergence of the 'presidential party' has been one of the most striking features of the Fifth Republic.[15] The election of an absolute PS majority in 1981 meant that for the first time a party of the Left occupied the status of being the presidential party. How did the PS react to its new status?

The post-1971 Socialist Party represented, among other things, an uneasy compromise between a *gaullien*-style presidential rally (inspired by Mitterrand's leadership), and a strong tradition of party organisation and self-sufficency (as embodied in the old SFIO, a party with deep traditions which could boast organisational continuity since 1905). The tension between traditions of party patriotism and the exigencies of presidentialism (notably Mitterrand's self-elevation above the party) was a constant feature of internal

PS dynamics during the decade of renewal (1971–81). By 1981, after a decade of skilful manoeuvring and considerable success, the PS had been firmly subordinated to Mitterrand's leadership.

Relations between President Mitterand and the PS after 1981 contained a number of novel departures by comparison with past president–party relations. These were incumbent upon the nature of the PS as a different style of party from the Gaullist UNR, or *giscardien* UDF; notably, a self-proclaimed mass party, rather than merely a personal appendage of a providential leader. Mitterrand's eventual mastery over the Socialist Party was achieved only after a hard-fought campaign during which he earned his spurs as a party leader of the type that de Gaulle professed to despise.

From the beginning of his mandate, Mitterrand insisted that the party had an important, but essentially subordinate function within the new regime. In his first message to PS deputies, the new President insisted that the *110 Propositions* were 'the charter of the government's activity, and therefore of your legislative programme'.[16] This principle of presidential initiative was constantly reiterated by Mitterrand throughout the 1980s: at successive PS congresses, President Mitterrand insisted that the role of the party was, above all, to support the government (therefore the President), rather than to propose alternative policies. The written address to the PS congress thus became a means of reasserting presidential supremacy over the party; the physical absence of the French President reaffirming the point that no French President can appear beholden to party, even when recalling party leaders to their duty.

The party's subordination to the President warranted several explanations. First, Mitterrand's early actions clearly reasserted the pattern of presidential supremacy that had characterised the Fifth Republic under previous presidents: quite simply, the party owed its 1981 parliamentary majority to Mitterrand. Second, the governmental system was largely dominated by *mitterrandistes*, who permeated all levels of government, the administration and even the parapublic sector (i.e. organisations dependent on the state). In theory, and to some extent in practice, this minimised conflict between the different layers of the Socialist power structure (presidency, government, parliamentary party and PS executive) and facilitated the subordination of the party to presidential directives. Mitterrand had coopted Lionel Jospin as PS leader in January 1981; his trusted allies controlled the parliamentary party (Pierre Joxe, and then André Billardon) and the presidency of the National Assembly (Louis Mermaz, 1981–86), as well as the important parliamentary committees. The replacement of Pierre Mauroy by Laurent Fabius as prime minister in July 1984 completed the domination of the *mitterrandistes*. But the sheer extent to which Mitterrand's supporters dominated created new problems. This was evident in relation both to rivalries among *mitterrandistes* themselves (especially between Fabius and Jospin), and animosity between *mitterrandistes* and factional rivals. The manner in which Mitterrand sought to set leading Socialist politicians against each other was indicative of one aspect of his governing style: divide and rule. This was scarcely designed to instil trust between Mitterrand and his lieutenants and finally proved counterproductive.

The subordination of the party to the executive also reflected a virtual osmosis between party and government. This was illustrated by the fact that prominent government ministers had the right to sit on the party's executive organs; that the composition of the party leadership was – until 1988 at least – heavily influenced by the Elysée, and that there was direct presidential involvement in the selection of PS candidates for parliamentary elections.[17] By a judicious use of political appointments, Mitterrand – like his predecessors – was able to ensure that loyal presidential appointees occupied the key positions within government, the administration and the party.[18] Party affiliation was an important consideration for political promotion at the beginning of Mitterrand's presidency, but diminished steadily in importance thereafter (see Chapter 6).

The PS leadership was clearly ill-at-ease with the subordinate position defined for the party by President Mitterrand in July 1981. It believed that the PS was different from other presidential parties of the Fifth Republic, and worried about the negative effects that presidentialism was having on the party's capacity to exist as an autonomous entity. The official definition of the correct role of the Socialist Party was given by its leader Jospin at the 1983 congress, when the PS appeared to come to terms with the constraints imposed by the political regime: 'It is not possible to oppose government policy (which is necessarily that of the President of the Republic) and to belong to the party leadership.'[19] In private, Jospin's attitude in relation to the role of the party was considerably less passive. In a confidental report presented to the party's Directing Committee in July 1985, Jospin complained:

> We have known for a long time that the PS cannot live with the institutions of the Fifth Republic in the same way as the UDR or the UDF used to. We are a different sort of party, a democratic Socialist Party.[20]

The implication was clear: the presidentialist basis of the Fifth Republic had deprived the PS of its capacity to act as a genuinely autonomous organisation. The party ran the danger of being reduced to a vehicle for rival presidential candidates and little else, a Gallic version of the American Democratic party. This sentiment was repeated in similar guises by other leading Socialists, such as Mauroy and Chevènement.

There was little doubt that the party *stricto sensu* was the subordinate partner of the governing triangle (president–government–party). But to a limited extent, new channels of influence on decision-making did evolve during the early reformist period. The major difference between Mitterrand's presidency and those of his predecessors lay in the large degree of access that PS leaders were initially given to the President. In the early stages of his presidency (1981–82), Mitterrand spent a minimum of two breakfasts and one dinner a week meeting representatives of the party leadership, the Prime Minister and selected ministers.[21] This reflected the fact that, more than any previous President, Mitterrand entered office as a *de facto* party leader himself. In this way, in the early stages at least, the party acted as an important semi-institutionalised interest, with various access points to the President of the Republic.

But the importance of party influence must not be exaggerated. Meetings with party leaders diminished in frequency after the early euphoric period. President Mitterrand had made it abundantly clear that, if it might occasionally be consulted, the party could only occupy a subordinate position if he were to respect the institutions of the Fifth Republic. It is clear that party considerations played a far less important role in the aftermath of the economic U-turn of March 1983 and the Catholic schools *débâcle* of 1984, and that the party exercised a marginal influence during the premiership of Laurent Fabius.[22] In fact, the supremacy of executive government in the Fifth Republic greatly limited the autonomy PS deputies could display. Mitterrand's preservation of the essentials of presidential power until 1986 gradually reduced the PS to the status of an observer, whose main function was a propaganda one: to support government policies in the country and to prepare for elections.

The ideological transformation of French Socialism

In the midst of the Mauroy government's turbulent conversion to economic realism, the party itself was largely absent, at least after the early reformist phase. It was indicative of the relationship which existed between the different partners of the Socialist power structure (president – government – party) that the Socialist Party's ideological *aggiornamento* followed rather than preceded the government's practical apprenticeship in the constraints involved in governing the country. This point can be illustrated by a brief overview of Socialist Party congresses during the period from 1981–86. At the congress of Valence in October 1981, leading Socialist orators created a highly detrimental effect by calling upon the government to radicalise its programme and by threatening reprisals against those hindering its application. Such a maximalist discourse was heard with a rare pleasure by PS activists, but with undisguised irritation by the government, anxious to reassure public (and world) opinion about the moderate nature of French socialism. This made Mitterrand determined to limit the party's autonomous means of expression in the future. Subsequently, the PS was rarely involved in crucial policy debates. The party was disoriented by the magnitude of the economic U-turn of 1982–83, and initially sought solace in the belief that the change in economic policy would only prove to be a temporary affair.[23] Once it became apparent that the *politique de rigueur* was henceforth to be a permanent feature of government policy, the party leadership reluctantly adjusted its message. In his speech to the 1983 Bourg congress, party leader Jospin affirmed: 'The party's attitude towards economic and social policy is clear: resolute support for the courageous action of the government, within the framework of the orientations fixed by the President of the Republic.'[24] In private, party leaders were far less sanguine: economic policy provided an enduring source of intra-party division which cut across the boundaries of the party's official factions. Constrained to support the government on economic policy, Socialist Party leaders sought and were offered ideological compensation elsewhere: for instance, PS-inspired amendments to the Education Bill of 1984 were forced upon the hapless Education minister Alain Savary by Mauroy's determination to satisfy the anti-clerical sentiment of the PS deputies.[25] This proved to be a destructive method of conducting government policy: these amendments in turn stimulated the pro-Catholic camp to ever-larger demonstrations, which incited Mitterrand to shelve the bill in July 1984. The failure of the Savary Bill, the fall of the Mauroy government and the advent of Laurent Fabius's administration in July 1984 diminished further party influence, at least until 1988.

The PS congress of Toulouse in 1985 represented a major landmark in the party's history. Drawing on the difficult experience of over four years of government, the party declared itself in theory what it had become in practice, a party committed to gradualist, social-democratic reform, rather than a rapid break with capitalism. This represented a break with the traditionally endemic conflict between a 'radical' political discourse aimed at party activists, and a 'realistic' governmental practice (a divergence initially inherited from the SFIO). The historic decline of the PCF, confirmed by its mediocre result in the 1984 European election, facilitated the party's evolution. The PS was no longer constrained to engage in crude ideological competition with the Communist Party in order to safeguard its left flank. Henceforth the party perceived its political credibility as being indissociably attached to portraying the image of a responsible party of government. The party fought the campaign for the 1986 legislative election as a party of government, which concentrated on defending its record of the previous five years.

MITTERRAND'S SECOND TERM

Relations between the directly elected President and his parliamentary supporters are always likely to be problematic. In part, this reflects the natural tensions caused in relations between the executive and its parliamentary supporters in all unitary political systems. The specificity of the French case rests upon its status as a semi-presidential system; the fact that the President is directly elected by a majority of voters on the vital second round of a presidential election confers an authority upon the French president which surpasses that of most other political leaders in western Europe. Once elected to the Elysée, the presidential candidate becomes head of state, with a constitutional and political duty to represent all French people. From the inception of the Fifth Republic, this has induced Presidents to distance themselves publicly from their parliamentary supporters.

Different presidents have, of course, sustained rather different relationships with their parliamentary majorities. The pattern established by the first three Presidents of the Fifth Republic (de Gaulle, Pompidou and Giscard d'Estaing) was to maintain a public aloofness in relation to their parliamentary supporters, but to move closer towards their parties throughout the course of their presidencies, especially in order to appeal for support during legislative election campaigns. In the case of François Mitterrand and the Socialists a reverse pattern appeared to occur: initially very close to his party, the fourth President gradually distanced himself from the PS. This process, which began in earnest under *cohabitation*, accelerated after Mitterrand's re-election in May 1988, and stemmed in part from the conditions of his re-election.

During his second presidential term, Mitterrand's capacity to dominate the Socialist Party appeared greatly diminished. On 13 May 1988, some five days only after his victorious re-election, members of the party's Directing Committee narrowly opted for Mauroy as their choice for party leader to succeed Jospin, who was named to serve in Rocard's first government. This was in preference to Fabius, Mitterrand's former premier and protégé. Such an apparent act of *lèse majesté* was of considerable importance, since it symbolised the dissolution of the pro-Mitterrand faction which had governed the party in various guises since 1971. Mitterrand's avowed supporters distributed their votes between Fabius and Mauroy. The hostility to the accession of a bourgeois *énarque* (Fabius) to the leadership, without any real internal party debate, explained the party's bad temper. The most probable explanation of Mauroy's accession was that it revealed an undercurrent of resentment to the subordination of the PS to Mitterrand's whims during the first *septennat*, to the centrist political thrust of Mitterrand's 1988 campaign, and to Mitterrand's leadership itself.[26] One effect of the latter had been to exacerbate tensions among his own protégés to such an extent that they outweighed any sense of common loyalty to Mitterrand.

There was evidence during Mitterrand's second term of a much more assertive party, one more determined to insist on its prerogatives, and more willing to advertise its differences with Mitterrand. At the level of party influence over policy and personnel, the pattern was rather an uneven one. Mitterrand's 1988 presidential campaign pledge in favour of 'an opening to the centre' involved a dilution of PS representation within the Rocard, Cresson and Bérégovoy governments, with Socialists holding only around 50 per cent of ministerial portfolios in each government. This was to the benefit either of non-Socialist 'presidential majority' centrists, such as J-P. Soissons or J-M. Rausch; or else personalities from 'civil society', such as B. Tapie or B. Kouchner. We should also signal the role performed by members of Mitterrand's presidential staff who subsequently became ministers, such as J-L. Bianco and S. Royal. All of these were, to some extent, to the detriment of the Socialist Party itself. On the other hand, the Rocard government (1988–91), with only a relative majority in the National Assembly, initially made a point of soliciting support from beyond the ranks of Socialist deputies in its mission to promote consensus politics. A greater willingness to accept amendments, both from PS and centrist deputies, was a natural extension of this.

During Mitterrand's second mandate, renewed factional infighting greatly contributed to the image of the Socialists as a divided ruling clique. Tensions were generated between party, executive and President, as well as within the party itself. They were illustrated starkly at the PS congress of Rennes in March 1990, when, for all of his manoeuvring, Mitterrand failed in his renewed attempt to replace Mauroy with Fabius. The re-emergence of factionalism, artifically suppressed during the first presidential term, was inescapable at the Rennes congress. At Rennes, the party split into two main coalitions (Fabius–Chevènement against Jospin–Mauroy–Rocard), divided far more in relation to rival ambitions and organisational imperatives than anything else. The congress of Rennes was remarkable for the animosity dividing hitherto loyal *mitterrandistes*. It was also remarkable for Mitterrand's refusal to allow Mauroy, Rocard and Jospin to create a new governing majority coalition within the party, which would have isolated Fabius in the minority. Such presidential intervention reaffirmed the indirect control Mitterrand could still exercise over the outcome of party conferences, but it created an additional source of tension within the party, as well as with his Prime Minister Rocard, who was forced to bow to the presidential will.

During the period from 1988–93, internal PS factional politics played a role in determining policy outcomes.[27] For instance, the government made substantial concessions to the Socialist group in the 1990 budget; this was in part an effort by the Finance Minister Bérégovoy (a supporter of Fabius) to fend off an attack by supporters of the main rival faction (Jospin–Mauroy) in the context of the forthcoming PS congress of Rennes.[28] We should not overestimate the influence of factionalism taken in isolation however: the fact that Béréovoy's initiative was supported by President Mitterrand helped to explain its success. The experience of the Rocard, Cresson and Bérégovoy govern ments also testified to the fact that even a government with only a relative majority of deputies was unlikely to be overthrown by the National Assembly, and that PS deputies could be counted upon to support the government on crucial votes of confidence. The repeated use of article 49, clause 3 of the 1958 constitution to force through legislation, often against the background of hostility from PS deputies themselves, increased the malaise separating the Socialist group in the National Assembly and the government. The disillusionment of Socialist deputies was aggravated by the prospect of near-certain defeat in the 1993 legislative elections.[29]

Mitterrand's former protégé Fabius finally did take over the party leadership in January 1992. But, by this stage, it was far from clear whether Fabius could still be considered primarily as a Mitterrand loyalist. The Fabius succession ought perhaps to be considered as one further indication of the post-Mitterrand sentiment sweeping the party.[30] Fabius was supported in his bid for the leadership by Michel Rocard, in exchange for the promise that Rocard be recognised as the party's 'virtual' presidential candidate. For his part, Mitterrand scarcely concealed his preference for Jacques Delors as Socialist candidate in the forthcoming presidential election, as opposed to Rocard whom he cordially detested.[31] The designation of Mitterrand's historic enemy Rocard as the 'natural' Socialist candidate by Mauroy, Jospin and Fabius at the extraordinary PS congress of Bordeaux in July 1992 virtually completed the party's emancipation from the President.

When it finally occurred in March 1993, the magnitude of the Socialists' electoral defeat exceeded even the most pessimistic predictions: with approximately 20 per cent of voters (20.2 per cent, including MRG and *divers gauche*), and a parliamentary group reduced from 282 to 70, the party obtained its lowest score since its re-formation at Epinay in 1971. The comparison with the true blue Assembly of 1968 was evoked by commentators, but this was misleading. In 1968, the PS/PCF/PSU total was over 40 per cent; in 1993, it was under 30 per cent. The extent of the party's lamentable performance was brutally recalled by several statistics. In 1993, the party polled just over one-half of its 1981 and 1988 totals. It did not quite manage to equal its 1973 total (20.7 per cent), despite the fact that the Communist electorate had more than halved since that date. In no single constituency did a Socialist candidate win on the first ballot, by comparison with 40 in 1988.[32] The party's lamentable performance in the March 1993 legislative elections reduced the PS to the level at which Mitterrand had inherited the party in 1971, and weakened further any lingering pro-Mitterrand sentiment within the PS. It is a rather cruel verdict on his twenty-year stewardship of the PS to observe that Mitterrand left the Socialist Party in almost as piteous a state as he found it in the early 1970s.

CONCLUSION

From the perspective of Mitterrand's career as a whole, the period as First Secretary of the Socialist Party would appear as somewhat of an exception. There was little doubt that Mitterrand excelled in the role of party leader during the 1970s, despite his long-standing distrust of organised political parties. Prior to his conquest of the PS leadership, Mitterrand had appeared as an independent-minded politician, too independent indeed to be constricted by the discipline and collective responsibility implied by belonging to a traditional party. This was one of the principal reasons for his early success: that he came from outside both of the main left-wing parties (PCF and SFIO) made him an acceptable presidential candidate in 1965 to the leaderships of both parties. As First Secretary of the PS after 1971, Mitterrand faced powerful constraints which should not be minimised: these included the internal factional balance within the PS and the commitments required by the alliance with the PCF. It was only in 1979 that he captured full control of the PS organisation. And yet, after the 1974 presidential election, Mitterrand ruled the party in a quasi-presidential manner, which short-circuited normal patterns of party management in several important respects.

This spirit of independence resurfaced after his election as President. From the inception, Mitterrand traced the limits to party influence in the new governing arrangements: the role of the party was to support the government. The party was constrained to support presidential or governmental initiatives over which it had little influence. When it dared to oppose the President, as during the Algerian Generals' affair of 1982, it was forced to retract and face presidential retaliation.[33] This deprived the party of the critical policy-making capacity essential for a genuinely independent existence, especially important for a party with a strong tradition of self-sufficiency such as the PS.

The reality of party influence during the Mitterrand presidency was an uneven one. At one level, there was evidence of real party input during the early reformist period. The degree of access accorded by Mitterrand to party leaders was unprecedented in the Fifth Republic. Anecdotal evidence relating to party leverage over specific policies confirmed the impression of an influential party.[34] On closer examination, however, Mitterrand's reliance on party networks was partial and short-lived. From 1982 onwards it gave way to dependence upon more classic bureaucratic structures, as illustrated within his presidential staff (see Chapter 7). Rather than party, Mitterrand's was a personal network: the key contacts were with *mitterrandistes* (assiduously cultivated) at all levels of party and government. This pattern assured an element of cohesion throughout the first presidency that revealed more about Mitterrand's personal governing style than it did about the party per se.

Throughout the period surveyed, Mitterrand's style of political leadership was one which purveyed a strong inclination for personalised mechanisms of control. This was apparent within the PS prior to 1981, when Mitterrand increasingly relied on his own advisers as a counterweight to the official executive: men such as Fabius and Attali were raised in this mould. This pattern was reasserted to some extent once Mitterrand was elected President, as revealed by the ties maintained with former close party associates. The breakdown of Mitterrand's ability to control these various networks after 1988 revealed his diminishing capacity to exercise unqualified personal leadership over his former lieutenants. This was itself a reflection on the limitations of Mitterrand's style of leadership. His inclination to use 'divide and rule' tactics to ensure that his protégés remained his subordinates ultimately backfired. Politicians such as Jospin and Fabius responded by marking their distance from Mitterrand, eventually by allying with Rocard, Mitterrand's historic adversary.

The President's detachment from his own party, especially during the course of his second presidential mandate, provided further insights into his political leadership. It is difficult to avoid the conclusion that Mitterrand became increasingly negligent of the interests of the political force through which he had reached high office. Not only did he purposely attempt to play off its leaders against each other, but he also revealed scant loyalty towards the organisation in other respects. For instance, from 1988 onwards Mitterrand attempted to distance himself from the PS by encouraging the creation of rival pro-presidential groups and personalities, such as J-P. Soisson's *France Unie*, and Brice Lalonde's *Génération Ecologie*, which directly threatened PS electoral fortunes.

The underlying reasons for the PS's electoral débâcle in 1993 ought not to be reduced solely to Mitterrand's leadership. There were more profound structural reasons, notably the perceived failure of Socialist economic management, the usury engendered by a decade in power, the desire for political alternation, and the impact of political corruption. Certain personalities close to Mitterrand were directly involved in scandals (such as Patrice Pélat in the Péchiney affair), although there was no evidence that directly linked Mitterrand with any financial abuse. Even Premier Bérégovoy succumbed to the suspicion of malpractice, in spite of his pledge to root out corruption.[35] The widespread perception of the Socialists as a corrupt and self-serving clique had a debilitating effect on the party's electoral fortunes in 1993.

These affairs transcended the personality of François Mitterrand. And yet, it would not appear too unjust to accuse Mitterrand of failing to offer the PS a coherent ideological vision or a positive role in recent years, save a vague commitment to republicanism, and an invitation to support governments nominated with scant reference to PS interests. Having been brought up as a political independent, the notion of loyalty to party was probably one that passed by Mitterrand.

Chapter 6

The President

It was revealed in Chapter 2 how Mitterrand's notoriety in the early Fifth Republic stemmed largely from his determined opposition to the creation of the new regime, a stance eloquently expressed in his 1964 work *Le coup d'état permanent*.[1] The consistency with which Mitterrand criticised 'personal power' was impressive. The leitmotif of his *Le coup d'état permanent* in 1964, the same theme reappeared fifteen years later on the eve of Mitterrand's election:

> It appears to us to be dangerous that the President of the Republic should concentrate the totality of powers within his hands, as is the case today. It would be even more dangerous if such a situation were to last indefinitely. We are no longer exactly in a Republic.[2]

In spite of such fine words, Mitterrand's attitude towards the Fifth Republic was peppered with ambiguities and inconsistencies. Although initially opposed to the new presidential institutions, Mitterrand was one of the first politicians to recognise the importance of the direct presidential election as a means of restoring the Left's fortunes (and as a means of rebuilding his own career). By his actions from 1965 onwards, Mitterrand became associated with an acceptance of the new presidential rules of political competition in the Fifth Republic. He was undoubtedly realistic to believe that the conquest of political power, if necessary via the presidential election, was an essential preliminary to any reform of the political institutions. Despite his early opposition to the 1958 constitution, Mitterrand asserted on several occasions prior to 1981 that the problem was not so much with the 1958 constitution itself, which he believed created a parliamentary regime, as with the manner in which the constitution had been interpreted by successive presidents.

There was, in the constitutional sphere as in others, a measure of discordance between Mitterrand's political discourse in opposition and his behaviour as President. It was typical of his enigmatic quality that Mitterrand's 1981 *110 Propositions* contained few references to the need for constitutional reform, despite his lyrical condemnation of 'personal power'. Mitterrand justified this caution with the defence that other priorities were far more pressing. The Socialist candidate's only firm commitment was to reform the presidential term of office, either to a renewable five-year mandate, or to a non-renewable *septennat*. This was not respected. In the words of one observer: 'François Mitterrand's virulent denunciations of presidentialism ceased the day he became president'.[3] The pattern of presidential supremacy was clearly reaffirmed by Mitterrand's early actions. This was illustrated by his dissolution of the conservative-dominated National Assembly, elected in 1978, and his call upon the French people to 'give me the means to govern'. The dual mechanism of dissolution and presidential involvement in elections for the National Assembly was wilily exploited by Mitterrand, as it had been by de Gaulle. In the circumstances, Mitterrand's actions appeared politically opportune: why should the Left deprive itself of the opportunity to maximise its power after two decades of conservative rule?

To conclude that Mitterrand abandoned his previous constitutional scruples in the pursuit of his narrow political interests would appear a logical deduction. He admitted in 1981 that: 'I have adapted to the institutions of the Fifth Republic because they have been accepted by the French people.'[4] Mitterrand's defence requires illustration that a different institutional practice materialised throughout the course of his presidency, and that this mitigated the absence of any serious constitutional reform. In the course of the present chapter we shall consider Mitterrand's presidential practice from several related angles: his relationship with his six prime ministers and their governments, with his own presidential staff, and with the civil service. We shall return to the issue of constitutional reform in the conclusion.

MITTERRAND'S PRIME MINISTERS

Interpretations of the hybrid French executive created by the 1958 constitution have been legion.[5] Underpinning most appreciations is the belief that, since de Gaulle, the Fifth Republic's executive has been centred around a strong directly-elected President. The presidency has acted as the key element of systemic legitimacy, which provides a measure of coherence to an otherwise obfuscated set of institutional arrangements. The prevailing presidential interpretation of the regime has tended to downplay (or ignore) the inputs of other institutional actors, such as the prime minister, individual ministers, bureaucratic elites, or interests.[6] It lies outside of the scope of this chapter to attempt an additional general definition of the French executive; rather, it is proposed to demonstrate how the presidential function (as well as Mitterrand's appreciation of it) varied throughout the course of the period 1981–93.

Ever since de Gaulle's celebrated press conference of 1964, during which the General asserted presidential pre-eminence, the 'principle of presidential initiative' (a phrase coined by Jean Charlot) has aptly delineated the underlying legitimacy of the Fifth Republican political system, with the exception of the two periods of *cohabitation*. Presidents have not only defined broad parameters of governmental action, but they have also reserved the right to intervene in any policy sphere. This does not mean that all presidents have been equally interventionist, or that presidents have been consistently interventionist. Presidential practice has in fact varied with each incumbent, as well as at different stages of each presidency. It is clear that presidents have chosen not to interfere in every aspect of detailed government policy. This is either because they do not possess the administrative resources or time to achieve this; or because of their personal political priorities.

Notwithstanding these qualifications, it will be argued that the principle of presidential initiative has essentially underpinned the Mitterrand presidency, except in the periods of *cohabitation*. This is consistent with interpretations of the French executive, which contend that the role of the prime minister has been underplayed in the academic literature. In fact, it is quite consistent to observe that the prime minister is far more involved than the president with the conduct of detailed government policy and the arbitration of intergovernmental disputes; and to reaffirm the principle of presidential initiative. Except during *cohabitation*, policy arbitration on exceptionally divisive issues occurred at the Elysée.[7] When conflicts occurred between President Mitterrand and his prime ministers, the former's view invariably prevailed. And the ultimate sanction of dismissal hung over each prime minister like the sword of Damocles, imposing constraints on prime ministerial autonomy.

Mitterrand's presidential practice varied at different stages of his presidency. This can be illustrated by an assessment of Mitterrand's relationship with his first six prime ministers. By common agreement, during the Mauroy premiership, there was a high incidence of presidential intervention in policy-making.[8] In an interview with the journal *Pouvoirs* Mitterrand himself admitted:

> After such a long absence from government, and in the light of the governmental inexperience of most ministers, Pierre Mauroy and I discovered that it was impossible to go as fast towards a more balanced constitutional practice as I had originally desired. The process was accelerated under Laurent Fabius.[9]

The newly elected President reiterated in his first message to Socialist deputies that the *110 Propositions* were to constitute the core of the government's activity. The broad parameters of governmental action were thereby clearly outlined by Mitterrand. As the personification of *Le Changement*, the new President was associated with the major reforms of the 1981–82 period, especially the form taken by the nationalisation programme. The available evidence suggests that many key decisions were taken by Mitterrand; this does not mean that the President involved himself in the minutiae of every policy. The most obvious examples of presidential arbitration during the 1981–86 period occurred during Mauroy's premiership. They were: nationalisation policy (June and September 1981), economic policy (June 1982 and March 1983 especially), reassertion of control over foreign policy (December 1982 and December 1985), the steel rationalisation programme (March 1984), the withdrawal of the Savary Education Bill (July 1984), and the adoption of proportional representation (April 1985). Many other lesser instances of presidential arbitration could be pointed to: such as the exclusion of works of art from the Wealth Tax, or the amnesty for rebellious generals in the Algerian War.[10]

One of the key functions of the French prime minister is to arbitrate in disputes between different government departments. In terms of settling interministerial disputes, the available evidence pointed to an increase in the activism of the Prime Minister during the 1981–82 period. This was itself a testament to the Left's charged reform programme. Jean Massot calculates that the number of arbitration meetings involving the Prime Minister's office (*comités interministériels*, and *réunions interministérielles*) reached 2,000 in 1982 (from 900 in 1979), before stabilising at 1,400 in 1983–84.[11] Well-placed sources suggest that policy committees chaired by the President (*conseils restreints*), which had proliferated at the early stage of Giscard d'Estaing's presidency, rapidly fell into disuse under Mitterrand, except in matters relating to defence and foreign policy.[12] Presidential arbitration under Mitterrand tended to occur either within the *conseil des ministres*, or else in bilateral informal meetings between the President and selected ministers.

This early stage might be characterised as one of presidential *and* prime ministerial activism. In the eyes of public opinion, President Mitterrand was clearly associated with the conduct of government policy. The President overlooked the desirability of allowing the prime minister to act as a buffer between himself and public opinion, thereby protecting the presidential function from adverse trends in public opinion. Mitterrand became personally associated with increasingly unpopular government policies. By November 1984, he had beaten all other records of unpopularity for presidents of the Fifth Republic. That this unpopularity was based upon his early presidential activism undoubtedly served as an important lesson.[13] Overt presidential involvement in unpopular government policies lay the President open to being criticised as a partisan political leader.

Mitterrand's most critical arbitration was that undertaken in March 1983 in favour of remaining within the EMS (see Chapter 7). This was followed by a period during which neither the President nor the Prime Minister was anxious to occupy the domestic limelight. Mitterrand sought to safeguard the presidency against further public discredit, and began to perfect the role of senior European statesman. This did not, however, prevent him from taking tough domestic decisions when unavoidable, such as that over the steel closures of March 1984. Prime Minister Mauroy suffered on account of his status as a lame-duck premier after the March 1983 drama. The 1984 Education Bill of Alain Savary illustrated Mitterrand's new more arbitral presidential style. Presidential intervention occurred only once after it became transformed into a major national crisis, as a form of crisis management at the ultimate stage of the policy process. The nature of Mitterrand's intervention in the crisis revealed both a new arbitral conception (Mitterrand withdrew a left-wing bill in the interests of national unity); and the highly personalised nature of presidential interventionism (the decision to withdraw the bill being announced at a press conference by Mitterrand alone, with no prior consultation with either Savary or Mauroy).[14] This decision sparked off the resignation of Savary, followed by that of Mauroy.

Mitterrand's nomination of Fabius as prime minister in July 1984 represented a further presidential withdrawal from the forefront of domestic policy-making, to safeguard the presidential function against the Left's likely defeat in the 1986 legislative election. In the words of one advisor, with the nomination of Fabius, 'Mitterrand began to cohabit with his prime ministers'. The modernisation policies of the Fabius administration, while inspired by Mitterrand's crucial choices of March 1983 and February 1984, were conceived in large measure by Fabius and his advisers. Open presidential involvement in the details of domestic policy-making became rarer and less public. But when Mitterrand chose to intervene directly, presidential supremacy was reasserted. This occurred, for example, in relation to Mitterrand's decision to create a new television channel *La Cinq* in the run-up to the 1986 election.

The new spirit of the relationship was articulated by the Prime Minister in September 1984, when he declared rather provocatively 'Lui, c'est lui, moi, c'est moi'.[15] Laurent Fabius imposed a managerial, technocratic style upon the operation of the premiership, in stark contrast to the amiable choas reigning under Mauroy.[16] Given Mitterrand's brief to Fabius, it was natural that policy coordination should be centred more on Matignon than the Elysée: the daily briefings for ministers inaugurated by Fabius provided testament for this. A more limited perception of the presidency under Fabius reflected not only Mitterrand's realisation of the dangers of excessive presidential exposure, but also his desire to consolidate his reputation as a major international statesman and architect of European union. The Fabius administration corresponded in some important respects to a prime ministerial model of executive power. But Mitterrand's second prime minister clearly overstepped the mark of prime ministerial autonomy on several occasions, leading to a deteriorating relationship with the President. Relations between the President and his young Prime Minister were embittered during the Greenpeace affair in the summer of 1985, as a result of which Mitterrand's co-conspirator Hernu was forced to resign as Defence Minister (see Chapter 3). The Prime Minister fell further out of grace with the President for publicly challenging the wisdom of Mitterrand's audience with General Jaruzelski in December 1985: the crucial error related to his questioning of the President's right to act as he pleased within the presidential sector of foreign policy. The brief Fabius premiership nonetheless served its essential function: it effaced the memory of Mitterrand's intense unpopularity from 1983–84, and (with Mitterrand's timely change to proportional representation for the 1986 legislative election) it rallied sufficient support to prevent an electoral rout in the 1986 election.

After the 1986–88 *cohabitation* (see Chapter 3) the Rocard premiership (1988–91) provided a case study of political endurance in the face of cross-cutting pressures. The nomination of Rocard as premier in 1988 corresponded to the political imperatives of the moment but there remained considerable animosity to Mitterrand's historic rival from within the ranks of government and party. In accordance with Mitterrand's 1988 campaign promises, the re-elected president largely confined himself to an arbitral role within the domestic sphere, intervening only to recall ultimate presidential supremacy in political and policy initiatives. The most spectacular example of this was his call for *un nouvel élan* shortly before Rocard's resignation.[17] This left Rocard in charge of coordination of government policy, a task within which he was ably assisted by a highly effective *cabinet*. That Rocard survived for three years bore testament to his durability; from the inception the Prime Minister had to face insidious pressures from within. These came from three directions: from the President, who on several occasions loftily criticised the Premier for lacking social ambition; from the party, whose deputies directed a barrage of criticism against Rocard throughout his premiership; and from members of his government (especially Bérégovoy, Jospin and Lang), who appealed to Mitterrand for support against unfavourable arbitrations by Matignon. Rocard left office not only the most popular of Mitterrand's prime ministers, but arguably the most effective in dealing with the bitter presidential embrace.

Presidential supremacy within the hybrid French executive was recalled with force in May 1991, when Mitterrand finally obliged Rocard to resign and named Edith Cresson in his place. The nomination of Cresson represented, among other things, a declaration of intent on behalf of President Mitterrand: in response to criticisms of uninterest for the fate of the French people, Mitterrand intended to exercise closer supervision over the conduct of domestic policy, after having been adeptly outmanoeuvred by Rocard for three years. The appointment of Cresson was a complete surprise (see Chapter 2). It was allegedly linked to a *policy* motivation; the appointment was heralded as the means of preparing France for the single market of 1993. In the light of this, it was rather incongruous that the Prime Minister was deprived of the means of effectively coordinating government policy, with Mitterrand and Bérégovoy forming an insuperable coalition to prevent her voluntarist industrial ideas from being put into practice.[18] Indeed, the Cresson administration approximated more than any other to a ministerial model of executive relations; key policy decisions were taken not by the Prime Minister, but by the Finance Minister Bérégovoy. Mitterrand's interventionism (the replacement of Rocard with Cresson) was openly censured by the electorate in the regional elections of March 1992: the President had little choice but to part with his fifth prime minister in a manner similar to his fourth.

Mitterrand's misadventure with Cresson left the President in a much weaker position in relation to Pierre Bérégovoy, a political heavyweight by any definition. The autonomy left to Bérégovoy's government recalled that of Fabius eight years earlier. The government's mission was to prepare for probable defeat in forthcoming elections in as honourable a manner as possible. The prestige accumulated from six years as Finance Minister gave Bérégovoy a strong pedestal from which to impose his control over the government. A strong premiership was not incompatible with a President who had recovered his taste for political manoeuvring. The 1992 referendum campaign (see Chapter 8) witnessed Mitterrand occupying the public lime-light in passionate defence of the Maastricht treaty. This confirmed not only that European affairs formed an inextricable part of the presidential sphere, but it provided further testimony to the penetration of the EC into internal French politics, blurring traditional distinctions between European and domestic policy. The Left's humiliating defeat in the National Assembly elections of March 1993 inaugurated a renewed period of *cohabitation*, when Mitterrand accepted the inevitable, and called upon the RPR's E. Balladur to become his seventh prime minister.

Generalities of the presidential–prime ministerial relationship under Mitterrand

Relations between presidents and prime ministers have been the subject of many rather simplistic assessments, which betray a complex reality.[19] No single model can account for the complexity of the presidential–prime ministerial relationship, which is simultaneously conflictual and cooperative, routine and non-static. There is effectively a perennial and institutionalised tension between the Elysée and Matignon. A host of influences can intervene to complicate further the inherently complex relations between the two heads of the French executive.

The ability of Mitterrand's prime ministers effectively to lead and co-ordinate government policy (their constitutional duty) was undermined by at least seven factors: their insecurity of tenure; presidential control over the composition of the government; the special relationship maintained by individual ministers with the President; the sporadic nature of presidential interventions; a presidentially inspired policy-agenda; the inputs of the presidential party; and rival strategies in relation to public opinion. These factors are limited to the internal dynamics of the president–prime minister relationship. The constraints on Mitterrand's freedom of manoeuvre as President (such as public opinion, the economic environment, societal para-meters, problems of policy implementation, etc.) applied all the more forcefully to his prime ministers on account of their ultimately subordinate position. Let us consider these variables in turn.

The appointment of the prime minister   The 1958 Constitution clearly stipulates that the president appoints the prime minister, but nowhere does it refer to the president's right to dismiss the premier. And yet in this sphere, as in others, Mitterrand inherited precise constitutional precedents. Ever since de Gaulle's 1964 press conference, presidents have reaffirmed their right to dismiss their prime ministers, and the latter have accepted presidential prerogatives in this sphere. Of Mitterrand's first six prime ministers, one (Mauroy) resigned in mid-term; three relinquished office as a result of electoral defeat (Fabius, Chirac and Bérégovoy) and two (Rocard and Cresson) were effectively dismissed by the President. In the case of Michel Rocard, the premier had made clear his desire to serve out a full legislative term only weeks before his 'resignation'. Cresson finally bowed out in April 1992 after attempting to cling tenaciously to office. That most prime ministers derive their political legitimacy from presidential patronage, rather than an independent elective mandate or party responsibilities, confirms their subordinate status, however much they might impress their mark on government policy. Stronger prime ministers (Rocard) are just as likely to be asked to resign as weaker ones (Cresson). Of Mitterrand's seven prime ministers, only Chirac and Balladur could claim a political legitimacy that was genuinely independent of the President.

The composition and control of government   The 1958 Constitution affirms that the president of the Republic appoints ministers 'upon the proposal of the prime minister'. In practice, the composition of government is subject to a bargaining procedure between the two: the key posts are nonetheless usually presidentially inspired. The president exercises almost a complete freedom of manoeuvre in relation to the 'reserved' sector of foreign policy, European affairs and defence. Even during the 1986–88 *cohabitation*, Mitterrand was able to ensure that Chirac's initial choices for these posts were vetoed.[20] Presidential patronage considerably weakens the control exercised by the prime minister over the composition of government. Edith Cresson, to take an obvious example, complained bitterly of the President's refusal to allow her to reshuffle her government in accordance with her own preferences. This key problem has affected all prime ministers in varying measures, and provides a permanent bone of contention.

Direct relations between ministers and the president   The hybrid semi-presidential regime discourages the notion of collective governmental responsibility in several ways. While bemoaning the lack of government cohesion, French presidents have in practice often encouraged prominent ministers to deal directly with them. This was more obvious under certain prime ministers (Mauroy, Rocard and Cresson) than others (Fabius or Bérégovoy). The direct appeal to the President to overturn unfavourable policy arbitrations was a tried and often successful tactic. The most cited example is that of Culture

Minister (1981–92) Jack Lang, who was consistently able to safeguard the Culture budget from the fiscal rigours of the Finance ministry. The prime minister can rarely count on absolute loyalty from ministerial colleagues, who often attempt to pursue an autonomous line with secret connivance from the President. In Mitterrand's case, this was particularly true of premiers Mauroy and Rocard, two men outside of the inner Mitterrand circle, and Cresson, whose *mitterandiste* credentials did not prevent serious policy divergences with the President.

The unpredictabality of presidential intervention   Ever since de Gaulle, presidents have reserved the right to intervene in any policy area, should the necessity arise. But, apart from areas of predictable and persistent presidential involvement, such intervention cannot always be foreseen. Mitterrand's announcement of the withdrawal of the Savary Education bill at a press conference in July 1984 was only the most spectacular example of this. Such intercessions can have a demoralising effect on the prime minister, especially when the latter learns of presidential initiatives at televised press conferences. The image of presidential withdrawal from domestic politics from the time of Fabius onwards can be exaggerated. In accordance with the principle that presidents can intervene randomly, Mitterrand displayed considerable interest in certain aspects of domestic policy: notably social policy, the environment, the media and cultural policy.[21]

A presidentially inspired policy agenda   This has been dealt with elsewhere (Chapters 3 and 5).

The influence of the party   The novelty of the Mitterrand presidency, in its early stages at least, was the degree of access to decision-making enjoyed by the PS leadership (Chapter 5). The party acted as an important institutionalised interest, on occasion influencing presidential thinking in a manner inimical to the prime minister. The factionalised nature of Socialist Party politics also played a role: that Pierre Mauroy had been on the 'wrong' side at the 1979 PS congress of Metz was a important consideration, encouraging pure *mitterandiste* ministers to appeal to the President over and above the Prime Minister. In addition, Mauroy faced stiff opposition on occasion from the Socialist parliamentary group, articulated by Pierre Joxe, a long-standing rival within the Socialist Party. Party considerations became less important, but continued to have a negative impact (from the prime ministerial perspective) during the Rocard premiership, when the President's *bête noire* came under attack from ostensibly friendly quarters.[22]

The 'presidential' factor   The personalisation of political competition encouraged by the Fifth Republic has made each premier into a potential future rival to the President himself. Prime ministers are nominated by presidents with a view to safeguarding them from public reprobation, which prime ministers are invited to assume in the event of government unpopularity. And yet, ambitious prime ministers often regard their position as a platform from which to launch a bid for the presidency, and might be unwilling to sacrifice their political capital for the sake of the incumbent president. The case of Rocard illustrates the point. As premier, Rocard was consistently more popular than Mitterrand: he thereby displayed a cautious approach towards policy, in order not to alienate any segment of public opinion that might be tempted to vote for him in a future presidential election. To some extent Fabius, although a *mitterrandiste*, fell into the same category. Ultimately, the potential for confrontation engendered by the hybrid French executive can erode the closest of political relationships: the experience of Fabius and Cresson, both stauch *mitterrandistes*, confirmed this. Prime ministers can become a liability if they are popular, for they risk overshadowing the president, as occurred to some extent during the Fabius and Rocard premierships. But they can be an even greater liability if too unpopular, as both Mauroy and Cresson found to their cost, since their unpopularity usually drags down the President.

These various constraints impinge upon the freedom of manoeuvre of prime ministers; but, even outside periods of *cohabitation* (when the system has largely reverted to being a prime ministerial, parliamentary model), their role has been far from minimal:

- Although there is no direct equation between resources and power (as demonstrated by the ineffective Italian presidency), the prime minister possesses far more administrative resources than the president. The president's Elysée staff pales by comparison with the expertise available to the prime minister. The prime minister also controls the services responsible for evaluating and monitoring government policy, notably the General Secretariat of the government (composed of elite civil servants). He is, moreover, assisted by a powerful private office (*cabinet*), responsible for intervening on his behalf in the work of other government departments and in assisting the head of government in the process of interministerial arbitration, and policy formulation.[24] The *cabinets* of certain premiers enjoyed a reputation as fearsome defenders of the prime minister's policy and political interests. This was notably the case for Rocard's *cabinet*, headed by the talented J-P. Huchon.[25]
- The prime minister usually performs a more important role than the president in coordinating specific governmental policies, although the president defines the general parameters of policy and can intervene at random. The prime minister (or his representative) chairs interdepartmental committees to arbitrate between government departments, although the Elysée's representatives will usually be present at important

meetings. As illustrated above, there is evidence that there was a lessening of presidential involvement in ironing out domestic policy disputes throughout the course of the Mitterrand presidency. The increased number of meetings chaired by the prime minister or a member of his staff did not necessarily signify presidential withdrawal, however: formal meetings of any variety might simply ratify decisions taken elsewhere, by definition impossible to measure accurately.

- Finally, the prime minister disposes of his own source of patronage, to some extent in competition with that of the President (see p. 99).

If we survey the Mitterrand presidency as a whole, there is little reason seriously to challenge a refined presidentialist interpretation of the Fifth Republic, except during the periods of *cohabitation*. The presidency remained the cornerstone of the institutional edifice: although other actors might often have been more involved with detailed policy-making (the prime minister, individual ministers, or bureaucratic elites), they ultimately derived their legitimacy from presidential preference, and could be removed by presidential edict.

THE ELYSÉE STAFF

French Presidents are assisted by their own presidential staff in the General Secretariat of the Elysée (SGE). It is not intended in this section to proceed with a detailed assessment of the sectoral organisation of the Elysée staff under Mitterrand; the interested reader will find this admirably developed elsewhere.[26] Rather, we shall illustrate how the changing composition and functions of the Elysée staff revealed how Mitterrand's notion of the presidency itself evolved in the course of his office. But, first, Mitterrand's presidential advisers must be placed in a comparative perspective.

Under Mitterrand, the size of the Elysée staff remained roughly comparable with that bequeathed by de Gaulle, Pompidou and Giscard. Definitive figures are difficult to establish, but no more than forty civilian and fewer than ten military advisers aided Mitterrand at any one time.[27] By comparison with the genuinely tentacular American presidency, these figures appear derisory.[28] In addition to the General Secretariat, the French president can rely upon the logistical support of various organs officially attached to the prime minister's office: the most important of these are the *Secrétariat général du Comité interministériel* (SGCI), the key organ dealing with European Affairs; and the *Secrétariat général de la Défense nationale* (SGDN), charged with co-ordinating defence policy. This modest presidential infrastructure, while more extensive than that at the disposal of a British prime minister, has to be set in the context of the extensive bureaucratic machine officially coordinated by the French prime minister, as well as the administrative capacity at the disposal of the larger government departments.[29]

Composition Whereas past presidents had drafted senior civil servants into the presidential staff, Mitterrand initially surrounded himself with writers, artists, party loyalists and university professors. The proportion of civil servants within Mitterrand's first Elysée cohort was 40 per cent, from 90 per cent under de Gaulle, 89 per cent under Giscard d'Estaing, and 73 per cent under Pompidou.[30] In symbolic terms, it was important to illustrate that a new elite had arrived in power: the presence of men such as Régis Debray in the Elysée achieved this effect.[31] A recurrent theme has been that as a political leader Mitterrand placed great importance upon proven personal loyalties among his subordinates. The overriding feature of Mitterrand's staff in 1981 was some element of personal connection to the President: men such as G. Beauchamps, F. de Grossouvre or G. Penne had been attached to the President for more than thirty years.

Once presidential rule became routinised, however, personal ties based on past loyalty became less important than demonstrable administrative competence. The early *compagnons de route* gradually left presidential service, often for a more direct political engagement. The replacement of P. Bérégovoy as General Secretary by J-L. Bianco in June 1982 was exemplary in this respect. Bianco's profile was far more typical of the traditional French politico-administrative elite than that of his predecessor.

This symbolised a more general return to established practices of elite recruitment in France, based upon selecting graduates from the *Ecole Nationale d'Administration* (ENA) and career civil servants. Mitterrand's later advisers largely shared the characteristics of the traditional French politico-administrative elite: prominent advisers such as J-L. Bianco, E. Guigou, G. Ménage, C. Salzman, and H. Védrine were all products of ENA. Indeed, recruitment to the presidential staff not only reverted to the established technocratic model, but became delegated to subordinates, notably Bianco, who selected ENA graduates previously unknown to the President. *Énarques* were ideal since their professional training gave them unrivalled knowledge of administrative procedures. By the time of Mitterrand's re-election in 1988, the presidential staff had become virtually 'depoliticised'. Presidential advisers were selected on grounds of merit rather than personal or political affinity, and the avenue of the Socialist Party, from being a favoured means of promotion, had become a virtual irrelevance.

As a general rule, Mitterrand was scrupulous about advancing the careers of his advisers once they had left his service.[32] Most returned to their origins within the career civil service, but a number of advisers used the Elysée as a springboard from which to launch a political career, a development unimaginable under de Gaulle, but practised by his successors. Mitterrand was insistent that those advisers seeking a political career should not benefit from undue presidential patronage, but should subject themselves to democratic election (whether at national or local level): no fewer than five advisers left presidential service in 1988 to contest constituencies in the 1988 National Assembly elections. The successful transition from presidential adviser to government minister was accomplished by several counsellors: Bianco, Royal, Guigou, Charasse, but others were less fortunate.[33]

Another notable feature of Mitterrand's style was his promotion of women and representatives of minority groups into positions of first rank importance. This was revealed with the increasing number of women appointed within the staff. In 1981, women accounted for about one quarter of the 40 presidential advisers in the Elysée; by 1991, they comprised about one half. In 1992, the youngest adviser – Anne Lauvergeon – was only thirty-two.[34] Prominent former women advisers, such as Elizabeth Guigou or Ségolène Royal, went on to occupy prestigious ministerial positions.[35] For one observer, Mitterrand's determination to facilitate the accession of previously excluded groups was genuine: this was typified by his promotion of women into prominent public positions, by his rejuvenation of the age profile of the presidential staff, and by his representation of minority ethnic and religious groups.[36] Indeed, Mitterrand proceeded with an unprecedented rejuvenation of presidential personnel, itself symbolic of his desire to associate younger generations with his enlightened, avuncular leadership.[37] By July 1992, only six of Mitterrand's original advisers remained in the presidential service.[38]

Functions   The role of the presidential advisers is to keep the President informed on all major areas of policy. During the early reformist period of the Mitterrand presidency, the Elysée advisers were reputedly highly interventionist, maintaining a ubiquitous presence at all levels of decision-making, although there is some dispute about this.[39] It has been contended, moreover, that Mitterrand's advisers initially freely 'interpreted' the presidential will in dealings with government departments, and routinely evoked presidential authority to arbitrate policy disputes in interministerial committees.[40] On occasion, relations between the Prime Minister and key presidential advisers have been severely strained, as they were between Attali and Mauroy. There is little doubt that their interventionist practice led to significant resentment from elsewhere within the state hierarchy, not least among government ministers. Mitterrand himself would on occasion be called upon to arbitrate between his adviser and a prominent minister.[41]

The economic U-turn of June 1982, followed by the replacement of Bérégovoy by J-L. Bianco in the key post of General Secretary of the Elysée ended this chaotic state of affairs. Under the control of Bianco the Elysée staff became more rationalised, more disciplined, less an extension of Mitterrand in his previous role as First Secretary of the Socialist Party. This was symbolised by a greater unwillingness to allow Elysée staff to intervene in spheres of domestic politics regarded as lying within the governmental domain. The type of adviser also changed: in 1984, a media communication section was established in the Elysée, led by Gérard Colé and Jacques Philan.[42] The growing influence of these two men occurred to the detriment of more established advisers. The new saliency of the experts in media-image and political communications reflected modified presidential ambitions, as policy concerns gave way to Mitterrand's positioning as the President of all the French from 1984 onwards. This reached its apogee during the 1986–88 *cohabitation*, during which Mitterrand's advisers were excluded from crucial policy arbitration meetings.[43] After Mitterrand's re-election, Elysée representatives again attended the major decision-making committees, but their presence was an unostentatious one. Mitterrand's key advisers during his second presidential term were within the sphere of foreign policy, European affairs and defence.[44] Throughout Mitterrand's presidency, an inner circle of advisers had regular contact with the President. Other advisers had less frequent, if any, direct access to Mitterrand and communicated with the President by means of written notes.[45]

Mitterrand's Elysée staff performed a relatively modest function. Any notion that the presidential staff constitutes an alternative government must be rejected: the staff is far too small, and the amount of work involved is enormous. The need to provide the President with daily support precludes the staff from being an alternative administration, even in very specific areas of policy where the President can call upon additional resources (notably Europe, aided by the SGCI, and defence, assisted by the SGDN). The influence of the staff is limited by the fact that none of the four presidents of the Fifth Republic has limited his contacts to staffers. Presidents will consult a wide range of opinions, Mitterrand more than any other. Direct contact with ministers, favoured especially by Mitterrand, acts as a counterweight to the presidential staff. The Elysée staff can accurately be described as the 'eyes and ears of the President' but their capacity for autonomous decision-making ought not to be overstated.

PATRONAGE: THE DISTRIBUTION OF THE SPOILS

Presidential powers of appointment extend well beyond the closed confines of the Elysée palace. The French president makes full use of his constitutional prerogatives of appointment, as well as those not explictly mentioned in the constitution. The French president disposes of the power of appointment in accordance with Article 13 of the 1958 Constitution: the top 300 or so posts are presented to the Council of Ministers (and require a prime ministerial, or ministerial counter-signature); others proceed by presidential decree alone. Presidential patronage extends beyond the de facto nomination of government ministers to include top civil servants, the heads of nationalised industries and banks, prominent positions within the media, university rectors, prefects, military officers, ambassadors and appointments to a myriad of governmental quangos.[46] A total of some 700 posts are at the disposition of the executive.

Upon his election in 1981, the new President proceeded to 'purify' the administration by replacing the most senior civil servants promoted under conservative administrations with more dependable bureaucrats close to the PS. Mitterrand also engaged in an extensive overhaul of positions in the parapublic sector. The heads of the new nationalised industries and banks in particular were reserved for politically dependable personalities close to the President. There was an undoubted element of mistrust on Mitterrand's part of existing bureaucratic elites, modelled by 25 years of right-wing governments. There was also a hint of provincial mistrust of Parisian technocracy.

This did not imply that Mitterrand was willing, or able, to relinquish the expertise provided by the French politico-administrative elite. The PS itself had attracted the services of numerous 'technocrats' before 1981, many of whom had worked in the party's commissions drafting future laws. Amongst Mitterrand's protégés, *énarques* figured prominently. Men such as Attali, Fabius or Jospin had all followed the classic path associated with France's elite: this involved attendance at the elitst *Ecole Nationale d'Administration*, followed by employment in the civil service before active political engagement. Any misgivings on Mitterrand's part towards *énarques* vanished once the complexities of policy making became clearer, and the technical expertise provided by politico-administrators came to be valued.

The notion of a spoils system is rather misleading in the French context. A comparison with the American system reveals several important differences. Unlike the American system, political appointments within the French bureaucracy are limited to the top elite, rather than reaching the middle ranks. Moreover, the permanent administration in France has proved remarkably effective at diffusing an administrative ethos among politicians, unlike its weak American counterpart. Third, there is a close interpenetration between political and administrative elites in France which is unparalleled in the US or UK. Finally, even where politicians can nominate freely to positions of public authority, they tend to choose top civil servants anyway, since they have expert knowledge of administrative procedures. This system has been characterised as a 'closed-circuit spoils system': in those spheres elucidated by the 1958 constitution, politicians can replace bureaucratic elites, but in practice they are usually forced to replace them with alternative bureaucratic elites.

Within these constraints, it can be seen that Mitterrand's 1981 'purification' was radical: from May 1981–July 1982, all prefects were either replaced or moved sideways, a measure unpredecented in its scope since the Liberation. During the period 1981–83, one third of directors (the senior-ranking career civil servants) were replaced annually.[47] After the nationalisation programme of 1982, only three out of 42 managing directors of public-sector firms preserved their posts. After the RPR/UDF victory in 1986, Chirac proceeded to undertake a cleansing of *l'Etat-PS* almost as radical in its scope as that executed by Mitterrand. Once re-elected in 1988, Mitterrand preserved in place many of those appointed by Chirac, as an indication of his new anxiety to exclude the civil service from political controversy.[48]

In practice, Mitterrand's discretionary power of appointment to top administrative posts was influenced by pressures to nominate from within the bureaucracy, or else face fierce corporative resistance from top civil servants. To take one example, Presidents can appoint whomsoever they please to the Council of state (*Conseil d'état*), but their choice will usually centre on trained administrators, thereby providing confirmation, according to critics, of the self-perpetuation of the politico-administrative elite. Mitterrand created an uproar in early March 1993 by nominating Pierre Joxe, a trusted lieutenant, to the post of President of the Court of Accounts (*Cour des comptes*), in anticipation of the Left's certain defeat days later; it was generally overlooked that Joxe had been a qualified magistrate attached to the Court before entering politics. This followed a series of similar moves of ministers or members of ministerial *cabinets* to posts in the administration or the parapublic sector.

Several examples illustrate that Mitterrand's prime ministers were also able to promote their pawns into powerful positions within the state machinery. As in other domains, the 1986–88 *cohabitation* reversed the normal order of priorities: nominations still resulted from a bargaining process, but the Prime minister now occupied the key strategic vantage points. Except in the limited sphere of defence policy, where he insisted upon compromise, Mitterrand agreed to Chirac's proposed nominations, in order better to castigate *L'Etat-RPR* during the 1988 presidential election campaign. Outside periods of *cohabitation*, the prime minister disposes of less patronage, but this remains significant: for instance, nominations falling within the prime ministerial sphere have included appointments to the position of *légion d'honneur*, to the *Cours des comptes*, and to the *Conseil d'état*; and the prime minister will usually be consulted over all senior bureaucratic appointments. Pierre Mauroy was known for pursuing the interests of *nordistes* within the civil service, as well as actively lobbying for regional funds to be allocated to the Nord-Pas de Calais region. Fabius created an uproar by nominating a lowly administrator in his own constituency (M. Lesouhaitier) to serve in the *Conseil d'état*. Rocard had less room for manoeuvre, coming as he did from outside of the President's habitual network: in the key ministries held by *mitterrandistes*, recognisable Rocard supporters were almost entirely excluded, but even Rocard was able to promote his appointees elsewhere.[49]

CONCLUSION: THE PRESIDENCY AND MITTERRAND'S LEADERSHIP

As surveyed in the course of this chapter, it appears obvious that the key to understanding Mitterrand's political leadership in the post-1981 period lay in his occupancy of the French presidency, the pinnacle of a generally hierarchical pattern of government. It has become modish to argue that the presidential institutions bequeathed by de Gaulle and his successors suited Mitterrand perfectly. This observation is not devoid of foundation, although it underplays the evolution of presidential practice under Mitterrand. It is difficult to contradict the notion that Mitterrand did not fundamentally challenge the *gaullien* institutional legacy, centred around a strong presidency. This was particularly the case in relation to foreign affairs, defence and Europe (see Chapter 9). Mitterrand's failure to introduce any measure of constitutional reform during the first twelve years of his presidency must be taken as proof of a lack of political audacity in this respect. The cause of constitutional reform became reduced to being a weapon in the presidential armoury, a part of an on-going game designed to destabilise his political adversaries. It was an unflattering observation on Mitterrand's leadership that a principal motive for his political action during the long years from 1958–81 was downplayed in such a cavalier fashion once he was elected President. Whatever his discourse in opposition, the *gaullien* model of presidential supremacy proved too seductive to be seriously challenged. When proposals for reform were finally presented one month before the 1993 National Assembly elections, they appeared destined to distract public opinion from the more immediate tasks at hand.

Mitterrand's defence rests upon his claim to have moderated the practice of the Fifth Republic. In 1987 he declared:

> Working in collaboration with Pierre Mauroy and then Laurent Fabius, I attempted to fulfil my duties in such a way that the President presides, the government governs, and parliament legislates. I have protected the major functions performed by the President, in particular the concentration on great national issues, which stem from the constitution and especially from article 5.[50]

Mitterrand referred repeatedly to this notion of restoring a correct institutional balance that had been disrupted by the presidentialist deviation of the Fifth Republic. In his 1988 campaign platform, the *Letter to the French*, Mitterrand portrayed his conception of the President as lying somewhere between the 'impotent President' of the Fourth Republic, and 'omnipotent' President of the Fifth.[51] As we observed above, a principle of presidential initiative essentially underpinned the Mitterrand presidency (excepting the periods of *cohabitation*). This was most obvious from 1981–86, but remained valid during the second presidential mandate, as evidenced by the fact that Premier Rocard referred repeatedly to Mitterrand's *Letter* as providing the legitimacy for the government's actions.

And yet, while Mitterrand continued ultimately to define the parameters of key policy choices (Europe, economic policy and so on), there was an evolution in Mitterrand's own perception of what the presidential function should comprise. There is a large measure of agreement that after the early reformist enthusiasm of 1981–83, Mitterrand adopted a more arbitral stance towards the supreme magistracy than any of his precedecessors, certainly since de Gaulle. But there remained a wide gulf between Mitterrand's discourse and his actions. For example, however sincere Mitterrand was in his quest to restore the authority of parliament, in the interest of more balanced institutions, it was undeniable that Socialist governments from 1981–86 and from 1988–93 made excessive use of the restrictive devices in the 1958 constitution to push through legislation without undue parliamentary scrutiny.[52] In this sphere, as in others, the record disappointed many of those who had swept Mitterrand to power in 1981.

Chapter 7

Mitterrand's governing style

The presidency of the French Fifth Republic has been likened to an elective monarchy.[1] Once established in the Elysée Palace (as French kings would previously install themselves at Versailles), French Presidents surround themselves with a network of advisers plotting intrigue and counter-intrigue, a latter-day monarchical court. Although comparisons should not be pushed too far, the monarchical metaphor does capture something of the essence of the French presidency. His formal status as head of state confers a prestige on the French President that surpasses that accorded to other European political leaders.

In this chapter, we shall attempt first to discern the outstanding features of Mitterrand's monarchical governing style as President, before appraising his media personality, his cultivation of a range of networks and clienteles, and finally considering how these contribute to our understanding of Mitterrand as a political leader.

MITTERRAND'S GOVERNING STYLE

In Chapter 4, an attempt was made to decipher Mitterrand's complex political persona. One recurrent theme was his enigmatic character, and the difficulty of interpreting the real Mitterrand. His personal characteristics would appear to some extent to be reflected in his mode of operating within the political system. A great amount of incidental research has been carried out in relation to Mitterrand's governing style, first as PS leader and later as President. This seems to converge in its main findings, which, perhaps of necessity, are often impressionistic and anecdotal. The prevalent features of the Mitterrand style involved patient reflection, the cultivation of plural sources of information and rival policy advisers, a taste for secrecy, an antipathy towards collective forms of expression, a sharp awareness of the balance of power in any given situation, and a proclivity for the counter-attack. We shall consider these in turn.

Patient reflection Mitterrand's celebrated maxim, *Il faut donner du temps au temps*, came to crystallise a distinctive governing style. He refused to be rushed into making rapid decisions, preferring patient reflection to precipitate decision-making. The advantage with this method was that Mitterrand gave the impression of being unlikely to act on impulse; even 'impulsive' actions, such as his startling visits to Beirut in 1983, or Sarajevo in 1992, had been carefully planned in advance. The disadvantage was that the President often gave the impression of uncertainty and hesitation. In such cases, Mitterrand was accused either of 'fiddling while Rome burns', or else concocting diabolic political manoeuvres to outwit his opponents.

In extreme circumstances, Mitterrand's style appeared to feed the media contention that there was a vacuum of power at the summit of the state, for lack of firm, decisive leadership. When, in mid-March 1983, Mitterrand was called upon to arbitrate on the major economic choices of his first presidency, his hesitations caused financial markets to panic. Ten days passed before the President finally confirmed his decision to devalue the franc and remain within the European Monetary System.[2] During this period even his closest advisers claimed to have been kept in the dark, so much so that contradictory statements were issued to the media. In fact, the coalitions advocating the rival options both believed at various stages that they had won the President over. For a full ten days, the sitting Prime Minister, Mauroy, was uncertain whether or not he was to remain at his post. The same was true for finance minister Jacques Delors, who on at least one occasion believed he was about to be named prime minister. The overall impression was one of confusion and uncertainty: even though the decision to remain within the EMS had reputedly been taken after three days, it was not made public until one week later.[3] Mitterrand's hesitation in nominating Pierre Bérégovoy as Prime minister in April 1992 was another case in point.

The style of political leadership exercised by Mitterrand (one of patient reflection, followed by endorsement of politically courageous, often un-popular decisions) appeared to be in stark contrast with that of a 'conviction politician' such as Margaret Thatcher in the UK. In spite of the fact that the major changes in policy direction were imposed upon him by complex forces outside of his control, Mitterrand personally contributed to their legitim-isation, by explicit endorsement of new directions taken. For instance, Mitterrand made repeated speeches throughout France in 1983 to drive home the message that he fully supported the new economic austerity policy.

Notwithstanding this legitimisation of new policy directions during his first presidency, on other occasions Mitterrand appeared to have been genuinely caught out by the evolution of history, most notably in relation to the East European revolutions of 1989, and the process of German re-unification. In these circumstances the maxim, *Il faut donner du temps au temps*, equated with indecision and vacillation. A natural tendency to hesitate before taking important decisions made Mitterrand appear unfavourable towards the events in Eastern Europe and contributed to the rather unjust image of him as one of the last cold war politicians (see Chapter 10).

Plural sources of information and rival policy advisers To be able to make informed decisions Mitterrand consistently exposed himself to conflicting sources of policy advice, a pattern firmly established in his role as First Secretary of the Socialist Party from 1971–81.[4] In the words of Schifres and Sarazin:

> No matter how apparently trivial the subject might be, François Mitterrand never relies on only one source of information, despite the fact that it might be the most complete and competent available. On the contrary, he will always multiply his contacts, conversations and research before making up his mind.[5]

Such duplication was in part inherent in the division of executive authority in the Fifth Republic; presidential advisers routinely paralleled the work of government ministers. But Mitterrand would also set two or more of his Elysée advisers to work on the same policy dossier, usually without informing them of their dual labour. Alternatively, he would call upon the services of outsiders to provide a different perspective. This division of labour suited Mitterrand's own Darwinian sense of selection. Far from being merely a presidential game, it avoided excessive hierarchy among his advisers, provided him with the fullest advice possible and reminded everybody that no one could take their position for granted.

For certain observers Mitterrand's governing style amounted to little more than a sophisticated form of divide and rule, blurring still further the already blurred lines of political responsibility with the French executive. This method created considerable, perhaps unnecessary, tensions among his close advisers, and between advisers and ministers. The example of the rivalry between Jospin (PS leader from 1981–88) and Fabius (prime minister from 1984–86) referred to in Chapter 4 proved a case in point.

A taste for secrecy Probably none of his advisers, not even Jacques Attali the 'special' adviser from 1981–91, could genuinely claim to be continually in the President's confidence, or to predict the way his mind was working. His advisers were on occasion so firmly convinced that the President had made a firm decision that they announced it as such to the media, only later to be reprimanded and fall into temporary disgrace. Mitterrand's secrecy had always formed an important part of his personality: it had explained, for instance, why he had refused to answer allegations relating to his behaviour in the scandals analysed above (pp. 11–12, 19–20). The secretive aspect to Mitterrand's personality (and his refusal to be baited by opponents) almost certainly allowed his rivals to portray him, sometimes unjustly, as a perennial manoeuvrer devoid of political transparency.

An antipathy towards collective forms of expression Unlike President Giscard d'Estaing, who regularly met with his advisers, Mitterrand dealt on a one-to-one basis with his, corresponding with the bulk of his advisers by means of written notes. In the course of his first presidency, Mitterrand reputedly met only once with his assembled Elysée staff.[6] This personalised form of relationship ensured that advisers were responsible to him alone, as befits a presidential style of authority. This was consistent with Mitterrand's distrust of rigid organisational formats, discussed in Chapter 5 in relation to political parties.

The balance of power and the counter-attack   Underpinning Mitterrand's actions was a finely developed sense of the balance of power, of the strength of the adversary, and of the realistic opportunities opened to him. It was argued in Chapter 2 that Mitterrand's capacity to rebound from seemingly hopeless political situations comprised a remarkable personal trait. Even during the darkest moments of his presidency, he preserved the ability to wrongfoot his political opponents by launching audacious counter-attacks, usually aimed at dividing the opposing political camp. In July 1984, at the height of the church schools crisis, Mitterrand coupled his withdrawal of the offending bill with a plan for a 'Referendum on the Referendum', which took the steam out the protest movement.[7] The entire period of the 1986–88 *cohabitation* might be considered as a subtle and shifting counter-attack, to recover his diminished political prestige prior to the 1988 presidential election. In June 1992, Mitterrand responded to manifest RPR/UDF divisions over Europe by announcing his decision to hold a referendum over ratification of the Maastricht treaty on European Union, causing a state of near-apoplexy within the neo-Gaullist RPR. On this occasion, the President disseminated the image of being too finely tuned a political strategist for his own good. The feeling that he was 'too clever by half' rebounded against Mitterrand in the Maastricht referendum, with the result that a pro-European electorate only narrowly approved a treaty Mitterrand considered vital for France's future. In this instance, his political judgement appeared impaired. Was he really willing to sacrifice perhaps his greatest European achievement for the pleasure of dividing the Right?

Apart from reflecting his personal qualities such as his secrecy and his individualism, Mitterrand's style developed from his political past as a parliamentary broker distrustful of excessive institutional rigidity, and from his original status as an outsider.

MITTERRAND'S MEDIA PERSONALITY

In the opinion of one observer: 'Of all of the Presidents of the Fifth Republic, only Mitterrand appears to have understood the need constantly to upgrade one's image while simultaneously grounding it in republican tradition'.[8] His grasp of the broadcasting medium was a gradual and imperfect process. Initially a poor television performer (notably in his 1974 televised duel with

Giscard d'Estaing), Mitterrand gradually mastered the technique, with the assistance of communications experts within the Socialist Party and among the Elysée staff. By 1988, Mitterrand was a past master in the art of political communication, adeptly outmanoeuvring his rival Chirac in that year's key presidential debate. As the incumbent president after 1981, Mitterrand exploited the whole panoply of media instruments at the disposal of French Presidents: the press conferences perfected by de Gaulle; the detailed face-to-face interviews (the format usually preferred by Mitterrand); and solemn presidential addresses. At a policy level, the audiovisual reforms introduced by Mitterrand's governments undoubtedly liberalised the tightly controlled broadcasting media, while retaining important elements of state control.[9]

In his media personality (as in his broader political persona), Mitterrand represented a novel synthesis of the old and the new. In the 1981 presidential campaign, for instance, the traditionalism of the Quiet Force (*la Force tranquille*) coexisted alongside the appeal for change embodied in the campaign slogan, *le changement*. The fusion of the old and new within Mitterrand was refined with considerable expertise throughout his first presidency. It culminated during the 1988 presidential campaign. Enjoying the advantage of presidental incumbency, Mitterrand portrayed himself as a man of state legitimised by his exercise of the presidential function. In his 1988 televised duel with Chirac, Mitterrand secured a clear tactical advantage by constantly referring to his opponent as Mr Prime Minister (*M. le premier ministre*), thereby emphasising his own political seniority and casting doubts upon Chirac's suitability for the presidential function. His 1988 campaign theme of a unified France (*La France unie*) responded lucidly to the 'centrist', non-ideological and symbolic stimulus of television as a political medium. The 'centrist' imperatives of political communication and the policy evolution of Mitterrrand's presidency thus appeared to combine. Mitterrand positioned himself as the crystallising force of France's rich Republican heritage and, exploiting his arbitral stance during the 1986–88 *cohabitation*, as the embodiment of national unity.

On other occasions, however, Mitterrand's poor television performance betrayed his diminishing grasp of political affairs. This was notably the case during the abortive *coup d'état* of August 1991 in the USSR: fearful of instability in the Soviet Union above anything else, Mitterrand appeared to recognise the coup in a televised press conference, only to seek to rectify this damaging impression the next day in a second address to the nation. This revealed the extent to which the direct presidential speech, especially in response to an international crisis, was fraught with danger. This was particularly the case for a President such as Mitterrand, who liked to demonstrate his control over events and ponder his options at length. An ability to cope with the media is one essential component of politcal leadership. In relation to this criterion, Mitterrand fared credibly, although his performance in this sphere was subject to a law of diminishing returns.

A SENSE OF FAMILY

Portrayals of Mitterrand as a republican monarch have claimed support for their theses by focusing on his use of patronage, especially his promotion of members of his own family to prominent positions in the public sector. Certain commentators have even evoked the notion of a Mitterrand dynasty. Mitterrand's relations with his family and close political associates are themselves highly informative of his political persona, and of his manner of operating within the political system. In this context, we shall consider first the role performed by Danielle Mitterrand, before assessing Mitterrand's sense of the importance of family and kinship as reliable networks, and finally going beyond family to evaluate the complex relationship binding Mitterrand and four generations of *mitterrandistes*.

Danielle Mitterrand   By definition, the influence brought to bear by the spouses of modern political leaders is difficult to assess, although certain examples spring to mind of instances where a great deal of covert influence has been attributed to them. The cases of Nancy Reagan or Hillary Clinton impose themselves. Such influence is, of course, virtually impossible to measure, but even anecdotal evidence is relevant, as it helps to inform public perceptions of political leadership.

It is generally accepted that Danielle Mitterrand is one of the few people to have had lasting influence on Mitterrand. She was born in 1924, and came from a different background from that of her husband. She was brought up in a strongly anti-clerical family, her father a freemason schoolteacher, and an SFIO activist. Mitterrand first met Danielle in Spring 1944, while both were involved in clandestine resistance activities. By marrying Danielle, Mitterrand further distanced himself from the narrow bourgeois provincialism of his upbringing. The influence of his spouse has been held up by most biographers as being one reason for Mitterrand's drift leftwards in the 1960s and 1970s. This plausible hypothesis is given a measure of credibility by Mitterrand himself.[10]

Danielle Mitterrand was far more politically active than any other presidential spouse since the creation of the Fifth Republic. She never abandoned her commitment to controversial political causes, not even when this brought her into conflict with the President himself. Her interest in Latin American politics in particular predated her husband's election to the Elysée. Mme Mitterrand had already sparked off the fury of the Americans in 1980, when she accompanied Régis Debray to El Salvador to denounce American imperialism. After Mitterrand's election, she took charge of the group *Association socialiste solidarité* (close to the PS), which expressed support for the Sandinistas in Nicaragua and the anti-US guerilla movement in El Salvador.[11] It has been speculated that it was due in part to the insistence of Danielle that President Mitterrand supported the Sandinistas in Nicaragua in August 1981, in the form of the joint Franco-Mexican declaration.[12]

Mitterrand's sons   If appraisal of Danielle provides interesting insights into Mitterrand's political leadership, his treatment of other members of his family is even more revealing of a particular political style. In the consideration of F-O. Giesbert, 'For Mitterrand, politics is often a family affair'.[13] Opponents have criticised Mitterrand for a sense of loyalty to family which borders on nepotism. Such accusations have been levelled particularly in relation to the President's two sons: Jean-Christophe and Gilbert.

Shortly after becoming President, Mitterrand appointed his eldest son Jean-Christophe to the Elysée staff, initially to serve as a researcher under Guy Penne, the President's special adviser on African affairs. After Penne's enforced departure in October 1986, Jean-Christophe became Mitterrand's African adviser. The symbolic importance of having the President's son in the African cell of the Elysée was considerable. Ever since de Gaulle, African affairs had always comprised the core of the presidential 'reserved sector', with other ministers excluded from effective influence. The departure of J-P. Cot in December 1982 as Minister for Overseas Cooperation illustrated the point that French Presidents would not tolerate criticisms of their activities in this sphere.[14] The presidential adviser for African affairs had always been a key appointment, acting as a de facto Minister for Africa, with direct access to heads of states of francophone Africa; in this sphere at least, the Elysée staff acted as the key power brokers on behalf of the President.[15] It has been alleged that once Jean-Christophe had been appointed, heads of francophone African states were anxious to bestow favours on Mitterrand's son, in order to further their cause with the President. Jean-Christophe rapidly acquired the nick-name 'Papamadit', on account of his alleged propensity for using his father's name to obtain favours.[16] Prior to his nomination in 1986, Jean-Christophe Mitterrand had developed extensive networks within francophone Africa, acquired during his tenure as an African specialist working for the *Agence France-Presse*, a career cut short by his father's election.

It was perhaps inevitable that accusations of exerting influence to obtain business favours should be levelled against Jean-Christophe Mitterrand, accusations which were promptly denied, but refused to disappear.[17] The case of Adefi-International, a public relations firm catering for the heads of francophone African states, was commonly cited. Adefi-International was headed by Jean-Pierre Fleury, a close friend of Jean-Christophe Mitterrand for 25 years. It rose to prominence only after Mitterrand junior arrived at the Elysée; its clients were limited to those states with which Jean-Christophe had close contacts. At least one African head of state complained of having been unfairly pressurised by Fleury to engage the services of Adefi-International. Thus, François Mitterrand's old associate Félix Houphouët-Boigny, President of the Ivory Coast, declined to continue with the services of Adefi-International, and claimed to have signed an initial contract after pressure from 'l'ami du fils Mitterrand' 'pour étre bien avec l'Elysée'. At the very least, Jean-Christophe Mitterrand allowed himself to be manipulated by friends engaged in a series of murky commercial deals. The boundaries between diplomacy, trade and *affairisme* have always been confused in relation to French African policy; the suspicion of scandal was likely to weigh upon any presidential counsellor. Whether, in these circumstances, Mitterrand's decision to appoint his own son to the controversial post was a wise one is questionable. Jean-Christophe finally resigned his position in July 1992, after having been directly accused of corruption (and of supporting authoritarian governments) by pro-democracy demonstrators in various francophone African states.[18]

Mitterrand's other son Gilbert was elected as a Socialist deputy in the Gironde in 1981.[19] His election was followed by routine accusations of nepotism, but, as Gilbert pointed out, his election in 1981 intervened after two unsuccessful attempts in 1973 and 1978.[20] The assistance accorded to Gilbert Mitterrand was less overt than that bestowed on Jean-Christophe; but the Mitterrand family name helped Gilbert to capture control of the PS Gironde Federation in March 1987. It is worth noting the contrast with de Gaulle, who insisted that his sons be invited to the Elysée no more than twice a year.

Revelations made by *Paris-Match* in 1994 that he had a 20-year-old daughter – Mazarine – were publicly acknowledged by President Mitterrand. Mazarine figured prominently at François Mitterrand's funeral in January 1996, in the front row of mourners alongside Danielle, Jean-Christophe and Gilbert Mitterrand, and her mother, Anne Pingeot.

Brothers and sisters   Other members of Mitterrand's family occasionally served as useful intermediaries for the President, especially in periods of crisis. His sister Geneviève served as a go-between in relation to the episcopal hierarchy during the 1984 church schools crisis. His younger brother, General Jacques Mitterrand, carried out at least one secret mission for the President and attempted to appease dissatisfaction with Mitterrand's presidency among high-ranking military officers. Relations between Jacques Mitterrand and brother François were subsequently soured by the General's criticism of the Left's nationalisation programme.[21] In defence against accusations of nepotism, François Mitterrand has pointed out that his brother Jacques was named president of the prestigious state firm Aerospatiale by President Giscard d'Estaing.

Mitterrand's closest relationship was with his older brother Robert, who had a history of past political engagement alongside him: notably as his *directeur du cabinet* during the Fourth Republic at the ministries of Ex-Servicemen and Information, and as General Secretary of the CIR from 1966–67.[22] Robert Mitterrand had pursued a successful career as an industrialist. Upon Mitterrand's election, Robert was given various secret missions for the President, including trips to Brazil and Eastern Europe. On 19 January 1982, Robert was appointed as a director of the *Centre français du commerce extérieur*, the same day that François Giscard d'Estaing, the ex-President's nephew, was ejected from his position as President of the *Banque française du commerce extérieur*.[23]

The relations maintained with his numerous brothers and sisters were based upon mutual benefit, as well as affection; as compensation for acting as intermediaries for the President, Mitterrand's siblings were offered official positions in the parapublic sector, or other rewards. Thus Jacques Mitterrand was named as president of the aerospace consortium GIFAS, a post bringing with it the possibility of earning large commissions; as stated above, Robert was appointed in 1982 to a top administrative post in the state commercial sector.[24] Mitterrand's youngest brother Philippe was awarded the ubiquitous *légion d'honneur*, while his sister Geneviève, although not sharing François' political views, benefited from presidential patronage to be nominated to the *Conseil économique et social*.[25] The *Conseil économique et social* was a favoured source of Mitterrand's largesse, the President being able to nominate one-third of its members by decree in the Council of Ministers: numerous friends and relations were named to serve in this prestigious but essentially honorific institution. The CES also served as a means of recompense for political services rendered. Quite apart from numerous Socialists of all tendencies, Mitterrand nominated B. Renouvin (a renowned monarchist), M. Rigout (a dissident Communist), and H. Désir (of SOS-racisme), all of whom had carried out 'favours' on behalf of the President.[26]

Kinship Mitterrand's endorsement of members of his own clan applied to the entire extended family, not just to close relatives (such as sons or siblings). Examples of President Mitterrand's sense of family are legion:

- Lydie Dulong, Jean-Christophe's mother-in-law, was named as a junior Minister for Agriculture, despite her lack of political experience. She was then conveniently found a position as *suppléant* to André Cellard in the 1988 legislative elections, acceding to the National Assembly when the latter was named as minister.
- Mitterrand's second cousin Jacques Bonnot was named to head *Crédit Agricole* in 1981, notwithstanding his lack of experience.[27]
- Roger Gouze, Danielle Mitterrand's brother, was named as a *conseiller technique* at the Quai d'Orsay in 1982; and later as a *chargé de mission* in another ministry. At 76 years old, Gouze thus became the oldest representative of any ministerial cabinet.
- Mitterrand's niece, Marie-Pierre Laudry, was nominated to serve in the Ombudsman's office.[28]

In other circumstances, the presidential connection worked in more subtle ways: thus, Mitterrand's sister Marie-Josèphe, a full-time painter for thirty-seven years, obtained her first exhibition in a Parisian art gallery shortly after her brother's election. Danielle Mitterrand's sister, Christine, witnessed her cinema production company take off after 1981. Mitterrand's nephew, Frédéric, was another relative whose media career was singularly boosted by his uncle's election.[29]

There were certain political disadvantages for Mitterrand in this method of appointing family members to positions of high authority. It led to accusations of nepotism. It also left family members open to the threat of manipulation, as in the case of Jean-Christophe. It might even on occasion have detracted from their considerable merits, as in the case of Robert and Jacques. And yet, it is unlikely that Mitterrand took such accusations seriously; as analysed above, the Mitterrand style relied on building personal contacts and varied networks. Family members could be relied upon to practise those virtues deemed primordial by Mitterrand: loyalty and reciprocity. Ultimately, members of Mitterrand's kinship group were rarely promoted above their station. The relationship maintained with Mitterrand's avowed disciples was, in a political sense, far more important.

THE MITTERRANDISTES

Mitterrand's treatment of members of his kinship group should not be considered in isolation. As Giesbert has observed, 'Faithful to blood relations, Mitterrand is also faithful to bonds of the heart.' His early promotion of *compagnons de route* within the government, the administration, the party, parliament and the presidential staff bore testimony to this. Even when close friends were eventually dispatched from prominent positions within the state, they were usually found positions offering adequate compensation elsewhere, especially in the administration, private businesses or the parapublic sector. The most obvious examples were all old friends from the Fourth or early Fifth Republic. These included François de Grossouvre, a highly influential adviser until his retirement in 1985, transformed into the president of Mitterrand's hunting committee; Guy Penne, Mitterrand's African adviser from 1981–86, turned Senator representing French people living abroad; André Rousselet, Mitterrand's *directeur du cabinet* until June 1982, then Managing Director of the communications group Havas; Georges Fillioud, ex-minister and the faithful Claude Estier, both appointed to the *Conseil d'État*.[30] It has been illustrated above how the *compagnons de route* gradually gave way to experts within Mitterrand's presidential staff. But there remained a special category of advisers which survived on account of Mitterrand's affective ties with them, such as Paule Dayan, the daughter of Mitterrand's old friend Georges Dayan; or Laurence Soudet, the widow of another Mitterrand acolyte.[31]

On a personal level, evidence from various close sources indicates his intense, even excessive feeling of loyalty towards friends, which led Mitterrand to retain their services longer than he ought to have done.[32] This sense of friendship and reciprocal loyalty on occasion went to extreme lengths. Thus, the President nominated a certain Christian Pallo to the *Cour des Comptes*: Pallo's chief merit was that he was the son-in-law of the owner of *Le Vieux Morvan*, the hotel in which Mitterrand habitually stayed when visiting Château-Chinon. In similar vein, the *légion d'honneur* was liberally awarded to Mitterrand's friends, accomplices and friends of accomplices: not least to Catherine Langeais, Mitterrand's one-time fiancée, and to numerous personalities in the cultural world to whom the President owed debts of gratitude.[33] Other contested nominations included: Hélène Hernu (the daughter of Charles Hernu, a long-time Mitterrand associate) to the post of sub-prefect, and the President's personal doctor, Claude Gubler, to an important administrative post within the Social Affairs ministry.[34]

Not the least of the paradoxes concerning Mitterrand is that the solitary individual succeeded in constructing a highly complex series of overlapping networks and clienteles, each focused on the personal relationship maintained with selected individuals by Mitterrand. These networks included (at various stages): family and kinship relations, political confidants from the resistance, the Fourth and early Fifth Republics; the *mitterrandiste sabras* of the 1970s' PS; a new elite pushed to the political forefront during the 1980s and early 1990s, and a range of extensive contacts outside of the narrow confines of politics. The importance of building personal networks testified to Mitterrand's status as an outsider for most of the period preceding his election as President. The construction of personal clienteles formed a part of a strategy for the conquest of power on behalf of an individual who initially lacked the infrastructure provided by a strong party, but who responded with clairvoyance to the political possibilities opened by the direct presidential election. Within the post-1971 Socialist Party, Mitterrand continued to promote close leader–follower ties, by personally promoting a new generation of cadres, in an attempt to consolidate his control over the PS. The prevalence of *compagnons de route* among the early presidential staff, and among government ministers represented a recognition by Mitterrand of the proven loyalty of several generations of *mitterrandistes*. Once comfortably installed as President in the Elysée, personal network building mattered less, since nobody could contest Mitterrand's position at the pinnacle of the institutional edifice, or dispute his need to appear as an ecumenical leader above the fray. The personal and party considerations manifested early on were scarcely compatible with the need to appear as President of all the French.

The importance of personal relations in Mitterrand's mode of operation has nonetheless been verified by most of his biographers: in a quasi-monarchical manner, loyalty has been rewarded and sedition punished. This personal aspect to Mitterrand's political persona remained important throughout his presidential term in office, although there was a greater professionalisation of personnel selection and criteria as time went on. That Mitterrand (initially) placed so much value on loyalty might have been because he had experienced at first hand so much disloyalty from *faux-amis*, such as during the Observatory Affair of 1959, or after the crisis of May 1968. For if Mitterrand attracted intense political loyalty from several generations of followers, he also provoked powerful enmities, not only among right-wing opponents. This is testified by the series of political scandals with which his adversaries attempted to implicate Mitterrand, from the 'leaks affair' of 1954 to the Péchiney scandal of 1989.

In a rather schematic manner, it is possible to identify successive generations of *mitterrandistes*, itself a testament to Mitterrand's capacity to attract followers towards him. An initial generation of *mitterrandistes* (often initially co-fighters in the resistance) gradually crystallised during the Fourth Republic, when Mitterrand led the UDSR. These included men such as Georges Dayan, Roland Dumas (Foreign Secretary from 1983–86 and 1988–93), Georges Beauchamps, Louis Mermaz, Patrice Pélat and others. The next generation of *mitterrandistes* were, not surprisingly, younger: their loyalty to Mitterrand was forged in the CIR in the early 1960s. This second group included Charles Hernu, Pierre Joxe, Claude Estier, Edith Cresson and Georges Fillioud.[35] The *conventionnels* were often suspicious of each other, as well as of the *sabras*, the new generation of Mitterrand's protégés who rose to prominence within the PS after 1971. The *sabras* were so named after the first generation of native Israelis: they had come to the PS as their first conventional political engagement and demonstrated a strong loyalty to Mitterrand.The most prominent *sabras* played a leading role in party and government during the Mitterrand years: they included Laurent Fabius (Prime Minister from 1984–86, elected leader of the Socialist Party in January 1992), Lionel Jospin (PS leader from 1981–88, Education minister, 1988–92), Jacques Attali (Mitterrand's special adviser from 1981–92, then President of the European Regional Development Bank), Paul Quilès (Interior minister, 1991–92) and a host of lesser figures. Finally, Mitterrand personally propelled a new generation of political figures into prominence throughout the course of his presidency, the most frequent route being from within the President's Elysée staff: Jean-Louis Bianco (Minister for Social Affairs, then Transport Minister), Elizabeth Guigou (Minister for European Affairs), Michel Charasse (Minister for the Budget), Ségolène Royal (Minister for the Environment). Several of these personalities had tenuous links at best with the party, deriving their early political legitimacy from their status as civil servants drafted into presidential service.

Relations between Mitterrand and these various generations altered somewhat according to circumstance. The early *compagnons de route* were the most likely to be personal friends, and to be accorded the equality of treatment this implied. For this reason, most preferred to leave presidential service after an early transitional phase, rather than be subjected to a changed relationship. Among the second and third generations, the leader–follower ties between Mitterrand and his lieutenants developed the aura of a patron–client relationship, which intensified once he had won the presidency. The *conventionnels* and the *sabras* were both conscious of the fact that they owed their positions of authority to Mitterrand; the legacy of this, throughout the first mandate at least, was obedient support for presidential initiatives. *Mitterrandiste* domination of the presidency, the government, and the party during the first five-year term helped explain why the various elements of the Socialist power structure remained relatively cohesive. The partial breakdown of this *personalised* ruling mechanism after 1988 (see Chapter 5) testified to Mitterrand's diminishing capacity to exercise effective political leadership during his second mandate. The most recent generation of *mitterrandistes*, while grateful for presidential advancement and fascinated by the personality of Mitterrand, did not rise through the party, and occupied a relatively weak position within it. In the aftermath of the Socialists' decisive electoral defeat in 1993, their future political prospects looked the least secure, although all were highly trained administrators liable to return to the administration.

Throughout his career, Mitterrand demanded loyalty from his aides and usually obtained it, although different lieutenants adopted differing approaches towards dealing with the President, reflecting their own personalities: Joxe was reputedly abrupt and direct; Mermaz more reverential.[36] Rivalries between different *mitterrandistes* were frequently intense, as each competed for the leader's favour. Mitterrand regarded such competition as healthy: it prevented any one politician from emerging as the dauphin and thereby potentially threatening his continued suzerainty. When one of Mitterrand's presumed heirs assumed that he was strong enough to contradict the leader, he was firmly cut down to size – as Fabius discovered to his cost in 1985–86. The counterpart to this was that, during the second mandate, Mitterrand was to some extent a lame-duck President, with limited potential for dispensing patronage in the future. This forced differences between Mitterrand's lieutenants out into the open, and revealed serious divergences of interest between the President and certain of his former protégés, such as Jospin. The patron–client relationship was thus shown to be subject to a law of diminishing returns, which weakened Mitterrand's (still considerable) control over the institutional edifice after his re-election in 1988 by comparison with his first term in office. Herein lay the weakness of an over-reliance on personal mechanisms for governing the country. This revealed an important limitation of Mitterrand's political style. Leader–follower ties demanded an element of reciprocal loyalty, but Mitterrand's sophisticated divide and rule tactics ultimately frustrated even his closest associates.

Mitterrand's cultivation of diverse constituencies brought within the presidential orbit not just different advisers, but also party contacts, personal friends, government ministers, civil servants, deputies, and outsiders from the world of business, or the arts. Mitterrand's extensive network was not confined to the ranks of the Left, nor limited to the world of politics. This was confirmed by his cultivation of student leaders (Isabelle Thomas), rock stars (Renaud), and sporting heroes. Special attention should be paid to Mitterrand's extensive business links, which predated his election in 1981. Throughout the course of the Mitterrand presidency, there emerged a new generation of politically active industrialists who supported Mitterrand (and, it was suspected, occasionally profited from association with the President). Bernard

Tapie represented the popular stereotype of the politically engaged industrialist, but the typical *mitterrandiste* businessman was an *énarque* who had
first served in a ministerial cabinet before leaving state service for more
lucrative positions in the private and parapublic sector. Mitterrand's cultivation of the business world was a matter of political necessity, especially after
1986: the President counted upon his business friends to help counter the
influence of right-wing industrialists appointed to the boards of the newly
privatised industries by the Chirac government.[37]

CONCLUSION

Personalised ties were initially privileged as a mechanism for governing firstly
the party, and secondly the nation. Mitterrand revealed a strong tendency for a
personalisation of decision-making: decisions were often arrived at by personal contacts, and by ad hoc arrangements rather than through formal
institutional channels. Family ties and proven political loyalties figured as
important considerations in making appointments. Mitterrand's propulsion
of his progeny in particular to positions of weighty political significance
illustrated not only his strong sense of family, but also the relative obscurity
and secrecy of presidential selection procedures in the Fifth Republic. Political
loyalties developed through successive generations of followers testified not
only to Mitterrand's longevity, but also to his seemingly timeless ability to
inspire fidelity. This was perhaps one means of measuring the importance of
Mitterrand as a political leader, by which standard he was surpassed only by
de Gaulle and Mendès-France. The promotion of loyal followers to the
highest ministries of state confirmed the relevance of applying a patron–client
analogy when analysing relations maintained between Mitterrand and his
closest lieutenants. It seems clear that Mitterrand possessed a capacity to
attract strong partisan loyalties; that these spanned across several generations,
and that genuine followers were rewarded handsomely for their loyalty. This
capacity to attract personal loyalties and the dedication of others is a necessary
prerequisite for success in a semi-presidential system. That Mitterrand was for
long able to govern in such a personalised manner reflected not only his own
predilections, but also the considerable personalisation of decision-making
that has occurred in the presidentialised Fifth Republic.

Chapter 8

The European statesman

More than any of his contemporary political leaders, in the 1980s and 1990s President François Mitterrand was in the forefront of European statesmen willing the EC member-states on to closer political and economic integration. In the present chapter, we shall attempt to retrace Mitterrand's evolving attitude towards Europe, aiming in addition to sketch the main lines of the changing European debate in France. In Chapter 10, we shall deal with Mitterrand's response to the post-1989 European order.

THE UNEVEN DEVELOPMENT OF MITTERRAND'S EUROPEAN IDEAL

Throughout the Fourth Republic, Mitterrand was far more interested in colonial affairs than in those of the old continent. His position was made clear in a report presented to the 1952 UDSR Congress.[1] While strongly approving postwar European initiatives by French governments, Mitterrand accused the same governments of having failed to secure allied recognition of France's supremacy in the Western Mediterranean. Mitterrand considered France to have a unique, historic role as leader of the Mediterranean nations, i.e. Southern Europe and North Africa, and that this was more important either than a non-existent European community, or than its status as a member of the Atlantic alliance. His hierarchy of diplomatic priorities was summarised in 1954 as 'the Western Mediterranean and Africa before Europe and the Atlantic. Europe before Asia'.[2]

Above all, Mitterrand feared that closer European integration would involve France abandoning its mission as the axis of a broad Franco-African community. There could be no question of France renouncing its control over its African colonies. Upon this condition, Mitterrand did not remain unmoved by developments in Europe. As a young deputy in 1948, he attended the European Congress at the Hague, at which Churchill, Adenauer, de Gasperi and others pleaded for the European cause.[3] He reiterated his belief that 'the twentieth century denies isolated nations the right to survive'.[4] In his advocacy of an enlarged French Union, as well as his support for moves towards closer European integration, Mitterrand evoked his belief that future French influence depended upon its ability to perform a leadership role within the context of wider groupings of nations.

In 1954, as Interior Minister in Mendès-France's government, Mitterrand abstained in the crucial vote on the creation of the European Defence Community, the 'European Army' envisaged by statesmen such as Schuman, Pleven and Adenauer. On several occasions Mitterrand had declared himself favourable to the EDC. It was as a token of solidarity with Mendès-France that Mitterrand abstained in the final vote, in order not to bring down the government. This act, taken as a sign of betrayal by Robert Schuman, ought not to be interpreted as an anti-European gesture on Mitterrand's part, as much as an act of pro-*mendèsiste* solidarity. In this respect, Mitterrand was far more European than Mendès-France, who was suspicious of and suspected by the Christian-democratic heads of state elsewhere in Western Europe. Mitterrand later justified his abstention by his opposition to a Europe of the Generals. Barely a decade after the Second World War, the creation of a European Army would have been dangerous without a strong political authority to control defence policy. On several subsequent occasions, Mitterrand pledged his support for closer European defence cooperation, notably during the 1974 presidential campaign.

Although Mitterrand supported the main moves towards greater European integration, culminating in the Treaty of Rome in 1957, he continued to stress the primordial importance of the French presence in Africa. In the final analysis, Europe occupied only a marginal place in the political preoccupations of François Mitterrand during the Fourth Republic. Although his European credentials were firmly established, others could claim the mantle of Jean Monnet rather more convincingly than Mitterrand.

With the collapse of the French colonial presence in Africa, sealed by Algerian independence in 1962, there was no place for Mitterrand's benevolent colonialism. A cautious Europeanism replaced his primary concern with Africa. Both of these sentiments testified to Mitterrand's patriotic reluctance to accept a diminution of French greatness in the postwar era. If we except his attitude towards the colonial problem, there was an underlying continuity in Mitterrand's approach towards the European Community from the 1950s onwards. There were also shifts of emphasis according to political circumstances and the dictates of political strategy, which blurred his essentially pro-European profile.

However strong Mitterrand's underlying beliefs, his pro-European emphasis varied to take account of the political imperatives of the moment. This should not imply inconsistency or mere expediency, as much as an awareness of varied political constraints and opportunities. In the course of the 1960s, Mitterrand's espousal of the cause of greater European integration was an efficient means of confirming his status as de Gaulle's chief political opponent. During the 1970s, in contrast, a less enthusiastic pro-European and a tougher anti-American stance helped to bring Mitterrand's PS closer to the PCF. If the tone of his discourse varied, Mitterrand was careful never seriously to question France's position at the heart of the European Community. Mitterrand's consistently pro-European attitude provided one source of cohesion throughout his career.

The 1960s   During the 1960s Mitterrand was one of the most prominent opponents of de Gaulle's European policy. He fiercely condemned de Gaulle's policy of the 'empty chair' decreed in 1965.[5] Such an attitude, according to Mitterrand, would encourage the resurgence of nationalism among member states, especially Germany, and facilitate American economic penetration of Europe.[6] Mitterrand was also critically opposed to de Gaulle's repeated vetoes of British membership of the EC (in 1963 and 1967). There were, however, subtle differences of opinion between Mitterrand and the SFIO leader Mollet on this subject. Whereas Mollet, a symbol of the SFIO's anglophile tradition, considered British entry to be desirable in itself, Mitterrand was more inclined to concentrate on the dangers of an Anglo-American bloc strengthening itself at the expense of continental Europe, should Britain be excluded from the EEC. Throughout the 1960s, Mitterrand occupied a median position within the Left in relation to Europe and foreign policy, equidistant from the supranationalism of the European Movement, and the harsh rhetoric of anti-Americanism and national independence employed by de Gaulle and the PCF.

The 1970s   The essence of Mitterrand's formal conception of Europe which prevailed throughout the 1970s was that: 'We do not want Europe for Europe's sake alone; we want Europe for Socialism'.[7] Mitterrand's alliance with the PCF forced traditional Socialist preoccupations with the construction of Europe into the background, to be replaced by hardline denunciations of American imperialism. For much of the period, it was difficult to disentangle Mitterrand's personal beliefs from the delicate role he was called upon to perform as party leader, and as embodiment of the PS–PCF alliance.[8]

Even in its Socialist guise, Mitterrand's European message combined a characteristic mixture of patriotism and pro-European sentiment. At the 1973 Bagnolet congress, Mitterrand secured the PS's commitment to the EC against left-wing opposition. In the final motion, it was asserted that: 'The future evolution of Europe towards socialism will depend upon the success or failure of the Socialists in France'.[9] There was a primary emphasis on the national character of the future French Socialist experience, as well as a *gaullien*-style belief in the superiority of the French experience over those of its European counterparts. The party was also stridently critical of the role of NATO as a vehicle for American imperialism. In its own fashion, Mitterrand's Socialist

Party thus contributed to expanding the Gaullist-inspired anti-Atlantic consensus of the 1970s.

Underlying Mitterrand's denunciations of American imperialism in the 1970s was a belief that only a more unified Europe could stand up to the economic and political superpowers. To some extent, the evolution of PS European policy under Mitterrand paralleled the evolution of the French government itself. The notion of Europe as being a strategic space potentially independent of the superpowers was in line with the Gaullist legacy of Europe, and of the role France was called upon to perform as the self-perceived leading nation of Europe. Concern with American monetary, economic and foreign policies was not limited to European Socialist parties, and lay behind a developing EC impetus for greater economic, political and monetary coordination, symbolised notably by the creation of the EMS in 1978. The belief in greater European independence was consistently repeated by Mitterrand throughout his career. It reappeared later on with his deter-mined efforts as President to push for closer European political and economic integration.

On the eve of his election as president, Mitterrand was not generally considered to be in the forefront of pro-European sentiment in France. But he had supported the main thrust of European integration and had carried his party with him. His continuing support for the Treaty of Rome and for the future strengthening of EC institutions, in spite of internal party and alliance pressures, proved Mitterrand's European credentials during the 1970s. Social-ist European policy was a delicate tightrope exercise throughout the 1970s. Mitterrand managed to tie the PS to a pro-European position which isolated manifest opponents of the EC, in the CERES faction and elsewhere, but which parted ways with traditional SFIO notions of supranationalism.

1981–86: PRESIDENT MITTERRAND'S EUROPEAN MISSION

Mitterrand's election as President represented the triumph of an outsider with no experience of European affairs, and with a priority interest in domestic policy: of Mitterrand's *110 Propositions*, only three were directly concerned with Europe. When it was considered, European policy was envisaged as an extension of domestic policy, with French solutions extrapolated to the wider European sphere. The new French government stressed its desire for a coordinated European economic relaunch, for increased social and industrial interventionism and for a move away from the liberal, free trade ethos which it diagnosed as underpinning the EC. These were all themes that had consistently been espoused by Mitterrand before his election as president.

A series of initiatives revealed French isolation after May 1981. At the Luxembourg summit of June 1981, Mitterrand's proposed creation of a 'social European space' was met with a mixture of indifference and veiled hostility by France's major European partners.[10] The next French initiative occurred in

October 1981, when André Chandernagor, the new junior minister for European Affairs, published his 'Memorandum for the economic relaunch of Europe'. Chandernagor's note called for united European action in a wide variety of spheres, including an expansionist economic policy, a coordinated anti-unemployment strategy, and common industrial and social policies. This intergovernmental note was treated with scepticism by most other EC governments. The notion of a coordinated European economic relaunch in particular ran directly counter to the economic orthodoxy prevalent in other European capitals.[11] The reception received by these proposals illustrated, inter alia, the tensions reigning between German Social-democracy, in the form of Helmut Schmidt, and French socialism: Mitterrand's proposal received no more sympathy from Schmidt than it did from Thatcher.

Upon his election in 1981, Mitterrand encountered an EC in crisis. The prevailing mood was one of 'Euro-pessimism': the combined issues of Britain's budgetary contribution and reform of the CAP led to a near-paralysis of the EC from 1979–84. In April 1982, the 9 overrode a UK veto on farm prices, challenging the national veto for the first time since the Luxembourg compromise of 1966. A common reaction against Margaret Thatcher's intransigent budgetary and CAP demands facilitated the termination of France's temporary isolation within the Community, notably by reasserting an essential community of interest on most matters with the Federal Republic. These related issues poisoned EC summits until the resolution over Britain's budgetary rebate at the Fontainebleau summit of June 1984, partly engineered by Mitterrand. The prospect of Spanish and Portuguese entry to the EC provided a further bone of contention. It was met with stiff resistance from sections of French and Italian public opinion. Mitterrand initially refused to countenance Spanish entry until French farmers were offered adequate safeguards against cheaper Spanish imports.

During the early period of his presidency, Mitterrand's interest in European affairs was overshadowed by his wider international role, notably with regard to France's relations with the superpowers and independent French initiatives in relation to the Third World (see Chapter 9). The failure of Mitterrand's early EC initiatives revealed unambiguously that French economic policy, facing grave problems domestically, was not for export. And yet, the European dimension was central to domestic economic policy. France's membership of the EC was perhaps the central policy choice of any French government. It appeared inconceivable that any French government would willingly endanger its status as a key Community player by disengaging from Europe (even in the name of national independence, a powerful symbolic rallying call since de Gaulle). Its economic policy was at variance with those of France's leading industrial partners. There was even some speculation that France might be forced to withdraw temporarily from the EC, in conformity with article 115 of the Treaty of Rome, in order to defend its vital economic interests.[12]

For most observers, unilateral Keynesian reflationary policies were no longer possible for a medium-sized nation such as France in an interdependent world economy. The attempt to reflate the French economy after 1981 had led to a severe disequilibrium of economic performance. Given the lack of enthusiasm for a coordinated European-wide economic relaunch, the French government had no alternative but to change economic course itself. Even the 'national protectionist' option advocated by Chevènement, Bérégovoy and others would have involved a tough deflationary package. The process whereby Mitterrand arbitrated in favour of a third devaluation within the European monetary system has been dealt with in Chapter 3. In retrospect, it appears surprising that the French President should have considered seriously the option of withdrawing from the EMS, taking account of the Franco-German authorship of the mechanism (created by joint decision of Schmidt and Giscard d'Estaing in 1978). Yet, to accept the stark consequences of remaining within the EMS was almost an equally unwelcome decision. It implied that (absolute) national economic sovereignty was illusory, a particularly bleak message for a politician who had always advocated economic voluntarism and stressed the French leadership role within Europe.

The European choice prevailed. The Delors plan adopted in March 1983 had a clear European dimension. This was in part because of the personality of its prime mover, but also because it implied a commitment to economic convergence with the leading industrial nations, most especially West Germany. The idea of the Socialist Europe was definitively buried with the third devaluation in March 1983. A determination to participate in European economic policy-making led Mitterrand later to accept the merits of a single European currency and a central European bank, where it was hoped France would be able to exert a powerful influence over monetary policy, which had become the appendage of the German Bundesbank.

Mitterrand drew a realistic conclusion from the abrupt U-turn in economic policy: that French influence within and beyond Europe depended upon close collaboration with its partners (especially the Federal Republic of Germany). The importance of the European dimension for French policy-making justified a more intensive presidential involvement. Europe had played a secondary role for Mitterrand not because of any disinterest, but because as the first Socialist President, his priority commitments had lain elsewhere, notably in the domestic sphere. This changed in 1983, after which Mitterrand personally supervised the direction of French European policy. In late 1983, Mitterrand replaced Chandernagor with his trusted confidant Roland Dumas as the fully-fledged Minister for European Affairs.[13] Dumas was regarded as Mitterrand's alter ego in foreign policy and European affairs. Although Claude Cheysson remained at the Quai d'Orsay until July 1984, Dumas henceforth represented France in intergovernmental EC meetings.

Mitterrand's closer involvement in European affairs stemmed from a mixture of sincere commitment to closer European integration, an aversion to

the avarices of domestic policy, and a far-sighted recognition of the importance of Europe for the pursuance of French objectives. Throughout the course
of 1982–84, Mitterrand refined his European vision, which combined a
mixture of idealism, realism and self-interest. Certain key steps towards more
active European engagement predated the economic U-turn of March 1983.
These included his call in November 1982 (via Defence minister Hernu) for a
European defence policy; the Franco-German summit of November 1982,
which reaffirmed traditional notions of the Paris–Bonn axis; and his speech to
the Bundestag in January 1983.[14] Quite apart from testifying to President
Mitterrand's reasoned Atlanticism (see Chapter 9), his Bundestag speech
signalled a new determination to relaunch the 'European dynamic'.[15] From
occupying a secondary role, Europe became the means through which
Mitterrand could internalise and rationalise the shift in domestic economic
policy, as well as claim a leading role for France in European affairs, and for
himself as artisan of European integration. This necessitated an unambiguous,
even an emphatic concentration on European issues, the counterpart to a
withdrawal from the finer details of domestic politics after 1983. However
sincerely felt, Mitterrand's European conviction was not devoid of domestic
considerations. The Left's sectarian image in the eyes of public opinion had
been confirmed by the episode of the Church schools: the issue of Europe
formed a part of the President's effort to recentre his political appeal, as well
as an attempt to deflect public opinion from (overwhelming) domestic issues.

Mitterrand's prominence in European affairs was assertively underlined
during the French presidency of the European Council, from January–June
1984. France took over the EC presidency at a time when the EC itself
appeared in grave crisis, particularly over the UK's budget contribution. The
Athens summit of December 1983 had led to stalemate on this issue.
Mitterrand's veto of the UK refund was greeted with intense hostility by the
Thatcher government. For the first time ever, there had been no final
communiqué at the summit: the European leaders had agreed upon virtually
nothing. The evidence pointed to a determined effort to relaunch the idea of
Europe during the French presidency, with notable results: a common fishing
policy was introduced in January 1984; discussions with Spain and Portugal
were re-opened in February 1984, with the objective of Spain joining the
Community by 1 January 1986; Mitterrand took the first steps towards
launching the ESPRIT and EUREKA programmes and placing the notion of
a Common Foreign and Security Policy onto the political agenda. The
enthusiasm and energy consecrated by Mitterrand to this first French
presidency were without precedent. Europe became an intensely *personal*
affair.

Mitterrand's style of presiding over the EC was an original one. It consisted
multiplying bilateral meetings with European leaders, rather than con-
voking a series of unnecessary summits, where disagreements were highly
publicised. In the space of six months, Mitterrand held no fewer than 30

meetings with fellow heads of state of the EC, in addition to statutory meetings of EC institutions. On rare occasions had the diplomatic role of the head of state been as personalised it was under Mitterrand in relation to Europe: the European crusade became associated with the personality of François Mitterrand himself. This was a high-risk strategy, since the effects of failure might have been total. Mitterrand's concentration on Europe also reflected the depths of unpopularity an interventionist President had reached during the first three years of the presidential mandate. Europe offered a less controversial, potentially more glamorous terrain for political activity.

The idealistic aspect to Mitterrand's new European discourse was articulated in a variety of proposals in spheres as varied as culture, education and industry. In a speech at the Hague in February 1984, the French President proposed the establishment of common policies for each important industrial sector (computers, telecommunications, biotechnology, transport infrastructure).[16] His most ambitious proposal was in the field of spatial research. Mitterrand suggested a programme of coordinated spatial research, with the objective of launching a manned space station. This initiative was Mitterrand's response to Reagan's call for Western European firms to collaborate in 'star wars' research under the aegis of American leadership. It was received cautiously by other EC leaders, but helped to establish Mitterrand's credentials as an undisputed European, especially in the typically French domain of promoting European technological independence.[17]

After threat and counter-threat, the Fontainebleau summit of June 1984 finally arrived at a formula for adjusting Britain's budget contributions, thereby ending the near-paralysis which had afflicted the Community since 1979. Both Mitterrand and Thatcher claimed the credit for this: while the obduracy of Mrs Thatcher undoubtedly constrained other European leaders to negotiate, the willingness of Mitterrand (and others) to compromise in the interests of relaunching the European enterprise was far-sighted. Mitterrand's determination to resolve the British budget issue revealed both a genuine sense of European idealism and a pertinent sense of self-interest: for as long as the EC remained paralysed by the British issue, there could be no moves forward in the direction of closer European integration. It is noteworthy at this stage that moves towards closer European integration and French national interest were considered as synonomous: the French were confident of exercising a leading influence on the conduct of European affairs. As a result of Mitterrand's pressure, the Fontainebleau summit also agreed to the creation of the Dooge Committee, an ad hoc body entrusted to deliberate upon institutional and policy reform (see pp. 126–127).

From 1984 onwards, Europe visibly became an issue of internal French politics, leading to the affirmation of a rather artificial consensus shared by the mainstream parties. French national interest was widely reinterpreted in terms of Europe: it was assumed by Mitterrand and others that by being in the forefront of the push towards European integration, France could reasonably hope to provide political leadership within the new European order. This marked a distinct move away from Gaullist conceptions of a Europe of nation-states, even if both de Gaulle's and Mitterrand's visions accorded France a leading role within Europe.

In January 1985, Mitterrand's ex-Finance Minister Jacques Delors was named as President of the EC Commission. The period stemming from the Delors nomination up to the election of March 1986 was one of exceptional activity for French diplomacy in Europe, coordinated by Delors and Mitterrand. The initiatives undertaken included: the launching of the EUREKA project (April 1985); support for the Single European Act (June 1985), Mitterrand's abortive proposals for referendums on Spanish and Portuguese entry into the EC; and the direct election of a European President. The first of these projects – EUREKA – represented a clear effort to pose as champion of European technological independence. Under the rubric of the EUREKA project, Mitterrand proposed increased technological cooperation between member-states across the whole range of high technology industries (including spatial research), and for this to take the form of an institutionalised EC policy. Mitterrand's proposal was eventually incorporated into the Single European Act of 1986.

To the extent that common EC industrial policies represented an extrapolation of the French *dirigiste* tradition to a European level, Mitterrand's EUREKA initiative was well within the legacy of past French governments.[18] Mitterrand's proposal that a referendum be held on Spanish and Portuguese entry to the EC appeared less European than that of less-affected countries such as the UK. Nonetheless, this position marked an evolution in contrast with that of 1981, when Mitterrand had refused to envisage Spanish entry: the proposed referendum vanished without trace, and France went along with Spanish–Portuguese entry in 1986. Mitterrand justified his support for entry in characteristically national terms: the accession of these two countries would further place France in the centre of gravity of Europe, a bridge between the Southern European democracies and the northern states.

The return of the Right in March 1986 meant an end to spectacular initiatives on the European scene, and a more careful cultivation of his image as a *grand européen* within France, a prelude to the presidential campaign of 1988.

FROM POLICIES TO INSTITUTIONS: TOWARDS THE SINGLE EUROPEAN ACT

In 1981, the Socialists were insistent that the central problems facing the Community were those of policies rather than institutions; by 1984, François Mitterrand had become the leading European statesman advocating institutional reform. During the early phase of the French Socialist government (1981–83), French policy was underpinned by attention to the prerogatives of national sovereignty. The issue of majority voting was particularly sensitive, since it appeared likely that majority votes during this period would go against France. The 1966 Luxembourg compromise, according to which any member-state could oppose its veto by declaring a matter to be of 'vital national interest', appeared to serve French national interests well, during a period in which France was relatively isolated within Europe. Throughout his presidency, Mitterrand remained favourable, *grosso modo*, to an inter-governmental model of EC decision-making, as had Presidents Giscard d'Estaing, Pompidou and de Gaulle before him. It was the responsibility of national leaders to 'preside and decide'.[19] The nature of the presidency itself, by any comparative measurement a key political office within the EC, incited French Presidents to favour vital national decisions being taken by national leaders. The length of the French presidential mandate, moreover, meant that the French President could be confident of following through his European initiatives to their fruition. And yet, in the interests of enhanced European integration and the pursuance of French policy objectives (notably in relation to social and monetary policy), Mitterrand proved more willing than any of his predecessors to consent to and indeed initiate reforms of the EC's institutional structures.

Prior to Mitterrand's Strasbourg speech of May 1984, the French Socialist government had consistently placed primary importance upon policies rather than institutions. Mitterrand was reluctant to support the Genscher–Colombo proposals of 1981 advocating EC institutional reform.[20] In addition, the French President was initially ill-disposed towards the so-called Spinelli initiative of 1982 calling for a new European Union Treaty to replace the Treaty of Rome.[21] To the dismay of the German government, the French (with the UK, Denmark, Ireland and Greece) also took a minimalist view of the powers of the European Parliament. The Genscher–Colombo proposals of 1981 were eventually limited to an anodyne *Solemn Declaration on European Union*, adopted at the Stuttgart summit in June 1983, which committed EC heads of government to a general pledge in favour of enhanced European integration, without undertaking any institutional reform. But as French domestic policy changed course, so did Mitterrand's attitude towards institutional reform.[22]

In a landmark speech to the European Parliament in May 1984, Mitterrand made an important, and rather unexpected statement of his European policy.[23] In what amounted to a conversion to European institutional reform, Mitterrand made a firm commitment to the European parliament's draft European Union Treaty (EUT) of February 1984, based on the 1982 Spinelli initiative. Whatever his motivations, Mitterrand appeared to MEPs as an unrivalled European statesman. Without his efforts, the draft EUT would almost certainly not have been debated by the Council. The rationale for Mitterrand's conversion has been subject to various interpretations. The sentiment had become widespread in France, as in other European capitals, that, faced with stifling budgetary problems and institutional paralysis, a new impetus must be given to the EC, or else the whole edifice would decline relentlessly. In addition, Mitterrand had consistently espoused the belief that Europe had to become a tighter economic bloc in order to respond to the challenges posed by the US and Japan: the single European market proposed in the EUT would comprise a first step towards this objective. Mitterrand's initiative was also an attempt to consolidate the Franco–German axis as the governing force within the EC, and to tie in the West Germans unambiguously to the Community at a time of powerful neutralist, unilateralist sentiment within their country. For cynics, Mitterrand's European crusade could not be divorced entirely from internal politics: it was intended to appeal to the federal instincts of the centrists, with the objective of preserving his competences in the field of foreign policy and defence after March 1986.

The Fontainebleau summit, at which the British budget issue was finally resolved, was deemed by all observers to be a success for Mitterrand. It acted as a spur for further EC integration, in that Mitterrand obtained the creation of an ad hoc committee to discuss institutional reform (the Dooge committee). Mitterrand subsequently repeated his determination to go ahead with enhanced political integration, even at the implied expense of the exclusion of some member states from a fast-track EC (notably Britain). The prospect of a two-tier Europe was held forth as a threat to force recalcitrant states into line.[24] The initial Dooge committee report called for the EC to become 'a genuine political entity', and proposed that an intergovernmental conference be held to negotiate a new European Union Treaty. By accepting the Dooge report, Mitterrand went further than any other French President in the direction of European integration. The text called for co-decision in certain matters for the parliament, as well as need to strengthen the Commission and the European Court of Justice, the other supranational EC institutions. The report also provided for enhanced majority voting and envisaged the eventual phasing out of the veto.

But the Dooge report was too radical for a minority of member states: after a failure to reach agreement at the Dublin summit of December 1984, a modified report was placed on the agenda at the Milan summit in June 1985. Under pressure from the Italian presidency, an intergovernmental conference (IGC) was called for at the Milan summit, in spite of the opposition of the UK, Denmark and Greece. Mitterrand felt constrained to go along with the Italian proposal, although this was to some extent at the expense of French prestige, since the final decision to call for an IGC had not been taken on Mitterrand's personal initiative. The results of the IGC on treaty revision were to be submitted to the Luxembourg summit in December 1985.

In the approach to the Luxembourg summit of December 1985, the French position on institutional reform appeared more reserved than that proposed by the EC Commission, as well as by European partners such as Germany and Italy. No French text went as far as the positions adopted by the German and Italian governments on the powers of the European parliament. Despite Mitterrand's initial acceptance of the Dooge report, moreover, the French government appeared later to back-pedal on its recommendation that the national veto should be phased out. The most reluctant Europeans were those French civil servants who feared that an increase in the EC's authority would occur at their expense. They were particularly prevalent within the Foreign Affairs Ministry (Quai d'Orsay), which had the most to lose from a more coordinated foreign policy structure.

Notwithstanding these pressures, the agreement on the Single European Act at the Luxembourg summit consolidated Mitterrand's status as a prime initiator of moves towards closer European integration. The initiatives taken by Mitterrand under the French presidency of the Council (January–June 1984) were crucial for the success of the process leading to the Single European Act, although the French President had to contend with rival ambitions of other European leaders, notably Thatcher, Kohl and Craxi. As on other such occasions, the Single European Act was a compromise between somewhat divergent national viewpoints. The Act reflected some French proposals, while going beyond the French viewpoint on others. The important point to retain was that Mitterrand again revealed his willingness to compromise in order to promote the cause of greater European integration, conceived to be vital for French policy interests. Indeed, Mitterrand recognised that the principle of majority voting was essential in order to proceed with his objectives in areas such as social or industrial policy, where opposition from the UK could be predicted. Acceptance of majority voting itself kept alive the idea of a two-or-more-speed Europe.

In essence, it was agreed at the Luxembourg summit that the parliament would have a power of co-decision-making in relation to the implementation of the directives contained in the Single European Act; and that the European Council would be able to oppose the parliament only by unanimous opposition to its decisions. Both provisions exceeded French proposals, and marked an important step in the direction of supranationality. The summit also suggested that the role of the Commission should be strengthened, an institution de Gaulle had sought to limit to a subordinate function.[25] Apart from these proposals, the institutional framework created by the Single European Act left largely intact the intergovernmental basis of decision-making within the Community: the Council of Ministers remained the key institution, and the rule of unanimity was retained for all matters except those relating to the Act. In practice, however, the momentum created by the Act led to the virtual abandoning of the unanimity rule, and the advent of majority voting as the norm within the European Council.

The Luxembourg summit represented Mitterrand's last major international rendezvous before the legislative elections of March 1986. His high profile on the European and international stage could not prevent the return of the Right.

EUROPE AND *COHABITATION*

The whole period of *cohabitation* – in some senses a permanent electoral campaign – was an image-building exercise for François Mitterrand. This was illustrated nowhere more transparently than in relation to Europe: the issue of Europe was propelled to centre-stage of domestic French politics, largely due to the efforts of Mitterrand during the preceding two years. The diffusion of the image of Mitterrand as a *grand européen* was essential, in order to replace that of sectarian left-wing leader inherited from the 1981–83 period.

Europe became an issue of (artificial) domestic consensus; the issue became not whether France should be in the forefront of European integration, but who was best qualified to lead the nation in this direction. The Mitterrand–Delors partnership had forged the powerful image within French public opinion that France's national interest coincided with the development of the EC, itself portrayed as a European extension of French leadership. Public opinion greatly appreciated the idea of a French tandem running the affairs of Europe. The fact that Mitterrand retained a high profile in European affairs throughout the period of *cohabitation* further enhanced the issue of Europe for the incumbent President. In fact, the popularity of Mitterrand's European policy forced other prominent leaders to silence their differences, notably Chirac, who had in the past voiced strong criticisms against the theme of closer European integration. Mitterrand appeared once again in his role as legitimator, imposing an enforced and fragile political consensus on the issue of European integration after having previously been ambivalent on this issue. The ratification of the Single European Act by the RPR–UDF-dominated National Assembly in September 1986 accelerated the quasi-unanimity expressed by mainstream French politicians in relation to Europe. The support for the single market among French business circles was overwhelming: this made it difficult for the RPR or UDF to express reservations in relation to developments in Europe.

Europe: the struggle for ascendency Europe had classically formed a part of the presidential 'reserved domain'; since de Gaulle, French Presidents had jealously guarded control over European affairs for themselves, and had resisted any encroachments in this sphere. Europe had such an impact on domestic affairs that it might be conceived of as lying somewhere between foreign and domestic policy. As prime minister, Chirac was unwilling to allow Mitterrand a free rein in terms of European policy: he argued, not without reason, that it was impossible to separate European affairs from domestic economic policy, and that the government had been elected in March 1986 to carry a programme of economic and political liberalisation. Chirac took a number of public initiatives designed to wrest control over European issues from Mitterrand: immediately prior to the Hague summit of June 1986, for example, Chirac declared that 'Community affairs are above all the responsibility of the prime minister'. This was met by the Elysée's proclamation that: 'European affairs are primarily the concern of the President of the Republic'.[26]

Specialist opinion is somewhat divided in relation to the distribution of powers in the traditional presidential sphere during the *cohabitation* of 1986–88. Cohen has postulated that three separate spheres of influence existed, with presidential authority tending to diminish in areas where the traditional reserved sector touched upon domestic policy. The 'predominantly govern-mental' sphere consisted of relations with francophone African states (with their obvious economic implications), the Middle East (with its anti-terrorist overtones), and commercial relations with foreign states. The predominantly presidential sphere related to defence, Franco-German relations and disarmament negotiations. These were spheres where the constitution, constitutional precedent, or else political realities personalised decision-making. Cohen asserts that there existed a third mixed sphere, where decisions were taken by cooperation between President and prime minister: EC policy-making was the foremost example of this.[27] Major EC decisions were co-managed, with both men anxious to preserve national unity on this issue for their own political purposes (the forthcoming presidential election). The daily management of EC affairs passed to the government. Mitterrand's European role was most obviously visible in relation to prestige operations, international summits (where he occupied a more prominent position than Premier Chirac) and face-to-face discussions with EC heads of government. This notion of a division of the presidential reserved sector is implicitly disputed by Howorth, who contends that the essential prerogatives on foreign policy and defence remained with François Mitterrand throughout *cohabitation*.[28] The evidence would tend towards the former interpretation.

Measures requiring legislative action (such as the ratification of the Single European Act) naturally fell within the governmental sphere. The government, able to rely on the permanent bureaucracy, also disposed of a major advantage in terms of information: Cohen (and others) contends that Matignon, the Quai d'Orsay and other relevant ministries initially refused to pass on all diplomatic telegrams and other relevant documentation to the Elysée, in an attempt to deprive the President of information vital to influencing decisions. This obstructionist attitude was gradually discontinued.[29] The precondition for Mitterrand's exercising his prestige function was that he launch no new European initiative that might lead to confrontation with his prime minister; this is the most plausible explanation why Mitterrand made no major policy initiatives during *cohabitation*. Whatever the realities, public opinion regarded Mitterrand, rather than Chirac, as being in charge of European policy.[30]

The 1988 Presidential Campaign   Mitterrand's promotion of a European consensus provided a subtle means of campaigning for the presidency: all other candidates were forced to deal with a European agenda which had largely been defined by the incumbent President. The theme of Europe dominated the presidential campaign of 1988. From the date of his official entry into the campaign, on 22 March 1988, Mitterrand made it clear that Europe was to be the central theme of his campaign: quite apart from its inherent importance, the issue of Europe forced other candidates to compare their records with that of Mitterrand.

In the course of the 1988 campaign, Mitterrand combined his characteristic mixture of idealism with pragmatic caution. The issue of Europe figured prominently in Mitterrand's *Lettre à tous les Français*: the central ideas contained in the Letter had never been so comprehensively vented before. Mitterrand called for political union, for a common defence policy, for a harmonised EC social policy, and for 'protection' for the single market of 1993. He insisted that the free trade opportunities opened for business must be complemented by active involvement on the part of governments in new EC policies: research, culture, education, environment, social protection. The theme of common European policies was again resurrected in a *dirigiste* approach towards Europe: there was a strong suspicion that the French President was unhappy with an exclusively liberal interpretation of the single market, such as that espoused by Mrs Thatcher in the UK. The Letter also served as an apologia for Mitterrand's European policy during the past seven years: an impartial reading of the Letter leaves the disinterested observer convinced that one man alone was responsible for progress towards greater European integration. The overriding impression was of an incumbent president attempting – rather successfully – to personalise the issue of Europe, necessarily claiming far more credit for a complex series of processes than was strictly justified. But by concentrating so exclusively on Europe, Mitterrand was, perhaps unwittingly, storing up problems for the future. The assumption that the French could shape Europe, *ipso facto*, greatly exaggerated his freedom of manoeuvre. Problems, and unforeseen circumstances might rebound against him. These themes will be considered in Chapter 11.

CONCLUSION: MITTERRAND'S EUROPE

The idea of Europe was propelled from one of secondary importance into becoming a guiding theme and justification for Mitterrand's political activity. Europe comprised the principal area in which Mitterrand could perform a proactive role. Far from being constrained merely to react to events, as in economic policy, the French President successfully promoted his own European agenda. European circumstances in the pre-1989 era were ideal for the pursuit of such an agenda by a French President. The self-imposed isolationism of Thatcher's Britain left the Franco-German partnership as the key driving force behind Community change. Within the Paris–Bonn axis, the French occupied the status at least of equals, occasionally of senior partners.

Political circumstances were fortuitous for the exercise of maximal influence by Mitterrand, once relations with other European countries had been normalised after the economic U-turn of March 1983. The skill of Mitterrand's political leadership in this sphere was to recognise this opportunity, and to provide a far-sighted vision of Europe's future which captured the imagination of European peoples well beyond France.

Several key European themes were reiterated throughout Mitterrand's career. These included the crucial significance of Franco-German reconciliation (see Chapter 10); the importance of building the EC as a means of safeguarding France's role as a leading world power, and the importance of Europe as a political, social, economic and military space with greater independence from the superpowers. Mitterrand's Europe was underpinned by a genuine commitment to closer European integration, allied to a patriotic sense of the need to enhance French influence as a primordial political force within the European family of nations. These concerns were complementary, rather than contradictory throughout the first presidential term. In terms of institutional structures, Mitterrand's Europe was conceived of as an intergovernmental rather than a federal entity, although he accepted more developments in the direction of supranationality than any of his predecessors. Finally, there were signs that Mitterrand preferred a compact, cohesive Community, based on a Franco-German directorate, rather than a broader nebulous association of less cohesive nations. There were already indications that the French President was more willing to entertain the notion of a several-speed Europe than were most other European heads of government.

Jean Monnet considered that Mitterrand was a 'sure value' in relation to European issues. Throughout his political career, Europe provided one source of continuity guiding his political action. His changing political discourse in relation to Europe reflected the contradictory situations Mitterrand was forced to deal with in the various leadership roles he performed. This was most evident in the 1970s, when Mitterrand was forced to tread a delicate tightrope between the various factions of the PS, and the reality of alliance with an anti-European Communist Party. Mitterrand was careful never to cede to the sirens of an anti-Europeanism strongly represented within the French left. As President, he lost no occasion during the 1980s to recall that he had been present at the earliest postwar gatherings of European statesmen since the late 1940s, and had consistently adopted a favourable attitude towards European integration. As Helen Drake observes: 'As a rhetorical tool, such references to his past clearly marked Mitterrand off from virtually all other European leaders: only he could claim such involvement in the history of the EC'.[31]

There remained a fundamental element of ambivalence in relation to Mitterrand's discourse on European integration. Mitterrand was the most European when it appeared as if the construction of Europe would magnify the glory of France (and therefore of himself). There remained elements of ambiguity and confusion about the relationship between European integration and national independence, regularly evoked by Mitterrand as imperatives in the same breath. These interrogations were pushed to the forefront during the course of Mitterrand's second presidential mandate.

Chapter 9

The world leader

Upon his election as President, Mitterrand could not profess any real competence in relation to contemporary foreign policy decision-making. Although his ministerial past had brought him into close contact with francophone Africa, the world had changed beyond recognition in the twenty-five years that had intervened since then. Along with other leaders of the opposition, Mitterrand had been excluded from detailed involvement in, or information about, foreign policy-making. This was in accordance with the marked presidentialisation of decision-making in foreign policy affairs from the period of de Gaulle onwards. But he had also been a President-in-waiting for almost twenty years, and this had enabled him to refine his command of foreign policy and defence issues. As de facto leader of the Left after 1965, Mitterrand was called upon to respond to the great foreign policy and defence issues of the 1960s and 1970s, such as the development of the French nuclear deterrent, de Gaulle's repeated vetoes of Britain's application for EC membership, the withdrawal from NATO, and the Arab–Israeli conflict. The near-systematic adoption of an anti-Gaullist stance on these issues in the 1960s gradually gave way in the course of the 1970s to the incorporation of key aspects of the Gaullist foreign policy legacy into Socialist doctrine. This occurred notably in relation to NATO, and the French nuclear deterrent. In this manner, Mitterrand contributed to the legitimisation of the Gaullist foreign policy legacy before his election as President.

This evolution was most marked in relation to the French nuclear deterrent, a development which conveniently enhanced Mitterrand's margins of manoeuvre once elected President. Mitterrand's PS initially took particular objection to the independent nuclear deterrent, in line with Socialist traditions of republican (i.e. conventional) defence. The PCFs spectacular U-turn in favour of the nuclear deterrent in May 1977 was imitated one year later by the PS. The Socialist reversal appeared to take place for reasons of political expediency: *gaullien* foreign policy concerns were widely accepted within French public opinion, fuelling the fear that an anti-nuclear left would never be elected. Moreover, support for the nuclear deterrent would lessen hostility from the military in the event of a left-wing victory in the 1978 elections. The party's shift in favour of nuclear deterrence also reflected a deeply rooted fear of Soviet military expansionism, which had caused less acute concern at the beginning of the decade, when the Socialists were primarily obsesssed with combating American economic imperialism. Finally, the change on nuclear policy represented the culmination of efforts by the future Defence Minister, Charles Hernu, to swing Mitterrand and the Socialist Party in this direction.[1]

Mitterrand's PS was also critical of NATO, and rallied to support de Gaulle's withdrawal from the integrated military command structure, initially contested in the 1960s. In Socialist Party documents throughout the 1970s, the belief was reiterated that American economic imperialism was more insidious than any military threat from the Soviet Union. The party repeatedly called for the simultaneous dissolution of NATO and the Warsaw Pact, a call repeated in Mitterrand's *110 Propositions*. One year before his election as President, Mitterrand affirmed that he was 'no more attached to the Atlantic Alliance than a Romanian or a Pole is to the Warsaw Pact'.[2] And yet, as with Europe, Mitterrand was careful to occupy a median stance on this issue within the PS, rejecting both the primary anti-Americanism of the CERES faction, and the enthusiastic Atlanticism of the old SFIO. Under Mitterrand's leadership, the party recognised that only the USSR had committed acts of aggression within the European theatre in the postwar period. His fierce rivalry with the PCF after 1977 incited Mitterrand to adopt a far harsher stance in relation to the Soviet Union than that espoused by the then incumbent French President, Valéry Giscard d'Estaing.

The bulk of the present chapter will concentrate upon the role performed by Mitterrand as the chief inspiration of French foreign policy from 1981–93. Prior to such an evaluation, however, it is indispensable to place Mitterrand's activity within the sphere of French foreign policy.

THE FRENCH FOREIGN POLICY ENVIRONMENT

The sphere of foreign policy, per se, is one where national political leaderships can enjoy limited autonomy in an interdependent world. The constraints faced by French presidents are similar to those encountered by chief executives in other comparable liberal democracies: these include inherited alliance structures, a powerful foreign policy community, a strong bureaucratic input, the existence of influential lobbies, and the unpredictable nature of political circumstances.[3] Political leaders operate within circumscribed limits that place strict boundaries upon their sovereignty. As will be illustrated, however, French presidents possess rather more autonomy than most other chief executives in this respect.

The sphere of foreign relations is also one where the personalisation of visible decision-making is most evident. In the French context, foreign affairs and defence have generally been considered to form part of a presidential 'reserved sector', where formal decision-making is primarily (although not exclusively) the responsibility of the president and his advisers. One specialist has described the French president as a nuclear monarch, who can declare war and peace unilaterally, conduct independent diplomacy, and who alone can trigger a nuclear weapon.[4] These powers stem from the legacy of General de Gaulle, from established precedents, and from general pressures towards the personalisation of foreign policy-making, rather than from unambiguous constitutional provisions.[5] They applied with less force during the 1986–88 *cohabitation*. But the general assertion of presidential supremacy in foreign policy-making does not mean that Mitterrand (or his predecessors) operated in a vacuum, or that foreign policy was reserved, strictly speaking, for the president. On the contrary, foreign policy-making is a highly complex affair. According to one close observer, the key governmental actors involved in foreign policy-making during the Mitterrand presidency were: the President, his foreign policy advisers (military and civilian) within the presidential staff; the prime minister and his foreign policy advisers; the foreign affairs minister and his advisers; the defence minister and his advisers; other ministers in pursuit of their foreign policy interests, and key civil servants within the Quai d'Orsay and other ministries. None of these units was entirely homogeneous, but contained varying viewpoints within their midsts.[6]

Although prominent figures such as the prime minister, the Foreign Affairs minister, and the defence minister are not devoid of bargaining power, the fact that the president personally supervises their activities tends to reinforce the perception of presidential supremacy in this sphere. In the case of disagreement between the president and his defence minister, for instance, the latter is expected to resign, as J-P. Chevènement learnt to his cost in January 1991 over his opposition to the Gulf War. In the case of Mitterrand, loyal personal acolytes usually occupied the ministerial portfolios connected with foreign policy decision-making, although this was not the case with Mitterrand's first Foreign Affairs Minister, Claude Cheysson. The replacement of Cheysson by Roland Dumas in 1984 signalled closer presidential supervision over foreign policy, with Dumas generally being regarded as the President's *alter ego*.[7] Apart from the instance of *cohabitation*, the Prime minister tends to defer to the presidential will in relation to foreign affairs: the self-effacement of Rocard during the Gulf War provides a case in point.

The president chairs all the important foreign policy and defence decision-making committees. Under Mitterrand, *conseils restreints* tended to be convoked on questions of foreign policy.[8] The technical expertise available to the presidency in the sphere of foreign policy, defence and European affairs is considerable. Although formally attached to the prime minister's office, the two key bureaucratic coordinating institutions, the SGDN (defence) and the SGCI (Europe), are responsible *de facto* to the president. And within the Elysée staff, the president can call upon the foreign policy expertise of a range of civilian and military advisers. The formulation of defence and foreign policy is shrouded in secrecy. The key civilian figures within the presidential entourage under Mitterrand included: Attali (Mitterrand's special adviser, 1981–92); Bianco (General Secretary of the Elysée staff, 1982–92); Penne (until 1986 Mitterrand's African adviser); Védrine (a diplomatic adviser, 1981–1992, General secretary after 1992), de Grossouvre (a close confidant, and a man of special missions). We should also mention the *chef d'état major particulier*, who is the chief military adviser within the presidential staff, a man attributed in interviews with significant influence. In addition, Mitterrand made wide use of the practice of naming personal appointees to fulfil specific secret missions for the president, not least members of his own family.

Foreign policy-making has tended to become increasingly personalised, at least on a formal level: the role of international summits, the symbolism associated with leaders as personally embodying national unity, and the personalisation induced by the mass media all contribute to this effect. Indeed, the French president possesses unrivalled resources compared with fellow chief-executives in comparable liberal democracies: these include the stability of presidential tenure in office; an inherited practice of presidential pre-eminence in the spheres of foreign policy and defence; a Gaullist foreign policy legacy of national independence; and the comparative weakness of countervailing domestic influences such as parliamentary, party or group pressures. An extensive consideration of these influences during the Mitterrand presidency would require a separate study, well beyond the confines of the present exercise. Whatever the extent of their influence, French presidents have acted as if France was a minor superpower capable of conducting an independent foreign policy.

GAULLISM BY ANY OTHER NAME?[9] MITTERRAND'S FOREIGN POLICY

The Gaullist legacy Attempts to assess French foreign policy from the vantage-point of Gaullism are fraught with difficulty. No-one can predict what de Gaulle's reactions to events would have been had he governed during the 1980s and 1990s. Gaullist foreign policy was itself multifaceted, contradictory and changeable according to the political conjuncture. And yet it is imperative to address this question, the object of several academic studies, although it is partially misplaced.

At the risk of considerable oversimplification, de Gaulle was the last of the great rhetoricians of twentieth-century French patriotism. At the core of de Gaulle's foreign policy lay the notion of rank; that France must be one among the great nations, however many there are of these at any one time. The vision of renewed French greatness under de Gaulle guided French foreign policy throughout the Fifth Republic and was consciously imitated by de Gaulle's successors. The positive psychological impact of de Gaulle's discourse upon the self-evaluation of the French people mattered as much as any objective restoration of French greatness. The Gaullist legacy might be charted in relation to five primordial spheres, although these are neither exclusive nor exhaustive: relations with the superpowers, policy towards the developing world, Europe, the rank of France, and defence policy. In the next section, we shall consider de Gaulle's legacy in these key areas of foreign policy, before assessing Mitterrand's initial objectives and subsequent activity in each of these spheres.

Relations with the superpowers The crucial Gaullist legacy was that of maximum national independence consistent with France's continuing membership of the western alliance. France's great power rank was to be restored by the construction of a nuclear deterrent, and the pursuit of an independent foreign policy. Gaullism was possible in the 1960s because there was no question of the Americans removing their nuclear guarantee over Western Europe, or their troops from West Germany. France needed the security offered by the western alliance, faced with the perceived threat from the USSR. Any genuine attempt to leave the western bloc would thus be undesirable and unfeasible; this acted as a powerful constraint on Gaullist foreign policy. Within this constraint, de Gaulle's policy oscillated between early attempts to enhance French influence within the Atlantic alliance (by means of securing French parity with the UK as an American ally); and later efforts to promote enhanced Western European security cooperation under the aegis of France's leadership. The former preoccupation explained de Gaulle's proposed three-power directorate (US, UK, France) over western Europe, but the latter strain prevailed throughout most of de Gaulle's presidency. The Franco-German friendship Treaty signed in 1963 not only consolidated the Franco-German partnership at the heart of Europe, but also contained (stillborn) clauses promoting western European defence collaboration.[10]

We have discussed how, as PS leader, Mitterrand adopted a median stance in relation to the US. After initial opposition, he had rallied to support de Gaulle's decision to withdraw from NATO, while reaffirming his commitment to the Atlantic alliance. In the *110 Propositions*, Mitterrand called for 'the withdrawal of the Soviet SS20s, coupled with the abandoning of the plan to install Pershing missiles upon European soil'.[11] This policy of subtle dosages contrasted subsequently with the strongly pro-Atlantic tone of Mitterrand's early term in office, notably with his determined support for the deployment of US Pershing missiles to counter the Soviet SS20s. His early Atlanticism was explicable in part by political circumstances, in part by conviction. Mitterrand had never articulated the primary anti-Americanism voiced by powerful strains of French public opinion. His commitment to basic Atlantic solidarity was never in doubt, although not always at the top of his hierarchy of priorities. What Mitterrand resented were American attempts to dominate Western Europe, and US support for military dictatorships throughout the Third World.

At key periods of crisis, Mitterrand was more resolutely pro-Atlantic than any of his Fifth Republican predecessors. This was illustrated by the Euromissile crisis of the early 1980s and the Gulf War of 1991. In both instances, Mitterrand was ready to accept American leadership, and to succumb to decisions taken by intergovernmental decision-making bodies dominated by the US (NATO and/or the UN). These events provided the two benchmarks of Mitterrand's Atlanticism. In his celebrated speech to the German Bundestag in January 1983, Mitterrand called upon the Federal Republic and Belgium to deploy US cruise and Pershing missiles, and to hold firm against domestic opposition.[12] The Euromissile crisis revealed that Mitterrand and Reagan shared many of the same preoccupations both in relation to Germany and the USSR. Mitterrand was determined to tie the Germans into the western alliance via the EC and NATO, and to retain the American security guarantee for Europe in an era of international tension. Atlanticism and Europeanism thus coincided perfectly at the beginning of Mitterrand's mandate, since the Federal Republic appeared dangerously tempted by the sirens of neutralism and pacifism. Mitterrand's repeated support for the Atlantic alliance, for the American presence in western Europe, and for the deployment of US Pershing missiles was essential to reassure the Americans over the participation of the Communist ministers in the Mauroy government. His firm stance over the deployment of the Pershing missiles set the French leader apart from majority sentiment within the German SPD, as well as the British Labour Party.

There were strict limits, however, to Mitterrand's Atlanticism. Support for the Atlantic alliance did not signify a willingness to re-enter NATO, to the proclaimed dismay of the Germans, the British and others. The French consensus on this issue was genuine. Moreover, certain of Mitterrand's announced foreign policy objectives were in stark contradiction with others. The image of Mitterrand as the Atlanticist was difficult to reconcile with the audacious tone of his Cancun declaration of 1981, however superficial the portrayal of Mitterrand as defender of the Third World transpired to be. As President, Mitterrand continued to criticise American behaviour in a range of spheres: its support for military dictatorships in Central and Latin America, its restrictive economic policies, its attempt to frustrate closer European union. The fundamental community of interests with the US during the cold war climate of the early 1980s did not exclude periodic disagreements: the most publicised of these related to the French sale of arms to the Nicaraguan Sandinistas in 1981.

As the international climate softened, after the deployment of the Euro-missiles and the advent to power of Gorbachev in the USSR, genuine divergences of interest proliferated between Paris and Washington. One consequence of this was Mitterrand's advocacy of closer European defence collaboration, confirmed by the creation of the Franco-German joint defence corps in 1987, and the defence clauses of the Maastricht Treaty of 1992 (see

Chapter 10). Mitterrand also sought actively to promote greater European technological independence from the US, notably in the form of the EUREKA project, symbolic of growing unease between Europeans and Americans (see Chapter 8). The Franco-American divergences over the GATT negotiations from 1986–93 provided another instance of different approaches between the two nations.

De Gaulle had been able to conduct an independent foreign policy in the 1960s in part because there were no obvious manifestations of aggressive Soviet designs within the European theatre, as there were in the early 1980s: in fact, the Soviet invasion of Czechoslovakia in 1968 revealed the tenuous bases upon which de Gaulle's *ostpolitik* was based. There is no accurate way of predicting whether de Gaulle would have displayed a comparable Atlanticist vigour faced with similar crises to those confronted by Mitterrand during the early 1980s.[13] This is logically impossible to deduct. It is true that, for all of his anti-American rhetoric, de Gaulle firmly supported Kennedy during the Cuban missile crisis of 1962. But it seems reasonable to conclude that Mitterrand's conduct of Atlantic policy differed from that of his predecessors, especially de Gaulle. This was illustrated by the fact that Mitterrand supported the continuing existence of NATO after the 1989 revolutions in eastern Europe, even after the dissolution of the Warsaw Pact. The value of intergovernmental organisations such as the United Nations, NATO, and the CSCE was deemed essential by Mitterrand to impose stability on a newly unstable world order.[14]

President Mitterrand's stance towards the USSR rested uneasily alongside de Gaulle's *ostpolitik*, or Giscard d'Estaing's complicity with the Soviet old-guard. Always uneasy, the invasion of Afghanistan in 1980 led to a further deterioration in Mitterrand's relations with the USSR, and it was an open secret that the Soviet leadership favoured Giscard d'Estaing's re-election. His firm attitude towards the USSR as a potential aggressor during the Euro-missiles crisis earned the French President the lasting enmity of the old Soviet leadership.[15] The ambiguity towards the USSR displayed by past French Presidents was notably absent. Mitterrand's visit to Moscow in June 1984 epitomised the new spirit of *désentente* between France and the USSR; the President broke with all rules of diplomatic precedence to denounce Soviet human rights abuses from within the Kremlin.[16] Relations with the USSR remained tender until the accession of Gorbachev in 1985. This was illustrated by the Soviet opposition to French initiatives in Chad or Libya. But, even at the height of cold war relations in the early 1980s, elements of the traditional French *politique de balancier* with regard to the superpowers remained: for instance, Mitterrand's firm response to the Soviets' shooting down of the South-Korean Boeing 747 in October 1983 did not prevent the French President from demanding favours from the USSR leadership with regard to French Middle Eastern policy.

The accession of Gorbachev, combined with the negative European reaction to Reagan's star wars initiative, provided the impetus for the resumption of a more traditional French foreign policy position. Mitterrand's firm support for Gorbachev throughout the period 1985–91 placed him in the mainstream of European statesmen: support for the reformist Russian leader became an article of faith for Bush, Mitterrand, Thatcher, Kohl and other leading statespeople. Mitterrand's reactions to events in Eastern Europe after the collapse of the Berlin Wall in 1989 are considered in the next chapter. On several occasions after October 1989, Mitterrand revealed his preference for the maintenance of existing political structures, rather than for the proliferation of new unstable states. This attitude led him to plead initially for the preservation of the USSR, and of the Yugoslav federation. In turn, this led Mitterrand to adopt an ambiguous stance during the August 1991 coup in the USSR, which served later to embitter his relations with Boris Yeltsin.[17] Indeed, throughout his second presidential mandate, Mitterrand appeared overwhelmed and disoriented by the new post-Communist world order.

Relations with the Third World   One key feature of Gaullist foreign policy was a conscious effort to engage in a dialogue with Third World leaders, in order to encourage them not to become satellites of either of the superpowers, and to look to France for guidance. The network of client states developed in sub-Saharan Africa out of the former French empire bore testament to the partial fruition of de Gaulle's efforts, although French influence was less marked elsewhere. De Gaulle's purpose was in part a symbolic one, to assert the independence of French foreign policy. However unreal, de Gaulle's approach allowed the French to maintain a dialogue with Third World leaders which was envied by other European nations such as the Federal Republic or the UK, who were more constrained to perserve alliance solidarity.

Foreign policy concerns occupied a relatively modest place in Mitterrand's 1981 campaign, but his most audacious and rhetorically compelling proposals concerned relations with the Third World. In the *110 Propositions*, candidate Mitterrand pledged to defend the rights of oppressed peoples everywhere, to champion a fairer system of international development and to work for world disarmament. He also made a number of more specific pledges, such as a moratorium on Third World debt, and an increase in the aid budget to 0.7 per cent of GNP.[18] With other avenues for meaningful French diplomacy temporarily blocked from 1981–82 (such as Europe, or East–West relations), Mitterrand's France fleetingly turned its attention to spectacular policy initiatives in the direction of the Third World. The joint Franco-Mexican declaration of August 1981, in favour of the Sandinista regime in Nicaragua, appeared specifically conceived to attract support for France as patron of the rights of third world countries. This initiative occurred in spite of the fierce opposition of the civil servants of the Quai d'Orsay.[19]

To the extent that France was portrayed as natural leader of Third World aspirations against the superpowers, Mitterrand's rhetoric lay squarely within

Gaullist traditions. During the period 1981–82, lip service was paid to the need to initiate a far-reaching dialogue with the more dynamic countries of the Third World, such as Algeria, Brazil, Mexico or India. But these fine words were largely without effect, and without any obvious link to policy. Ideas of co-development were rapidly abandoned as unrealistic and too expensive. By the end of 1982, attention to the 'Third World' was once again largely confined to the francophone states of sub-Saharan Africa.

Quite apart from his spectacular declarations, Mitterrand's choice of foreign policy personnel perplexed France's allies. His selection of Régis Debray as a presidential adviser troubled the Americans almost as much as the PCF's participation in government.[20] The nomination of Claude Cheysson as Foreign Affairs Minister (1981–84) had a similar effect: in Cheysson, Mitterrand appointed someone reputed for his pro-Arab, pro-Third World, anti-American views. It was obvious that Mitterrand drew satisfaction from the portrayal of Socialist France as defender of the rights of man throughout the world. Upon closer examination, one is forced to undertake an unfavourable comparison between Mitterrand's lyrical rhetoric and the substance of policy. None of Mitterrand's 1981 pledges achieved fruition. The pledge to support 'oppressed peoples' was selectively interpreted in order not to damage France's real political interests, especially in Africa (see pp. 143–145). The commitment to increasing the aid budget to 0.7 per cent of GNP was quietly abandoned, a victim of the government's financial austerity after 1982. The pledge in favour of adopting a moral approach towards arms sales suffered a similar fate, in the interests of realpolitik.

The most charitable interpretation of Mitterrand's Third World policy was that the constraints of the international economic and political system rendered illusory efforts to inaugurate a 'new model of development'. In this sphere, as in others, Mitterrand lacked the means for his ambitions.[21] Once the myth of France as the natural spokesman for developing countries had evaporated, Mitterrand's presidency was marked by a downplaying of efforts to encourage Third World countries to escape from tutelage by either of the superpowers (a prominent characteristic of de Gaulle's presidency), and a reversion to traditional patterns of French activity in its former colonies in Africa.

Europe   Mitterrand's attitude and behaviour towards Europe clearly marked out the fourth President of the Fifth Republic as distinct from the first. It was argued in Chapter 8 that Europe provided one source of cohesion and continuity throughout Mitterrand's career. The rhetoric and behaviour of Mitterrand as President could not easily be squared with de Gaulle's Europe of Nation-States. The theme of Europe is developed in detail in Chapters 8 and 10.

The rank of France   The guiding theme of classical Gaullism had been the need to preserve France's rank as a great power. There existed clear elements of continuity between de Gaulle and Mitterrand in this sphere. Thus,

Mitterrand stressed on several occasions the imperative of maintaining France's 'rank' as the 'third military power of the world', whereas President Giscard d'Estaing had declared himself satisfied to be 'top of the league of middle ranking nations'.[22] The preoccupation with retaining France's permanent seat at the UN might be interpreted as an incidence of Mitterrand's *gaullien* obsession with 'great power' status. After the allied victory in the Gulf War, Dumas publicly defended the fact that France and the UK each had a permanent seat on the UN Security Council because they were the 'victorious powers' in the Second World War. Several of his actions as President revealed the conception the French President retained of France as a great power. These included his unilateral initiatives in relation to Latin America, especially at the early stages of his presidency; the French peace-keeping mission in Lebanon in 1982–83; the involvement in the Gulf War, and unilateral military actions in Africa (notably in Chad).

The notion of France as a first-rank power also underpinned Mitterrand's Middle Eastern policy. A firm pro-Israeli stance had marked out Mitterrand's instinctive reactions to the crucial Middle East problem since the creation of the Jewish State in 1948. As President of the FGDS in 1967, for instance, Mitterrand unyieldingly backed the Israelis against Arab aggression, and against the unholy alliance of de Gaulle and the PCF.[23] Yet, the delicate balancing operations of the type in which Mitterrand succeeded so well in domestic politics were fruitless in the harsh realities of the Middle East. His belief that Arab recognition of Israel's right to exist should be accompanied by Israeli guarantees for a Palestinian homeland was laudable in theory, representing a marked dialectical evolution away from the pro-Arab stance adopted by de Gaulle and his successors. And yet, Mitterrand's complete failure to secure an evolution of Israel's hard-line position under Premier Shamir rapidly disillusioned the French President. This was in spite of the fact that he had been the first western leader to address the Knesset in March 1982. A medium-sized nation such as France lacked the means for the ambitions of its policies, especially in a region where there were other major antagonistic players present. This conclusion was also valid for a country of traditional French influence such as the Lebanon. Mitterrand's assertion that Lebanon had the right to be unified and independent was impotent when faced with the centrifugal realities of the country. The deployment in 1983 of a large French force as part of the UN contingent resulted in many French deaths, without satisfying Christian Lebanese sentiment. The French were powerless to assist the Lebanese Christian community when faced with Syrian bombardment in 1990.[24]

The 1991 war against Iraq also alienated one of France's closest Middle Eastern Arab allies, to whom French governments had sold vast quantities of arms, and upon whom rested traditionally pro-Arab French policy. The Middle East revealed that France could no longer act effectively as a minor superpower in the region, and that its influence depended upon being a part of an allied coalition. By the end of Mitterrand's presidency, France had lost much of its prestige with key Middle Eastern governments, Israeli and Arab alike. The main players in the Middle East no longer included the French, who nonetheless retained more than a residual influence.

The claim to represent a first-rank power was far more credible in relation to Africa, where previous French Presidents had coupled generous aid packages with military logistical support, to carve themselves out a position of unrivalled influence for a medium-sized nation such as France. Although decolonisation was completed in 1962, close relations have been maintained between metropolitan France and its former African dependencies. One of the canons of Gaullism was that, in order to maintain its influence in post-colonial Africa (hence its rank as a great power), metropolitan French governments had to offer financial, military, economic and political support to friendly African regimes. Under de Gaulle and Pompidou, African policy comprised the very core of the presidential reserved sphere; the African adviser, Jacques Foccart, became the key figure, maintaining direct relations with African heads of state.[25] Suspicions of the peddling of influence, clientelism and commercial exploitation were never far from the surface. Although Giscard d'Estaing dispensed with the services of Foccart, African policy remained a presidential preoccupation. In total, President Giscard d'Estaing engaged in twelve separate military interventions in Africa in the course of his term in office.[26] The President's acceptance of a gift of diamonds from the Emperor of the Central African Republic, Bokassa, contributed to his downfall.

Africa had been an area of intense personal interest to Mitterrand since his Fourth Republican ministerial past. French African policy, particularly the notion of France as a gendarme to maintain regional stability, had been harshly criticised by Mitterrand's Socialists in opposition. During the first year in office, Mitterrand's *tiers-mondiste* discourse was to some extent reflected in governmental actions. For an eighteen-month period, J-P. Cot, the Minister-delegate in charge of Cooperation and Development, attempted with some success to coordinate French aid policy in relation to the developing countries, and to improve the conduct of French relations with African states. This attempt to encourage a new model of development did not endure. By the end of 1982, African policy reverted to *gaullien* norms observed by Mitterrand's predecessors. In the words of one qualified observer:

A policy of subsidized exports of arms and equipment was pursued, and a small group of private advisers to the president saw to it that the bulk of French development aid would continue to flow into the pockets of those African heads of state who had always proved faithful friends though not necessarily effective developers of their countries.[27]

The resignation of Cot in December 1982 signalled a return to a more classical neo-interventionist policy, coordinated from the Elysée. The fact that Mitterrand nominated one of his closest lieutenants (Guy Penne) and later his own son as his personal adviser on African affairs testified to the interest the President manifested in the continent.

A detailed assessment of Mitterrand's African policy lies outside the scope of this study: the interested reader will find this dealt with elsewhere.[28] The example of Chad will serve as a model for general developments among francophone African states during Mitterrand's presidency. The conflict with Colonel Gaddafi in Chad provided a classical example of French neo-interventionism. Ever since the independence of Chad in 1960, the French government had provided extensive assistance to a series of pro-French military governments. Paris had helped these governments to survive, latterly against the threat represented by Gaddafi's Libya and the presence of Libyan troops in the Northern band of the country. President Giscard had withdrawn the most recent convoy of French troops in 1980. Thus Mitterrand inherited a neo-colonial situation in Chad (and elsewhere in francophone Africa), and a range of expectations from client states concerning the former colonial power. These expectations severely curtailed the freedom of manoeuvre of any French government if France was to retain its undisputed influence in sub-Saharan Africa. After at first refusing the Chadian leader Hissène Habré's demand for French troops (in October 1981), the government finally succumbed in the summer of 1983, faced with evidence of large-scale Libyan backing for Habré's opponent, Goukouni. As Kolodziej observes: 'France risked losing much of its influence and standing among francophone African states if it failed to act'.[29]

In the case of Chad, the Gaullist inheritance imposed itself upon a rather reluctant Mitterrand. In October 1983, Mitterrand agreed to the launch of *Opération Manta*: 3,000 troops were sent to Chad, with orders to aid Habré's forces, but not to engage directly in combat. These troops were withdrawn in September 1984, after a meeting occurred between Mitterrand and Gaddafi in Crete, which resulted in a mutual troop withdrawal agreement. This episode resulted in considerable embarrassment for Mitterrand, since US space satellites proved that Gaddafi had not respected the terms of the agreement. In February 1986, Mitterrand was forced to backtrack, and to dispatch a new force to Chad, a force enlarged by the Chirac government in February 1987. Eventually, in 1991 the French refused to prevent dissatisfied army officers from staging a coup against Habré. Coming shortly after Mitterrand's La Baule speech of June 1990, this signalled the new rules of the game in post-cold war francophone Africa. Friendly, but inefficient and repressive regimes could no longer automatically count upon the support of the French government.

Despite the obvious continuities, Mitterrand's African policy did evolve in important respects by comparison with that of his predecessors. There was less compulsion to intervene to arbitrate in strictly regional disputes; and, as the example of Chad finally illustrated, there was less tolerance of repressive dictatorships, with French governments increasingly tying aid to the adoption of liberal democratic political systems.[30] At the Franco-African summit of La Baule in June 1990, Mitterrand made an explicit link between aid and democratisation. It is worth noting that the wave of National Democratic Conventions which proliferated throughout Africa during the period 1989–92 occurred disproportionately in francophone African states. But we should also note France's failure to come to the aid of democratising states when they ran into difficulty. By March 1993, one close presidential adviser could point with satisfaction to the fact that a dozen francophone African states had engaged in a process of democratic reform, whereas in 1981 only Senegal possessed a rudimentary democratic system.[31]

Defence and the nuclear presidency   The centrepiece of de Gaulle's defence policy was the French independent nuclear deterrent, initially derided by the Left as de Gaulle's *bombinette*, but in time accepted by Communists and Socialists alike as an indispensable guarantee of national independence.[32] Defence policy provided one indisputable element of continuity throughout the Fifth Republic. Mitterrand's stout refusal to engage the French nuclear deterrent in disarmament negotiations was in line with the General's heritage. The doctrine of the *défense du faible au fort* (the weak's defence against the strong) remained in place; this stipulated that even a small nuclear capacity would act as a deterrent to any potential aggressor. At the heart of Gaullist nuclear doctrine lay the idea of the nation as a unique protected sanctuary; national independence prevented nuclear guarantees being extended to France's allies. Giscard d'Estaing developed the doctrine of the extended sanctuary: tactical nuclear, as well as conventional forces, could be deployed to protect West Germany from a Soviet invasion; the strategic deterrent would be reserved for any attack on France itself. This marked a move away from classic Gaullist formulations, towards NATO's strategy of flexible response.[33] The canons of Gaullist defence policy rejected NATO's flexible response because it implied external alliance constraints on the deployment of nuclear weapons; and because it informed the enemy of the West's intentions. In the Gaullist formulation, the President of the Republic alone would decide where and when a French nuclear riposte would be forthcoming, keeping a potential aggressor in a state of uncertainty. By refusing NATO's flexible response, as well as Giscard's concept of the 'extended sanctuary', Mitterrand reasserted de Gaulle's contention that it was impossible to extend the protection provided by the French *force de frappe* to Germany. To this extent, Mitterrand lay more squarely within the Gaullist tradition than his predecessor Giscard d'Estaing.

The credibility of the independent nuclear arm depended upon a potential aggressor having no doubt about the French President's willingness, if necessary, to unleash a nuclear attack. Mitterrand appeared to accept the logic of the independent deterrent more forcefully than Giscard d'Estaing: he repeated on more than one occasion that he would not hesitate before releasing France's nuclear weapon, whereas Giscard d'Estaing had publicly faltered at the prospect.[34] Mitterrand's refusal to rejoin the command structure of NATO represented another key element of the Gaullist heritage, although the French President participated in a more open manner in NATO meetings than his predecessors. Finally, Mitterrand's reaffirmation of the French presidency as a 'nuclear monarchy', even during the 1986–88 *cohabitation*, marked the greatest continuity with Gaullist policy: the President reasserted his absolute right alone to decide whether to unleash a nuclear attack.[35]

The major departure from the Gaullist legacy in terms of defence lay in the extent to which the French were willing to cooperate with their main European allies. Traditional French notions of autonomy, though largely intact, were to some extent modified by a new willingness to subordinate operational command of a European defence corps to the WEU, as the Maastricht defence agreement illustrated (Chapter 11).

MITTERRAND'S FOREIGN POLICY-MAKING STYLE

Referring to Mitterrand's manner of conducting foreign affairs, one commentator condemned 'the defects of a leadership style that has preferred to encourage multiple and even contradictory voices and policies as a technique of placating, diverting or seducing diverse domestic and foreign interests'.[36] While this judgement is excessively harsh, there was a distinctive Mitterrand style in foreign policy-making. The principal features of Mitterrand's foreign policy style were the spectacular political gesture, the taste for subtle dosages, and the righteous crusade.

- *The spectacular political gesture* formed a part of Mitterrand's foreign policy armoury, as it had for de Gaulle. Mitterrand's meeting with Gaddafi in Crete in June 1984 was a case in point: by sheer political willpower, Mitterrand hoped to achieve a breakthrough over the Chadian conflict. In this instance, Mitterrand's spectacular gesture misfired, leaving the President open to accusations of duplicity and naivety. On other occasions as well the spectacular gesture caused unnecessary problems for Mitterrand: this was evidenced by the French President's meeting with the Polish leader General Jaruzelski in December 1985. His motivations were not always clear: one of the dangers for a perennial manoeuvrer lay in the possibility of being outmanoeuvred or duped, as in the case of Gaddafi. Another danger lay in being misunderstood or distrusted. On a more positive note, Mitterrand's lightning visits to Beirut (1983), or Sarajevo (1992) testified not only to the President's personal courage, but also to his profound humanism which struck a chord with public opinion.

- Mitterrand retained the *taste for subtle dosages*, an extension into the foreign policy sphere of his successful mediating skills illustrated as party leader, or arbitral President. Typically, this involved an attempt to occupy the *juste milieu* in a conflict, a style which suited the *gaullien* illusion of national independence in foreign policy. This style worked well in traditional areas of foreign policy, such as relations with the superpowers, where it was possible to engage in the *politique du balancier*. But it functioned less well where there was scant room for compromise. This was best illustrated in the Middle East, where, through his inability to mould the main players to his ambitions, Mitterrand ended up with diminished prestige on all sides. Another example appertained to Yugoslavia. Mitterrand for long resisted recognising Croatian and Slovenian (and then Bosnian) independence, before being pressurised into this course of action by Chancellor Kohl in January and April 1992.[37] Convinced that the preservation of the Yugoslavian federation was the only alternative to civil war, the French President for long refused to designate Serbia (traditionally a French ally) as the major protagonist. It must be stressed that Mitterrand was not alone in this respect, and that his unwillingness to become involved was widely shared in other European capitals, especially London. One result of this style was to give the image of ambiguity, even when foreign policy objectives were clear.

• On occasion, Mitterrand could also appear as a visionary leader on issues he deemed of vital importance. His foreign policy activity was the most impressive when the French President campaigned tirelessly in pursuit of unambiguous objectives, such as the need for western vigilance during the Euromissile crisis, the vision displayed by the European statesman from the mid-1980s onwards, or the solitary wartime leader during the Gulf War.

CONCLUSION

Foreign policy under Mitterrand seemed permeated by contradictions and ambiguities. This was to some extent inevitable, given the diverse goals pursued by foreign policy-makers, and the fact that situations themselves were contradictory. The policies towards the Middle East, for instance, were inherently irreconcilable because of the intractable nature of the problems involved, not because of any cunning on Mitterrand's behalf. If anything, the great axes of Mitterrand's foreign policy were more consistent than those of his predecessors. These included a consistent commitment to the process of European integration, a more balanced relationship with the erstwhile superpowers, the acceptance of the Gaullist heritage in key areas such as defence, and the modification of de Gaulle's legacy in other spheres.

The importance of foreign policy issues for Mitterrand was initially uncertain. Few declared foreign policy objectives permeated Mitterrand's 1981 campaign, the Socialist candidate being motivated primarily by domestic concerns. From the perspective of Mitterrand as PS candidate in 1981, the most obvious failure related to his espousal of a new model of development, and his advocacy of a more vigorous moral stand towards relations with the Third World. Mitterrand's action in this sphere amounted to little more than rhetorical exhortations, which had little relationship with policy. The most obvious success for which the French President could claim some credit related to the commitment to enhance European cohesion. It would be a rather artificial exercise, however, to measure Mitterrand's foreign policy achievements merely by reference to his 1981 campaign platform. Election manifestos address issues prevalent at a particular point in time; they can in no sense predict the evolution of circumstances, especially in foreign policy situations beyond the control of national governments. It was contended earlier in this chapter that the constraints on political leaders elaborating a genuine innovative foreign policy were extremely powerful, perhaps more so in France than elsewhere on account of the particular Gaullist legacy in this domain. Evaluation of stated objectives drawn up while in opposition must form only one part of any appraisal of Mitterrand's foreign policy. It is probably more meaningful to evaluate the fundamental choices made by Mitterrand while President, the skill with which he performed the role of foreign policy leader, and the extent to which he modified the Gaullist legacy in this sphere.

The Gaullist legacy was visible in a number of spheres during Mitterrand's presidency: the ritual evocation of national independence in foreign policy-making and defence; the assertion that France remained a first-rank power; the observance of the canons of Gaullist nuclear doctrine; the refusal to return to the military command structure of NATO; the preservation of a priority relationship with Germany within Europe; the maintenance of neo-colonial relations with francophone African states (until 1990 at least), and the concentration of foreign policy-making within the presidential sphere. In certain respects, however, Mitterrand went beyond the Gaullist foreign policy model. This occurred notably in relation to his European policy; his closer cooperation with NATO; his difficult relationship with the USSR and the countries of eastern Europe; and his belated attempt to promote a democratic evolution in francophone states of sub-Saharan Africa.

Throughout the course of his presidency, François Mitterrand was called upon to adopt various roles. His leadership skills were illustrated by the fact that he appeared equally convincing as the cold war warrior of the period from 1981–84 as he did as the architect of European Union from 1984 onwards. His leadership appeared distinctly less attuned to political circumstances in the post-1989 period, when he had to deal with the completely unexpected (from his perspective) breakdown of the post-1945 cold war division of Europe (Chapter 10). The visionary streak in Mitterrand's political persona expressed itself most cogently in foreign policy terms when the French President espoused clear-cut causes and offered firm leadership which contributed towards visible results, such as during the Euromissile crisis, or the Gulf War. A similar quality would be accorded to the political leadership offered by

Margaret Thatcher as the Iron Lady of the west, or as the supreme commander of the Falklands War. And yet, unlike Thatcher, Mitterrand had the ability to don more than one guise. His ability to adapt to changing circumstances in domestic policy was one of his most formidable traits. To a lesser extent, this was also the case in relation to foreign policy. By the second presidential term, however, Mitterrand appeared less at ease with the development of history, less proactive in most respects, above all, less powerful with the break-up of the cold war security system, and the emergence of a unified Germany.

Mitterrand's contribution was considerable. He helped to legitimise key aspects of the Gaullist foreign policy legacy, and in some senses left office a more *gaullien* figure than his predecessor Giscard d'Estaing. He superseded the Gaullist straightjacket in other areas, opening a new margin of manoeuvre for French foreign policy too long subordinated to the dogmas of Gaullism. Mitterrand's role during the Gulf War was crucial in this respect. The Gulf War instigated a direct relationship between the President and the French people, with crisis foreign policy-making the absolute preserve of Mitterrand, forcing all other actors into a background role.[38] Mitterrand's decision to engage France in the Gulf War – arguably against its own interests in the Middle East and North Africa – illustrated that the freedom of manoeuvre for French foreign policy was limited; and that, contrary to the central theme of Gaullist foreign policy, France could not really perform as a major world player in a crisis situation outside an Allied coalition. It has been contended that the Gulf conflict did for French foreign policy what the 1982–83 economic U-turn had done for economic policy: it brought France into line with her European neighbours, thereby signifying the end of the 'French exception'. While this assessment is rather too straightforward, it is clear that the Gulf War called into question a number of key tenets of French foreign policy, such as anti-Americanism, national independence, and France's traditionally pro-Arab stance, which paled beside the necessity to form an active part of the western coalition. The Gulf War also revealed that, while France had accepted American leadership, its independent initiatives had had relatively little success. And whereas de Gaulle had criticised the UN, Mitterrand constantly referred to the organisation in order to justify French intervention in the Gulf. In this manner, Mitterrand was able to loosen the shadow cast by de Gaulle, and to adapt foreign policy to changed political circumstances. To this extent, at least, the conclusion that Mitterrand's foreign policy was 'Gaullism by any other name' appears rather unsatisfactory.

Chapter 10

François Mitterrand and the new Europe

Mitterrand's canonisation as a great European statesman in the 1988 presidential campaign reflected the extent of his achievement in the sphere of European policy in the preceding seven years. Most observers agreed that Mitterrand's political career had been characterised by a consistent espousal of the cause of European integration. It would be futile to deny the sincerity of his European engagement, but it is clear that Europe was viewed by Mitterrand in gallic tradition, where French interests were regarded as inseparable from those of Europe itself. Europe was perceived as a surrogate nation-state, the vehicle through which the French genius could manifest itself, for the benefit of the other peoples of Europe. To this extent at least, de Gaulle's and Mitterrand's views of Europe were shaped by a common patrimony.

In the period immediately following his re-election, Mitterrand appeared to backpedal somewhat on the theme of European integration. This mood was communicated in his first press conference of the second presidential term in May 1989. The President called for the need to preserve 'the rank of France', which recalled de Gaulle's determination to claim a role of political leadership for the French within Europe. It appears likely that one aspect of Mitterrand's personal philosophy was expressed in this speech; it was the speech of a patriot deeply imbued with the eternal, universal values of French culture.[1] Herein lay one of the dilemmas relating to Mitterrand: a President who so typified French culture was determined to go down in history as one of the great builders of Europe. Naturally, these two conceptions occasionally conflicted with each other, notwithstanding Mitterrand's remarkable efforts at synthesising both within his own person. The European project proposed by Mitterrand during the period 1981–88 was a planned, progressive and methodic enterprise, which reflected many French priorities, and within which (for reasons explained in Chapter 8) the French President was able to perform a leading role. Events in Europe in 1989 displaced the centre of European gravity further to the East, and rendered the process of the building of Europe more aleatory. This theme will become apparent in the course of this chapter.

MITTERRAND AND GERMAN UNIFICATION

It was somewhat ironic that the tumultuous events of 1989 should occur during the French presidency of the European Council, and the bicentennial celebrations of the French Revolution. Whereas the first French presidency had been highly successfully stage-managed, during the second (July–December 1989) history conspired to rob Mitterrand of the world spotlight, at least after the excesses of the bicentennial celebrations. It was undoubtedly true that Mitterrand drew considerable prestige from the bicentennial celebrations: for three days (13–16 July 1989), Paris was transformed into the diplomatic capital of the world, when the bicentennial celebrations were combined with the G7 meeting of the leaders of the world's main industrial nations. From August 1989 onwards, however, world attention was firmly rooted in developments in Eastern Europe, as Hungary, Czechoslovakia and Romania in turn shook off the shackles of Communism. The breaching of the Berlin wall on 9 November was the key historical event of this chaotic year which radically reshaped the European and international world orders.

The new European configuration was far less predictable or manageable than the pre-1989 system. It lies outside of the parameters of this chapter to consider Mitterrand's reactions to each of the 1989 revolutions; to events in Yugoslavia, or to the process of change in the Soviet Union, culminating in the replacement of Gorbachev by Yeltsin in December 1991. It is proposed to consider German unification as representative of Mitterrand's (remarkably similar) reactions to these various movements, in order to illustrate how the French President appeared impotent to master the complexities of the post-cold war period. The German example has the additional advantage of revealing the changing balance of power within the European Community itself after unification. In the ensuing section we shall consider general French attitudes towards the prospect of a unified Germany, before assessing Mitterrand's reactions to the events leading up to unification.

There was, of course, no single coherent French attitude towards the prospect of German unification; opinions differed according to function, political affiliation, degree of awareness and elite or mass opinion. But a number of underlying themes surfaced in the debate surrounding unification; these preoccupations dominated the campaign for the Maastricht referendum two years later.

- The geo-political position occupied by Germany continued to raise French suspicions of German intentions. Germany was, in certain French circles (including within the foreign affairs ministry), permanently suspected of a potential drift towards neutralism, and towards a preference for an independent central European strategy, or even for a German–Russian entente, at the expense of a commitment to the EC. In short, French policy-makers were anxious lest Germany engage in Gaullist practices in its own foreign policy. One essential objective of postwar French foreign policy was thus to tie the Germans into the western alliance, via the EC and, to a lesser extent, NATO. On no account were the Germans to enjoy the same degree of independence and autonomy in foreign policy-making as the French. In turn, German policy-makers were irritated by French suspicions of their European credentials.[2]

- Underlying French anxieties also lay calculations of the economic weight of a unified Germany, a state already enjoying massive commercial surpluses with its main European trading partners (France, UK, Italy, Spain). Many French politicians and commentators already judged that the Franco-German relationship had become progressively more one-sided with the increase in German economic power.[3] French policy-makers had come to the conclusion that, given Germany's uncontested economic power, the best means of retaining political influence lay in a more integrated EC. Mitterrand shared this view. The real fear of unification, according to the French ambassador in a remarkably frank admission, was that it 'would give birth to a Europe dominated by Germany, which no one, in the east or west, wants'.[4]

François Mitterrand's attitude towards German unification was above all determined by the Gaullist notion of the balance of power and the need to preserve France's self-perceived rank as the pre-eminent political power in Europe. Postwar Franco-German collaboration, especially since the co-operation treaty of 1963, had been based upon an overall equilibrium between the two countries, according to which German economic suprem-acy was counterbalanced by French political pre-eminence within Europe. The prospect of a unified German state threatened to shatter this delicate balance. In spite of Mitterrand's *gaullien* claim that France wanted to 'escape from the legacy of Yalta', the events surrounding German unification strongly suggested that the French President remained attached to a bipolar vision of the world, shaped by an inability to escape from the logic of the cold war, and an incomprehension of the revolutionary changes in eastern Europe. This became apparent with Mitterrand's reaction to the events leading to German unification.

In a press conference held several days before 9 November, Mitterrand forecast: 'I would be extremely surprised if a fundamentally new European structure does not materialise within the next ten years': this statement gives some idea of the unpreparedness of the French government for the cataclysmic events that were to follow.[5] François Mitterrand's immediate reaction to the collapse of the Berlin wall was widely interpreted as a cultivated refusal to acknowledge that the European balance of power had changed. As on many other occasions, Mitterrand's attitude was aptly expressed by his alter ego,

Foreign Minister Dumas: some six days after the fall of the Berlin wall, Dumas asserted that the issue of German unification was 'not an issue of current concern'. To this failure to appreciate the speed at which events were moving was added a doubt as to the genuine desires of the German people: the French President questioned whether the Germans really aspired to unity within the boundaries of a single state, or whether they would prefer 'a different solution yet to be determined'?[6]

The manner in which the European debate on German unification proceeded after 9 November caused some degree of bitterness between the FRG and its European allies. A number of countries – including France, but also the Netherlands and the UK – expressed irritation at being presented with a series of *faits accomplis* by Kohl. The German Chancellor's Ten Point Plan for unification was presented to the Bundestag in November 1989 without any prior consultation with Germany's allies. The most flagrant example was Kohl's initial refusal to rule out changes to the Oder–Neisse border with Poland, a decision announced unilaterally without any international consultation, and only withdrawn after the East German election of March 1990. While Kohl accepted Mitterrand's attempt at the Strasbourg summit in December 1989 to link progress towards German unification and European union, the German Chancellor continued in practice to give precedence to immediate national priorities (unification and its financial consequences) over European ones, which would have to wait. Initial French reactions to the perspective of German reunification were largely shared throughout Europe: in the USSR, Gorbachev's spokesman Gennady Gerasimov dismissed unification as 'an intellectual exercise'; whereas George Bush, while welcoming the principle, carefully avoided being more specific. In London, Mrs Thatcher dismissed any notion of unification in the immediate future. Indeed, within Germany itself, most politicians initially declared themselves hostile to any precipitate move towards unification. This changed once Helmut Kohl – responding to public pressure and fearful of the political credit the extreme-right Republicans might draw should he hesitate – began openly to espouse a rapid move towards unification.

François Mitterrand alternated between three alternative approaches in attempting to define French policy towards the prospect of a unified Germany: first, an alliance with Germany's eastern neighbours (Russia and Poland); second, cooperation with the Anglo-Saxons in order to attempt to limit German influence within continental Europe; third, an attempt to draw Germany into an intangible relationship with France.[7] The first two options (especially the first) were implausible, given geo-political realities and past French strategic developments; the third was the natural prolongation of Franco-German postwar relations, but ultimately Mitterrand had to accept that the balance of power within the Franco-German relationship had shifted in favour of Germany. A rather desparate oscillation between these three strategies was evident in the response offered by Mitterrand to the prospect of German unification.

In response to Kohl's Ten Point Plan of November 1989, Mitterrand appeared to make a blatant attempt to resurrect a Franco–Russian axis to frustrate aspirations for German unity. On 6 December 1989, Mitterrand and Gorbachev made public a joint declaration in Kiev which stipulated that any altering of European borders was premature and would have a destabilising effect. Mitterrand also made highly symbolic visits to Poland and to East Germany: the latter (in December 1989) particularly irritated Helmut Kohl, who was incensed by Mitterrand's statement that Hans Modrow, the interim East German leader, was destined to perform a vital role in the construction of Europe. Indeed, Mitterrand's visit to East Germany appeared openly provocative, as did his vaunting on East German television of the 'East German identity'. Mitterrand's courting of Gorbachev was fundamentally flawed; subsequent events showed that the official French belief that France could outbid Germany in terms of relations with the east overestimated French influence within Eastern Europe. In particular, the USSR would always consider relations with Germany as being more important than those with France. If Germany was an end of Soviet policy, France was at best a means to this end. Mitterrand's proposed European confederation (see below) bore marked similarities to Gorbachev's Common European Home and could be interpreted as a conscious effort to build bridges with the Russian President.

The notion of a European Confederation, associating existing EC member-states, the EFTANS and the new Eastern European democracies (including the USSR), was first raised in December 1989, as Mitterrand's response to the events in Eastern Europe.[8] The format of the confederation would allow the new democracies to associate themselves with the EC, without threatening the cohesion of the existing EC structure. The idea of a confederation evoked symbols of a two-(or more) speed Europe, within which a nucleus of member-states would provide a core around which successive layers of lesser European states might form. This proposal was revealing of Mitterrand's preference for a cohesive, compact European Community, dominated by a Franco–German axis, rather than a broader more nebulous assortment of nations. In relation to the new East European democracies, Mitterrand's assessment was undoubtedly a realistic one. The French President did finally accept in mid-1991 that the East European democracies should sign treaties of association with the EC, but envisaged their eventual membership only 'in tens and tens of years'. The fate of Mitterrand's proposed confederation illustrated, *inter alia*, that the balance of power within the Franco-German partnership had changed, and that French initiatives were not certain to receive a favourable reaction from other member-states.[9]

With the benefit of hindsight, it appears certain that Mitterrand misjudged both the political strategy of Helmut Kohl, and the genuine desire for unification felt by most Germans. The French President was not alone in this respect. In characteristic fashion, Mitterrand appeared to adopt a new type of double language: this involved proclamations of faith in the principle of German unification, accompanied by efforts to frustrate its realisation. For the French President's real intention was to slow down the movement towards unification, an attitude summed up in December in an interview with the French weekly *Paris-Match*, when he declared: 'Even if unification forms part of the dream of Germans, which is legitimate, the process will take far longer than certain people imagine.'[10] His belief – that the German people did not really want unification – combined with a series of tactical manoeuvres to embitter temporarily the previously close relations between Kohl and Mitterrand.

It was hardly surprising that the imminent prospect of German unification (rather than its theoretical long-term possibility) was unlikely to find favour with a French president, given the changing European balance of power it was likely to produce. Once it became clear that German unification would go ahead anyway – whatever the French attitude – Mitterrand drew the logical consequence from this, and officially welcomed the process. But it must be stressed that the Franco-German special relationship had virtually no impact on the process of German unification. Far more important were: the decisions taken by Mikhail Gorbachev (the acceptance that a unified Germany would be in NATO); the role played by the US; and, of course, the determination illustrated by Kohl himself to exploit the issue of unification for its maximum political benefit. Attempts by Mitterrand and other European statesmen to influence events were largely without consequence. Herein lay one of the minor paradoxes of German unification: despite widespread calls for European political union (EPU) and common security and defence policies, the real leverage on the Federal Republic continued to be exercised by the two superpowers.

Official French attitudes changed after the results of the March 1990 election in East Germany: there could no longer be any doubt that Germans were massively in favour of unification. Mitterrand's reaction to the results of 18 March 1990 was a gracious 'good luck to Germany', and an acceptance of the mechanism of article 23, hitherto treated with suspicion.[11] Once unification had become inevitable, the French attempted to ensure that the unified state would be tied as closely as possible to the EC, and that the Franco–German axis would continue to provide an effective co-direction of the Community. The accelerated integration of the EC was important for the French both because it would help to discourage any threat of German isolationism, and it would help to preserve an arrangement – the Franco-German partnership – which had always benefited France politically, even if the new balance had altered somewhat in favour of Germany. From the German perspective, Kohl was determined to illustrate that Germany would remain irrevocably tied to the EC, and that fears of a neutralist drift were unfounded. Thus, there was a direct link between German unification, and the new drive towards greater European political and economic integration leading to the Maastricht summit (see next section). There was, moreover, evidence of a growing anxiety among French public opinion about the implications of German unification.[12] In this context, the European dimension provided, among other things, a means of reassuring French public opinion that nothing had really changed.

Mitterrand had not foreseen German unification. But the French President was able to extract some political advantage out of German unification, even if the global balance sheet was a negative one. This was illustrated by the series of joint Franco-German EC policy initiatives from December 1989 to November 1991, which helped to consolidate Mitterrand's image as a European statesman. For this reason, it would be inaccurate to argue that Paris had simply missed a 'historic' occasion; rather, it had contributed towards re-centring the terms of the debate away from a near-total preoccupation with German unification and focusing on a radical new departure in European policy. But the prevailing perception within both French and German corridors of power was that the nature of the Franco-German relationship was bound to change after unification. The subtle disequilibrium in favour of France, which had characterised the Franco-German relationship bequeathed by the historical circumstances of the Second World War, had now to change in favour of Germany.

MAASTRICHT AND BEYOND

One effect of the Franco-German dispute during the months October 1989–April 1990 was that the commitment on both sides to the European ideal emerged strengthened, and that more practical steps were taken towards European monetary and political union than might otherwise have been the case. The willingness to keep alive the Franco-German entente over Europe was illustrated by the two letters signed by Kohl and Mitterrand preceding the European summits in April and December 1990. Franco-German pressures lay firmly behind moves towards the new Treaty of European Union negotiated at the Maastricht summit in December 1991. In the run up to Maastricht, it became clear that France and Germany (among others) held rather different views as to what Europe should comprise. These subtle differences of approach tended to be overshadowed by the British question, but they were arguably of greater importance for the future evolution of the EC. It was testament to the continuing efficacy of the Franco-German partnership that they received scant media attention and proved no obstacle to a historic compromise being agreed at Maastricht in the form of the Treaty on European Union, formally signed by member-states in February 1992. The rejection of the Maastricht treaty by a small majority of Danish voters in June 1992 introduced a new element of uncertainty into the ratification process. Mitterrand's June 1992 decision to call for a referendum on ratification of the

Maastricht treaty further complicated the issue. In the next section, we shall consider the provisions of the Maastricht treaty with special reference to political and economic union and foreign policy, and finally the French referendum on Maastricht of September 1992.

Political and economic union   The word Federal figured prominently in the approach to the Maastricht summit. The debate centred on John Major's insistence that the 'F-word' be removed from the final Treaty; this caused Mitterrand little inconvenience, in contrast to certain other European leaders.[13] Indeed, the French President had been careful never to tie his European vision in with 'federalist dogma', notwithstanding his occasional flights of rhetorical fantasy. The French version of an enhanced political union continued to be formulated largely in intergovernmental terms.[14] In fact, Mitterrand and Britian's Prime Minister Major were objective allies in more senses than they cared to admit: neither the British nor the French leaders were prepared to allow supranational EC institutions (the Commission and the European Parliament) too great an influence. Indeed, among Mitterrand's advisers there was even a determination to limit the supranational aspirations of the Commission President, Jacques Delors, as well as to resist attempts to make the European Parliament more democratic and to extend the scope of its competence unduly. At the Maastricht summit of December 1991, Mitterrand accepted *some* strengthening of the Commission and the European parliament.[15] But this was more than counterbalanced by the summit's expressed aim of moving towards a single European currency by 1999 and provisions for the new common foreign and security policy, the effect of both being to strengthen the role of the European Council, rather than that of the Commission.[16] Paris was thus determined not only to increase the EC's capacity for intervention where it suited French interests (for instance, in foreign policy), but also to maintain effective political control in the hands of the – intergovernmental – Council of Ministers.

Definite moves towards monetary union, the creation of a European Central Bank and a single currency were the primary French economic objectives at Maastricht. Mitterrand calculated that a single currency and a European Central Bank would allow the French a greater influence over monetary policy, currently monopolised by the German Bundesbank. In the words of one wry commentator: 'The European Central Bank would replace the Bundesbank, and France and its allies, rather than the Germans, could run monetary policy'.[17] The commitment to economic union illustrated the extent to which Mitterrand had fully integrated the European constraint into his conception of France and Europe: it testified to the irreversible nature of the U-turn undertaken in 1983 and to the new confidence felt in future French economic performance. On economic and monetary union, Mitterrand had every reason to be satisfied: the fixing of a staged timetable for the creation of a single currency by 1999 at the latest was Mitterrand's greatest summit achievement, far outweighing any setbacks in areas such as industrial policy, or the British opt-out on the social chapter. The final treaty locked the EC more firmly into economic integration (the objective of a single currency by 1999) than it made real concessions to the principle of political union. To this extent, it responded more accurately to French priorities than to German ones, notwithstanding the pivotal role performed by Helmut Kohl in the run-up to the summit.

In their detailed research into economic and monetary union (EMU), Dyson and Featherstone demonstrate the paradoxical quality of Mitterrand's stance in the Maastricht negotiations.[18] The French President was above all preoccupied with preserving French presidential prerogatives in the process leading up to monetary union. Internally, this meant that Mitterrand was the principal move behind the decision to pursue monetary union; this was against the lobbying of the *Trésor* division within the Finance ministry. On a European level, Mitterrand was determined that heads of government would decide which countries met the economic convergence criteria to participate in a single European currency. Mitterrand failed to impose one of his central policy objectives, however: that an 'economic government', composed of political representatives of member-states, would provide democratic safeguards against the financial hegemony of a future European central bank. This met with a flat refusal from Chancellor Kohl, for whom the sacrifice of the German Bundesbank could only occur if a future central bank enjoyed complete autonomy from political interference. Moreover, it became clear that it was in the nature of the EMU decision itself to diminish the influence of all political actors over future economic policy.

Foreign policy   Franco-German military cooperation had provided a cornerstone of Mitterrand's first presidential term, culminating in the creation of the joint Franco-German bridge in 1987 (composed initially of some 4,200 troops) and the Franco-German Defence and Security Council in January 1988.[19] These two institutions were envisaged by Mitterrand as the core of an embryonic European defence pillar. The realm of foreign policy is one in which the French have often claimed a leadership role within Europe, which the Germans have found difficult to match. The Federal Republic of Germany has had little experience of playing a top-level role in the field of international relations: the Gulf War painfully illustrated this fact. The Gulf War revealed that, while France could still pretend to great power status through an active military participation, the new Germany remained incapable of formulating a coherent military strategy, as well as being constitutionally barred from deploying troops outside the NATO area. France continued to possess a diplomatic prestige in the military sphere which outweighed that of Germany.

Notwithstanding their increased military cooperation, there remained various areas of contention between the two nations. Mitterrand's decision to construct the short-range HADES missile – seen as an essential component of the French nuclear deterrent – had caused substantial problems with the

German government: the range of the HADES missile (480 km) meant that if ever deployed it would fall on German territory. Its deployment had met with stiff opposition from public opinion in the Federal Republic. In his September 1991 press conference, Mitterrand announced that France would manufacture only 30 short-range HADES missiles (as opposed to 120, then 40); moreover, these would not be operational, but would be stockpiled. The French President also announced that the short-range Pluton missiles would be withdrawn from service by 1993–94.[20]

The Gulf crisis illustrated unambiguously the inexistence of Europe as a coordinated foreign policy unit. The French position was, arguably, one of the least pro-European, relying on older traditions of autonomy and independent diplomacy: the French success was interpreted by certain political commentators as Mitterrand's revenge on Kohl for forcing an acceptance of unification. Different conclusions could, of course, be drawn from the lack of European presence during the Gulf crisis. Either this made it imperative for the EC states to adopt a common foreign policy, or else it proved that national responses continued to have the most relevance. The FRG drew the conclusion from the Gulf War (and later from the crisis in Yugoslavia) that the EC states must move towards a common foreign and security policy; this position had been consistently espoused by Mitterrand since 1981. The joint Franco-German defence paper of October 1991 represented a compromise between the two nations, with which each had cause for contentment. The defence paper proposed the creation of a joint European defence corps based upon the existing Franco-German brigade under French leadership, but enlarged to include forces from other European countries. This force would be responsible to the West European Union (WEU), which would in turn answer to the EC (rather than to NATO). The defence paper also advocated qualified majority voting on certain issues of foreign and security policy.[21] It satisfied Germany's need to respect existing alliances, insofar as it could be interpreted as drawing in the French into a European pillar of the Atlantic alliance, separate from the NATO command structure.[22] No other plan had managed to obtain as much French subordination to an international authority (the WEU); in this sense, it was regarded as a break with the Gaullist foreign policy legacy of maximum national autonomy in all circumstances.

From the French point of view the proposed joint European defence force would anchor Germany firmly into the western alliance, thereby lessening the spectre of German neutrality, and offer France military leadership of the 'European army', a form of military compensation for developments elsewhere in NATO from which she had been excluded.[23] It would, finally, ensure that France was not absent from the West European security debate at a critical stage in European development. François Mitterrand had reason for satisfaction with the defence agreement signed at the Maastricht summit. The British agreed to two important principles at Maastricht: that majority voting could occur at the later stages of commonly agreed foreign and security policies; that the WEU should be accepted as the core of a common defence identity. The Maastricht treaty also inaugurated a European defence corps, based initially on the existing Franco-German brigade but open to other countries, which would be answerable to the WEU. In fact, the defence agreement was so ambiguous that every major player at Maastricht claimed a degree of satisfaction.[24] The events in former Yugoslavia in the course of 1991–93, and the inability of the European Community to formulate a coherent response augured ill for a coherent common foreign and security policy.[25]

The French referendum on Maastricht   By common agreement, Mitterrand's decision to subject the Maastricht treaty to a referendum after the Danish defeat was a typical hand of presidential poker. According to viewpoint, the artist was to be congratulated for an astute political move, or the manoeuvrer to be condemned for subjecting Europe's future to an uncertain electoral verdict. Mitterrand's goals were widely depicted as machiavellian. These were to cleave further the chronically divided RPR, possibly causing a formal split within its ranks (with the additional advantage of setting Chirac against his troops); and to secure an electoral victory only six months away from the legislative elections, after an unprecedented period of governmental unpopularity. A more noble interpretation was that the French President felt the urgent need for a popular ratification of the treaty to set the European train back on the rails after the Danish defeat. The call for a referendum was the far-sighted act of Europe's elder statesman. This interpretation was favoured neither within France, nor among France's EC partners, whose domestic problems were greatly increased by Mitterrand's actions. If this were indeed the motivation, Mitterrand's political judgement appeared rather impaired: the pinnacle of achievement of Mitterrand's second *septennat* was to be subjected to the vagaries of a notoriously volatile and dissatisfied electorate, which the opinion poll evidence portrayed as anxious to condemn an administration tainted by the exercise of power. The notion that the pro-European French electorate might reject Maastricht was not initially accorded much credence.

The decision to call a referendum on Maastricht seemed an unnecessary gamble to most observers, including those close to the President and within the PS leadership.[26] It should be recalled that, in constitutional terms, the referendum was unnecessary: after a judgement from the Constitutional Council, the Bérégovoy government had introduced a bill to reform three articles of the French constitution, to enable the transfers of sovereignty foreseen in the Maastricht treaty. These were accepted by 89 per cent of all parliamentarians, meeting as the joint Congress at Versailles; only a sizeable fraction of the RPR voted against the amendment paving the way for consideration of the Maastricht treaty.[27]

The referendum campaign itself was highly illustrative of the position in which the French nation perceived itself to be within the new Europe. The key theme dominating the campaign, for supporters and opponents of the treaty alike, was how to control the unified Germany, and prevent German political and economic domination of the European continent. Supporters of Maastricht contended that the treaty provided the most efficient means of tying the unified state within the corset of a powerful European Union; they predicted that the proposed monetary union would dilute German economic domination over Europe, by allowing other EC states (especially France) an input into controlling economic policy. These arguments were resisted by opponents of the treaty, who formed an unwritten and unholy alliance stretching from the PCF on the Left, to the FN on the extreme-right, and encompassing dissident Socialists, a fraction of the Greens, most RPR politicians (but not J. Chirac) and a leading UDF personality.[28] Both sides had a fixation with Germany, revealing deep-seated fears that had lain dormant for decades. There could be little doubt that Franco-German relations were soured, albeit temporarily, by the ritualistic allegations relating to Germany's expansionist tendencies coming from both sides of the French argument. The outbreak of a spate of racially motivated attacks in former East Germany was held to confirm the stereotypes portrayed by the media.

The role performed by Mitterrand himself during the campaign revealed that the senior European statesman had lost none of his pugnacity, notwithstanding the revelation of his serious illness several days before the vote. From the outset, Mitterrand made it clear that he would not resign as president in the event of a No vote; the verdict on Maastricht was to be dissassociated from his continuation as president. This marked a departure from de Gaulle's practice of insisting upon popular ratification as a test of confidence in his leadership. In the circumstances, such caution was advisable. The early complacency of the Yes campaign during June and July was transformed into a sense of foreboding by the end of August 1992, as three successive opinion polls predicted a No victory, after a dramatic erosion of support for the treaty. Mitterrand was reputed to have believed that the Yes camp was saved by his own intervention in the campaign, in the form of a three-hour televised debate with Philippe Séguin, during which the President fought courageously for political survival by appearing as a dignified, ardent defender of the Maastricht treaty. The narrow victory of the Yes (51.1 against 48.9) on 20 September 1992 obtained a temporary reprieve for the Maastricht treaty, and dampened calls for Mitterrand's resignation as president. The fact that Mitterrand won the Maastricht referendum, in spite of his unpopularity, testified to the strength of pro-EC sentiment within France, at least among the dynamic sections of the population, which outweighed the desire to precipitate Mitterrand's departure. And yet, the President could not interpret the result of the referendum as in any sense a personal vote of confidence.

Prolonged attention to the sociological profile of the two camps clearly falls outside of the confines of this chapter.[29] But it is clear that France was once again divided into sociologically differentiated camps: to use Hoffmann's phraseology, a 'dynamic' and a 'static' France. The dynamic France that voted

Yes consisted of a majority of salaried non-manual workers, of the inhabitants of large cities, of most frontier regions. The static France that voted No appeared to consist of victims of the economic recession, or of probable future victims: a majority of manual workers, of farmers, of small businessmen, and of the unemployed responded negatively. The common perception was that the sociological profile of the Yes vote was, in political terms, that of the moderate Right, whereas a large proportion of Mitterrand's 1981 left-wing electorate (especially among industrial workers) found themselves in the No camp, disillusioned with the causes espoused by the President. The fears articulated by the No camp were on occasion irrational: Maastricht became the scapegoat for a variety of real and imagined economic ills. But they reflected the fact that the mutation of contemporary France towards a classless, prosperous and more egalitarian society was far from complete. The strength of the agricultural protest against Maastricht in particular reflected the anger against CAP reforms, and bore testament to the continuing importance of the farming lobby, with which any French government must come to terms. The tough stance adopted by French negotiators towards the GATT talks before the US presidential election confirmed that, in an attempt to limit the Socialists' virtually certain defeat in the 1993 elections, Mitterrand was willing to cede to the pressure of the farming lobby even at the expense of provoking international tensions.

CONCLUSION: MITTERRAND AND THE NEW EUROPE

On repeated occasions throughout the course of his second term in office, François Mitterrand adopted a rather awkward posture, faced with the development of history. This was most obviously illustrated in relation to German unification, which the French President neither predicted, nor understood, nor really accepted.

Mitterrand's foreign policy activity was the most coherent during periods of relative international stability, when the behaviour of leading actors could be predicted and initiatives carefully planned. In the context of rapid change in international relations after 1989, Mitterrand seemed rather disoriented, unfamiliar with the emerging world order, and distrustful of the emerging nationalism in central and Eastern Europe. Faced with the challenge of uncertainty, Mitterrand appeared to favour the preservation of the status quo wherever possible, and revealed himself highly critical of the process of micro-state formation out of the ashes of the former USSR and Yugoslavia.[30] In February 1993, for instance, he more or less explicitly affirmed his view that the EC's recognition of the independence of Croatia, Slovenia and Bosnia-Herzegovina had been premature, forced upon a reluctant Community by German pressure.[31] In fairness to Mitterrand, we should point out that the French President's tendency to support existing states and structures was shared by several of France's leading allies, bewildered by the speed of change and the collapse of the old world order. And Mitterrand's response of strengthening the cohesion of the EC was entirely appropriate, far-sighted even, given the new instability in Europe and elsewhere.

After unification, the Franco-German partnership remained the most important relationship within the European Community. The efficiency of this alliance revealed itself at the Maastricht summit. Although subtle differences of approach existed between the two leaders, Mitterrand and Kohl were determined that everything necessary should be done to foster an agreement, which both leaders valued as an act of faith in closer future European integration. Initially reserved, Mitterrand came to regard the Franco-German partnership as *the* key reference point, in spite of (or as a result of) his fear of Germany's potential influence.[32] Unlike Jacques Delors, or even Helmut Kohl, Mitterrand conceived of the EC far more in terms of a privileged Franco-German partnership than as an evolving federal entity. Mitterrand's Europe remained far from being the supranational entity dreamed of by Jean Monnet.

In the post-Gaullist period, the European Community gradually became a source of artificial near-consensus among mainstream French politicians, in part because it had proved to be an effective means of promoting national interests under the veneer of *communautaire* rhetoric. The French were fervent Europeans, because they exercised substantial influence within Europe. As Mitterrand asserted in September 1991, France would contribute its genius to the construction of Europe. But the objective bases for French influence within Europe were weakened by events after 1989; the unified German state looked set to exercise a considerably enhanced influence, if not to dominate the new Europe. The near-consensus over Europe among France's politicians, above all within French public opinion, was shattered by the Maastricht referendum campaign, which at least had the merit of engaging a genuine discussion of European issues usually reserved for the elite. This was to Mitterrand's credit, even if it was an unintended consequence of his decision to call a referendum on Maastricht. It seemed clear that, despite Mitterrand's successes at the Maastricht summit of December 1991 and his narrow victory in the referendum of September 1992, the new Europe in the process of being born would not be altogether to French tastes, or shaped entirely according to French influence.

Chapter 11

Mitterrand's political leadership

THE ACADEMIC DEBATE OVER POLITICAL LEADERSHIP

As opposed to traditions of European sociology (Weber and charismatic leadership) or history, mainstream political science traditionally reserved little place for the concept of political leadership. The prominent political science paradigms of the 1960s were concerned with impersonal processes and structures, rather than individuals. There was an instinctive distrust of leadership as fostering a Great Man approach, an approach which supports the view that 'historical events are caused by, or bear the imprint of, or would have been very different but for, the unique personalities of leading actors'.[1] The Great Man interpretation tends to produce a leader-centred approach, which invariably minimises impersonal processes, structures and systems: ideally, a great man could be great in a variety of different contexts.

Leadership studies are multidisciplinary, attracting work in the fields of psychology, management studies, organisational theory, and history, as well as from political scientists. A renewed interest in leadership has flowed in part from an interest in a rediscovery of political institutions since the mid-1980s, although the study of political leadership is not associated with any particular school of contemporary political science.[2] Universal propositions about political leadership have been advanced in the academic literature, as well as more limited, usually national, frameworks.[3] As Edinger points out, general theories of political leadership 'tend to be conceptually and propositionally too narrowly tailored to fit the explicit or implicit theoretical biases of their authors to gain wider acceptance'.[4] Most attention has been centred upon the institutional offices or positions occupied by leaders, the personality traits associated with leadership (what distinguishes leaders from routine office-holders, for instance), the governing and policy environment within which political leaders operate (notably, their interpersonal and interdependent relations with other decision-makers) and the variable dimensions of political leadership (supra-national, 'core executive', local).[5]

For institutionalist analyses, concentrating upon the institutional positions or offices occupied by politicians, leadership is equated with formal control over the political institutions: attention is centred on presidents and prime ministers, and their interactions with other institutions such as parties, bureaucracies and parliaments. This facet of leadership is central to any serious endeavour; however personally remarkable or otherwise they are, in stable liberal democracies we evaluate individual political leaders on account of the institutional positions they have occupied.[6] Only rare political leaders rise above the constraints associated with a particular office to assume an historic stature. Position or office is thereby a key aspect of leadership, but not its only dimension.

Rejecting a narrowly institutionalist approach, Jean Blondel asserts that 'leadership is a behavioural concept'. Blondel urges a distinction between formal institutional hierarchies, and the exercise of real, or 'behavioural' leadership: the 'real leader of a constituted organisation may well be someone who does not occupy a formal position in the group'.[7] Behavioural analysis illuminates certain qualities of leadership (for instance the relationship between leaders and followers), but underplays the interactions of leaders and followers with the wider political system, and the structuring qualities of institutions. The study of political leadership should reject any uni-dimensional explanations. It should draw upon institutionalist and be-haviouralist explanations of leadership, both of which contain important insights.

Other types of leadership analysis also have their shortcomings. Political biographies usually emphasise the distinctive personality traits of leaders, without always demonstrating how these affect their capacity for *political* leadership. The genre of the psychobiography is especially revealing in this respect. At its best psychobiography can give interesting insights into the personality traits of political leaders, the reasons underlying their political involvement, the driving force which motivates their pursuit of high office.[8] To the extent that leaders matter, such analysis can be illuminating, especially in relation to whether political leaders possess the requisite qualities and skills normally associated with leadership.[9] At its worst, psychobiography can be totally misleading, partly because it makes unwarranted extrapolations re-lating to political behaviour from private life, but also because it can easily misrepresent the latter. Formative experiences are subjectively selected, and automatic associations established with little hard evidence. In one example of the genre, Margaret Thatcher, Ronald Reagan and Malcolm Fraser are blandly portrayed as victims of the divide and rule experience of the Oedipal conflict: this is advanced as the key to understanding their activity as political leaders.[10] Such psychological determinism is highly misleading. Political outcomes are analysed in terms of the resolution of internal personality conflicts, with scant reference to the political environment. This is not to deny that personal beliefs and character traits are of considerable importance in explaining subsequent behaviour patterns and influencing political beliefs: the former UK premier, Margaret Thatcher, frequently referred to the fact that she was a grocer's daughter. At the other extreme, those emphasising the political environment have tended to underplay, or reject altogether, the notion of political leadership. The leaders-do-not-matter school believe that leaders are unimportant: the key to understanding historical and political change lies in environmental factors such as social movements, socio-economic forces, institutional constraints and cultural patterns; at best, leaders come to articulate historical movements outside their control.

The study of political leadership should draw on insights from these various schools, rejecting the temptation for a unidimensional explanation. The study of political leadership necessitates an appreciation of political structure, human agency, and the relationship between the two. It involves observing individual leaders in action, evaluating the resources at their disposal at any one time, as well as the constraints which weigh on their action, charting their relations with other influential decision-makers (at home and abroad), and realistically appraising the opportunity structure which conditions their action.

The study of political leadership assumes that leaders do make a difference: individual political leaders exploit opportunities created by particular sets of circumstances, make choices from a number of different available options, and exercise such unfathomable personal characteristics as political skill, courage and intelligence. Set against this, political leaderships in all advanced liberal democratic polities have to function within the context of powerful constraints, which limit their margins of manoeuvre. These include constraints relating to the domestic political system, such as the nature of the executive, the power of bureaucratic elites, the party and elective structures, the parliamentary configuration, the constitutional set-up, and corporatist factors. They also involve constraints relating to the economy (notably the interdependent relations between developed economies); the social structure (the limits to political activity imposed by the tolerance of society itself); and not least the international system and pattern of alliances. These constraints impinge heavily upon the freedom of manoeuvre of even the most powerful chief executives, although leaders do vary considerably in their capacity to deal with these constraints, and in the extent to which they admit their existence. What we have labelled as constraints can themselves be regarded as potential resources: in the French case, the constitutional set-up, the parliamentary configuration, the party and elective systems, even the nature of the politico-administrative elite have tended to strengthen the cohesion of political leadership, whereas the same variables have greatly weakened the executive in Italy.

From the preceding chapters, it emerges that political leadership, even of the routine, institutionalised variety, can be important in a variety of spheres: for instance, the definition of goals, the formulation of policy initiatives, the intermediation of conflicting interests, and the mobilisation of support. From an institutional perspective, presidents and prime ministers are the most obviously recognisable political leaders. The study of political leadership has particular relevance in a regime such as the French Fifth Republic, with traditionally strong presidential leadership that certain analysts have likened to a republican monarchy.

Rather than attempt to provide an additional all-encompassing definition of what political leadership comprises, the framework for reference presented in Table 11.1 proposes a series of variables that ought be considered when

Table 11.1 Political leadership within liberal democracies: a framework for reference

Personal characteristics	Positional characteristics
political skill clarity of goals capacity for mobilisation	longevity/mode of election constitutional framework interactions within core executive
communication skills	interactions with other institutions (bureaucracy, parliament, parties, groups)
political intelligence	Leader as decision-taker/policy coordinator/power broker?
personal attributes (e.g. courage, ruthlessness, stamina)	Appointments and dismissals
political style (e.g. reactive, conviction, pragmatic)	Configuration of party system
Multi-role capacity	Control over policy process
Internal constraints	**Internal opportunities**
socio-economic equilibrium cultural traditions	ability to define internal constrains as opportunities
social constraints (limited tolerance of society) judicial constraints political constraints (diminishing political returns? party constraints?)	
External constraints	**External opportunities**
prestige of the nation in international system role of supra-national bodies (e.g. EC, NATO) interdependency of the international economy	personalising tendencies in foreign policy-making international summitry
bureaucratic influences in foreign policy-making	control over nuclear deterrent?
past policy choices and alliance structures	ability to define external constraints as opportunities

attempting to evaluate a particular political leadership. This list does not pretend to be exhaustive, but to point the direction for future research into comparative political leadership. The framework for reference regroups various features such as personal characteristics, positional context and environmental constraints and opportunities. We shall now consider Mitterrand's leadership from the perspective of these variables.

EVALUATING MITTERRAND'S LEADERSHIP

In accordance with the criteria established by the framework of reference, Mitterrand's political leadership will now be evaluated by considering his personal characteristics, positional resources and internal and external constraints and opportunities.

I: Personal characteristics

At the level of personal characteristics, there can be little dispute that Mitterrand displayed consummate political skill, resolute physical and political courage, and demonstrated a vivid intelligence, all features associated with successful political leadership. But these personal qualities were not consistently demonstrated. Mitterrand also revealed a capacity for miscalculation, for example in May 1968, as well as a diminishing tendency for astute political judgement throughout the course of his second presidential term in office.

However difficult it is evaluate elusive concepts such as political skill, intelligence or capacity for mobilisation, the evidence presented in the preceding chapters demonstrates that Mitterrand's personal characteristics had a notable impact upon his manner of operating within the political system, especially via his cultivation of leader–follower ties and his building of personal networks upon which to base his authority. In the case of Mitterrand, explanations laying stress on the importance of leader–follower ties appear particularly cogent in an overall assessment of his political leadership. Mitterrand's personal political persona is considered in more detail in Chapter 12.

Attitudes, behaviour and goals　There is often a fundamental divergence between expressed attitudes and the practical behaviour of political leaders in government. Even where attitudes are firmly held and internally consistent, they have to contend with countervailing influences – or environmental constraints – which are liable to impose an element of inconsistency between beliefs on the one hand, and the possiblities of political action within government on the other. Attitudes should not, therefore, necessarily be relied upon as a good measurement of behaviour. This can be illustrated in relation to President Mitterrand, whose refined sense of the need for tactical shifts make it an extremely hazardous exercise to seek to understand his political persona by attempting to verify the consistency of his attitudes. This exercise would appear less hazardous for a leader such as Margaret Thatcher, whose political credibility was built on being a conviction politician, but even here there is considerable doubt: the lady was forced to turn far more often than she publicly admitted.

Blondel has urged that the concept of leadership goals should be adopted as the basis for appraising achievements.[11] There are various problems with this notion: how are goals gauged? How are they prioritised? Are they internally consistent? Are they subject to change? It is unclear whether goals can be accurately measured. Goals might shift and be redefined. Public goals (the reduction of injustice) might serve as a pretext for less avowable intentions (the pursuance of power). It is possible that the pursuit of policy goals can be measured by comparing presidential or party manifestos with policies enacted in the course of a given administration; however, such measurement is likely to be crude. The concept of leadership goals is an interesting one, since it comprises attitudes, strategy, and expectations of behaviour. It is clear that Mitterrand's goals varied during the period after 1971 (the year he captured control of the Socialist Party). Political circumstances themselves were not static.

Mitterrand's overriding goals of the 1970s, avowed or otherwise, were to reduce the dominant position of the PCF amongst the left-wing electorate, to rebuild a great Socialist Party, and to mould the Socialists as a presidential rally behind his leadership and as a powerful vehicle for the capture of the presidency. With the benefit of hindsight, Mitterrand appeared remarkably successful in pursuance of these goals, although the restoration of Socialist fortunes and the decline of the PCF stemmed from far more immutable structural factors than Mitterrand's personality.

In the case of Mitterrand as President, it often appeared as if the greatest impact was felt in spheres unrelated to the initial goals. His early policy goals as President, as elucidated in the *110 Propositions*, comprised: an economic reflation via a relaunch in popular consumption; the priority objective of combatting unemployment; the erection of the state as an instrument of industrial policy via nationalisations, and as a dispenser of social justice through welfare reforms. None of these goals were successful, at least not in the sense originally envisaged by Mitterrand. There were unintended consequences of policy. The failed economic relaunch of 1981–82, for instance, forced a 'learning process' on the Socialist government which transformed the French government into one of the faithful exponents of economic monetarism in Europe. This had not been one of the original goals but it was, arguably, one of the major achievements. The policy of the strong franc associated with Bérégovoy left the French government as one of a handful of European governments likely to fulfil the economic convergence conditions for membership of a single European currency, as stipulated in the Maastricht

Treaty. Similar conclusions might be drawn, *inter alia*, in relation to industrial policy, and Socialist foreign policy: the achievements of the Mitterrand presidency were real in each of these spheres, but they were not those originally anticipated. It was also clear that Mitterrand's goals varied throughout the course of his presidency. From an early preoccupation with domestic policy, Mitterrand later immersed himself in European affairs and foreign policy.

Flexibility versus consistency   Traditional prescriptive models of leadership valued consistency and single-mindedness as cardinal virtues.[12] A strong case can be made, however, that adaptability to changing situations might prove to be a better recipe for the retention of effective power. The ability to respond credibly to changing political circumstances might be a more accurate gauge of effective political leadership than unswerving conviction. This depends upon political circumstances, and the responses called for by particular historical situations: it is impossible to judge this in an abstract manner without reference to specific types of situation. The most accurate assessment of François Mitterrand in power must be that of a flexible political leader able to react well to the development of events: not even his most ardently sympathetic biographers would seriously pretend that he controlled the run of events.

Leadership roles   The success of political leadership in complex liberal democracies probably depends upon the ability to perform different roles appropriate to variable contexts. Mitterrand displayed immense political skill in adapting his leadership to a variety of roles, many of which he had not been prepared for beforehand. After his presidential bid in 1965, Mitterrand came to excel in the role of party leader during the 1970s, for which his political past had scarcely equipped him: his epitomisation as defender of the *vieille maison* against the modernist challenge posed by Michel Rocard for the 1981 PS presidential nomination illustrated this. Once he had been elected President, a new set of roles had to be mastered; it was obvious that Mitterrand was more comfortable in certain of these roles than in others. He was never particularly convincing on economic issues, for instance, despite his willingness to legitimise the fundamental choice adopted in March 1983. He took immediately to the gravitas associated with the presidential office, but it must be admitted that Mitterrand performed the role of the arbitral President of *cohabitation* (1986–88) rather more convincingly than he did the omnipresent chief executive of the early reformist period (1981–83). In part, this was because the former was an easier role to perform than the latter; in part because Mitterrand had greatly increased his experience as President in the meanwhile. It might also have been the case that Mitterrand preferred the arbitral role. The most effective roles performed by Mitterrand were within the traditional presidential sector of foreign policy, European affairs and defence, activities favoured by chief executives everywhere. As European statesman, Mitterrand found an outlet for the idealistic traits of his political persona; the fervour with which he promoted closer European integration recalled that earlier deployed in defence of francophone Africa. As crisis leader during the Gulf War, Mitterrand took refuge in the solitary exercise of decision-making that left no one in any doubt over the impulsion of French policy. As Commander-in-Chief of the armed forces, Mitterrand solemnly reaffirmed his absolute control over the French nuclear deterrent. Mitterrand undoubtedly displayed great political skill in adapting to these various, rather different roles, but these roles themselves were predicated upon the strength of the French presidency as an institution rather than Mitterrand's inherent virtues.

II: Positional context

From 1981 onwards, Mitterrand derived his authority from his occupancy of the French presidency, one of the key political institutions in western liberal democracies. His margins of manoeuvre were shaped in a large measure by the possibilities opened by this office. One manner of demonstrating the strength of Mitterrand's leadership position is by contrasting the resources and opportunities available to executive leaders in several comparable nations. In this manner, we shall appraise Mitterrand's leadership in relation to the criteria outlined in Table 11.1 such as longevity, popularity, constitutional authority, party structures, personnel selection, and policy implementation. Although the positional context does not provide for precise measurements of the impact of leaders, it does offer evidence for balanced judgements in this sense. The fact that Mitterrand exercised 'more' power than any one of a string of Italian prime ministers during his presidency cannot seriously be doubted. In this spirit, the leadership resources available to Mitterrand might be compared with those of comparable European leaders such as the British Prime Minister, the German Chancellor, or the Italian Prime Minister.[13]

The *duration of the presidential mandate* sets the French President apart from his European counterparts. Alone amongst European chief executives, the French President is directly elected for a seven-year term of office; alone amongst French presidents, Mitterrand was twice directly elected as President.[14] The longevity of Mitterrand's rule stemmed mainly from the length of the French presidential term-in-office, rather than his expertise at winning elections; after all, Thatcher and Kohl outscored Mitterrand in terms of electoral victories, and neither the British nor German leaders had to deal with an equivalent of *cohabitation*.

The resources disposed of by Mitterrand as President were considerable. At the beginning of his first presidential term, the French President exercised a degree of mastery over key resources rare even for a French President. These included: a direct elective mandate; a seven-year term-in-office; an established constitutional precedent in favour of a strong presidency as the pinnacle of systemic legitimacy; a principle of presidential initiative in policy formulation and personnel selection; a strong presidential bargaining position in relation to other key institutions (bureaucracy, government, parliament, parties, interest groups); an absolute majority for the President's supporters in parliament; and a sympathetic public opinion. Mitterrand's early political credit was rapidly dissipated: within one year, public opinion had become wary of *la vie en rose*, and the full force of constraints facing the new government had become apparent. The loss of a sympathetic parliamentary majority to support the President in 1986 accentuated a process of presidential withdrawal from domestic politics that had been gathering pace since 1983. The arbitral interpretation of the presidency (forcibly) espoused by Mitterrand during the 1986–88 *cohabitation* was carried over in a modified form to his second presidential term after 1988, when the Socialists disposed only of a relative majority within the National Assembly. The Socialists' shattering defeat in the National Assembly elections of 1993 removed Mitterrand's last remaining source of political legitimacy and virtually reduced the President to observer status.

Mitterrand's presidency was thus subject to a law of diminishing returns of power that had characterised previous French presidential terms. The French President became a diminished President during his second presidential term. His control over his governments and the Socialist Party lessened, as did his capacity to influence his own succession. His political judgement was called into question on several occasions, notably by nominating Edith Cresson as premier in May 1991. And he had to cope with the wearing-down effects of power, as well as the results of the ageing process: Mitterrand's extraordinary mental agility could not prevent public disclosure of his illness in 1992.

Linked to his institutional longevity is the *virtual irremovability* of the French President while in office. Unlike the German Chancellor or British and Italian premiers, the French President does not answer directly to an elected Assembly; nor can he be formally removed by that Assembly, unlike in Germany, Britain or Italy. Direct presidential accountability to the electorate leads to elements of comparison with the US President, although the French President habitually suffers few of the systemic checks and balances that regularly hamper his US counterpart: instances of *cohabitation* (1986–88, 1993–95) provide the obvious exception to this rule. It is in the sphere of foreign policy that the comparison between the French and US Presidents is the most cogent. The Gulf War revealed Mitterrand as a crisis-President with an uncontested and highly personalised control of foreign policy, rather similar to that enjoyed by President Bush in the US. Mitterrand's personalised control over foreign policy decision-making extended beyond crisis situations providing a major element of continuity with his predecessors. While certain similarities can be drawn between the French and US presidents in foreign policy terms, most US presidents appear severely constrained in domestic politics in contrast with their French counterparts.

The complement to his longevity of tenure and his virtual irremovability while in office is the French President's power of dissolution. This accords the French head of state formidable leverage over the elected Assembly, in a manner quite alien to the US system of government, where the function of Congress is to check the exercise of executive power. In this instance, the more apt comparison is with Britain, rather than the US, although the French President enjoys a considerably freer hand than the British premier. The weapon of dissolution was used with great effect by Mitterrand on two occasions, in 1981 and 1988. In 1981, President Mitterrand dissolved the conservative National Assembly elected in 1978 and urged the French people to elect his supporters; the Socialist parliamentary majority returned in June 1981 thus owed its existence largely to Mitterrand. The proximity of the presidential and parliamentary elections strengthened the dependence on the latter on the result of the former. A similar pattern prevailed in 1988, although only a relative majority ensued from the parliamentary election following the dissolution. Following the indecisive 1988 verdict, the experience of the 1988–93 governments illustrated that, even without a parliamentary majority, the governments led by Rocard, Cresson and Bérégovoy could count upon the passage of government legislation by exploiting various devices in the 1958 constitution designed to weaken the legislature.[15] By a delightful irony, the imposing powers vested with the executive in de Gaulle's 1958 constitution were marshalled to their maximum effect during the Mitterrand presidency.

French presidents have generally observed fewer constraints than their European counterparts in terms of *appointments and dismissals* of government ministers. Mitterrand enjoyed complete freedom with regard to appointments within his immediate entourage, although he delegated responsibility for minor apppointments to the general secretary of the presidential staff. He also performed a major role in appointing and dismissing government ministers, and exercised a large measure of control over appointments of top civil servants and parapublic posts. Mitterrand not only appointed his prime ministers with reference to his own criteria, but dispensed with their services (Rocard, Cresson) with minimal notice. The fourth President illustrated a marked continuity with his predecessors in this respect. In relation to other key ministries, government formation resulted from a bargaining process between President and Prime Minister, with the former usually having a larger input than the latter. The French President's ability to dismiss prime ministers had no comparison in Germany, the UK, or Italy, although strong British prime ministers have proved equally ruthless in ridding themselves of undesirable ministers. No direct comparison exists in the German system, where the Chancellor, although a strong figure, has to respect a tradition of strong ministerial autonomy. In Italy, prime ministers have been sub-ordinated to the mechanics of coalitional decision-making, as well as to their chronic insecurity of tenure.

Mitterrand's control over personnel selection was predicated upon a political balance of power which was not static and which could turn against the President, as in 1986 and 1993. During the first period of *cohabitation*, government appointments, as well as those within the administration and the parapublic sector, were largely the preserve of Prime Minister Chirac. We should point out also that, in terms of the bureaucratic apparatus, Mitterrand was constrained to accept the perpetuation of a politico-administrative technostructure he implicitly distrusted, and initially attempted to modify.

Throughout Mitterrand's presidency, a principle of presidential initiative prevailed in policy-making, personnel selection and elections. This did not signify that Mitterrand personally involved himself in all aspects of policy; after an early interventionist phase, he withdrew into a more arbitral conception of his role during the Fabius premiership that he maintained thereafter. Although the principle of the President's right to intervene in policy formulation and orientation remained intact, after 1983 Mitterrand's interventions were increasingly restricted to the traditional sector of foreign policy, defence and European affairs, in conjunction with other areas of intense presidential interest such as culture and architecture.

The renewed presidential caution stemmed in part from *difficulties of implementation* of early policy goals: for instance, economic reflation, the anti-unemployment economic priority, or the reform of church schools. Difficulties of implementation stemmed partly from unrealistic policy goals (notably in relation to unemployment or industrial policy), but also from resistance from within the administration, as well as amongst powerful social groups (the failure of the Savary bill), and from the international community (notably the US and France's EU partners). The difficulty of policy imple-mentation during the early reformist period gave way post-1983 to an overwhelming prevalence of macro-economic considerations thereafter, to the extent that finance minister (then premier) Bérégovoy became associated with the defence of a strong franc to the virtual exclusion of all other policy interests. Implementation difficulties continued into the second presidential mandate, notably in relation to sectoral professional interests such as farmers (CAP reform), nurses, teachers, and lorry drivers. This testified both to the resilience of direct action as a form of protest in France (employed by many of the Socialists' erstwhile supporters), and to the weakness of neo-corporatist bargaining techniques, along with the impermeability of the French civil service.

The *configuration of the party system* acted, *grosso modo*, as a source of strength for Mitterrand. The existence of a relatively disciplined PS majority from 1981–86, which directly owed its existence to Mitterrand, ensured a large measure of subordination to the President, notwithstanding early rumbustiousness by PS deputies. To the institutional link between party and President were added the personal leader–follower ties which united the President and many prominent Socialist leaders, such as Fabius, Jospin, Quilès, Joxe and Hernu. The legacy of pre-1981 factionalism served to strengthen the President's control over the party, since his avowed supporters were placed in prominent positions in party, parliamentary group and the government. The party remained subordinated to its presidential leader even when the Socialists had returned to opposition in 1986, but relations deteriorated steadily throughout the second presidential mandate. To some extent, the post-*mitterrandiste* phase of French politics began upon his re-election as President in 1988: since it was evident that Mitterrand would not stand for the presidency again, his strategic influence was diminished.

The PS gradually became more autonomous with regard to Mitterrand; even with the President's former protégé Fabius in charge in 1992, the party's interests were no longer felt to coincide automatically with those of the President. This was consistent with the model of a diminution of power during Mitterrand's second mandate. The PS was too weak to act as a mobilising force; it became reduced to a catch-all party deserted by its troops, and discredited by the corruption of many second-rank leaders. But it must be admitted that the party acted as a minimal constraint on the President's freedom of manoeuvre for most of the period, unlike in Italy (where the strength of parties equated directly with the weakness of executives), the UK (where Margaret Thatcher was eventually overthrown by a cabal within the Conservative Party), or Germany (where SPD Chancellor Schmidt was overthrown in 1982 by the FDP's decision to desert the Social-Democrats in favour of Kohl's CDU). Thus, the party configuration helped to maximise presidential impact at the level of the executive, while representing a minimal constraint upon Mitterrand's freedom of manoeuvre, except during the periods of *cohabitation*.

By any comparative measurement, however crude or inexact, it would appear as if Mitterrand occupied a strong leadership position amongst his counterparts in comparable liberal democracies. The strength of this location reflected the strength of the French presidency, far more than it did Mitterrand's personal qualities, however impressive or otherwise. Combined with the strength of his institutional position, Mitterrand faced powerful constraints upon his freedom of manoeuvre which shall now be considered.

III: Internal and external constraints and opportunities

Thus far, we have considered the resources available to Mitterrand as a political leader, in terms firstly of personal characteristics, secondly of institutional context. Mitterrand's governments were subject to severe economic, political, social, and international constraints. On the level of internal constraints, we might enumerate the following: the need to respect economic equilibrium, the weight of cultural traditions, the natural parameters represented by society, the limitations imposed by the judicial system, and the internal dynamics of the political system itself (as above). On the level of external constraints, we would specify, *inter alia*: the place of France in the international system, the heritage of past foreign policy-making (in particular the legacy of Gaullism), the role of the EU and the Franco-German partnership, the nature of the international economy, and bureaucratic influences in foreign policy-making. An exhaustive recapitulation of these environmental constraints would lie outside of the limits of this chapter. Certain examples suffice to illustrate the point that the capacity for genuinely independent choice for governments of medium-sized nations such as France or the UK is limited, whatever their formal political structures:

Economic policy   The most obvious domestic and external constraint related to economic policy. From 1981–82, the left in power introduced Keynesian reflationary economic policies which contrasted starkly with the macroeconomic policies being pursued by France's principal trading partners. The failure of Socialist reflation from 1981–82 revealed the pressures for convergence between French economic policies and those of its main competitors, especially Germany. The pursuance of the original economic policy would have exacerbated already spiralling trade and budget deficits, forced France out of the European monetary system (EMS) and thereby endangered France's role at the heart of the European Community. In a critical policy arbitration in March 1983, President Mitterrand opted for France to remain within the EMS, to devalue the franc, and to adopt monetarist-style economic policies consistent with those of France's European partners. Economic policy provided a prime example of constraints becoming opportunities: the French Socialists gained considerably in economic credibility as a result of Mitterrand's 1983 policy arbitration. The French commitment to economic and monetary union at the Maastricht summit of 1991 illustrated the extent to which Mitterrand had fully integrated the economic constraint into his conception of France and Europe.

Social equilibrium   The decision to abandon an increasingly unpopular economic policy, and to moderate an ambitious programme of social reform in 1982–83 also reflected the importance of public opinion, and of organised group opposition. The most convincing example of a policy reversal occasioned by public hostility was that of the Education Bill of 1984. The overwhelming public opposition to this moderately anti-clerical measure not only forced the retreat of the proposed legislation, but also brought down the Mauroy government. In general terms, mobilised public opinion acted as a powerful constraining factor on the freedom of manoeuvre of Mitterrand's governments: full blooded reform of the 1981–82 variety was simply not on the agenda from 1983 onwards. The President's steep decline in popularity after 1983 acted as a signal for a reorientation of his political efforts in the direction of foreign policy, European affairs and defence, henceforth substituted for an apparent presidential disinterest in domestic politics. During Mitterrand's second presidential term, the politics of modesty replaced those of messianism: the cautious reformism of Rocard's premiership (1988–91) was itself consistent with Mitterrand's 1988 'Letter to the French People', which had invited a new compromise between left and right after a decade of ideological turbulence.

Europe   Critical to Mitterrand's decision to remain within the EMS in 1983, the European constraint became progressively more important throughout the course of his presidency. At the same time, Europe developed into a source of considerable internal benefit for Mitterrand. It was undoutedly the case that Mitterrand's proactive European policy facilitated his re-election in 1988, as well as enabling French governments to play a leading role in moves towards closer European political and economic integration. The Maastricht treaty itself represented the pinnacle of Mitterrand's achievement in this sphere: moves towards monetary union were foisted upon a reluctant Chancellor Kohl by Mitterrand.

Closely allied to the theme of European Union, the need for a close Franco-German partnership imposed itself as an imperative for any French President. In spite of his early misgivings, Mitterrand came to regard the Franco-German partnership as the key European relationship. From 1983 onwards, Mitterrand assiduously cultivated relations with Chancellor Kohl. The imbalance in relations between France and Germany occasioned by German unification in October 1990 weakened the position of the French President *vis-à-vis* his German counterpart, but both leaders reaffirmed the centrality of the Franco-German partnership for future European integration. The advantages of cooperation with Germany are such that any French leader is impelled to promote close relations between the two nations.

Foreign policy   The constraints on foreign policy-making are, if anything, more imposing than in the sphere of domestic politics. As surveyed in Chapter 9, these include the consequences of past foreign policy decisions, the need to respect existing alliance structures, the pressures of foreign governments, and an important bureaucratic input into foreign policy-making. While Mitterrand managed to surpass the Gaullist legacy in certain respects, French foreign policy remained predominantly shaped by key policy choices taken by Mitterrand's predecessors.

From these examples, it is clear that no individual political leader operates in isolation. Assessment of Mitterrand as a political leader must be tied in with a broader recognition of structural and environmental aspects of the French polity.

CONCLUSION

The study of political leadership, in France and elsewhere, must be appreciated in terms of the interaction between leadership resources (personal and positional) on the one hand, and the constraints imposed and opportunities opened by particular socio-economic and political systems and sets of historical circumstances on the other. Any framework can only be indicative: for this reason, it would be rather artificial to discriminate in an abstract manner between personal characteristics, positional context and environmental constraints without referring these to specific case studies.[16] Understanding Mitterrand's personal characteristics is undoubtedly important to an appreciation of his method of operating within the political system (especially his cultivation of leader–follower ties), and his capacity for endurance, ruthlessness, patience and courage. But the extent to which, as a political leader, Mitterrand shaped events is open to doubt: even personal triumphs (such as his electoral victory in 1981) were brought about by deeper movements beyond his control. The main achievements of the Mitterrand presidency bore little relationship to the initial goals personally espoused by the President. Mitterrand's personal policy preferences ran up against powerful economic and international constraints that imposed a gradual process of policy redefinition. But Mitterrand exercised considerable personal skill in redefining constraints as potential opportunities. This was notably the case in European affairs and economic policy.

Within western European polities, political leaders derive their authority from their occupancy of one of several key political offices or positions. The resources possessed and opportunities open to chief political leaders are variable according to the type of executive structure involved, as well as the interaction of the political executive with the other variables outlined in the framework for reference (particularly the party system, constitutional rules, bureaucratic inputs, and forms of political and social mobilisation). Especially in foreign policy terms, the importance of the country involved also has a major bearing upon the resources at the disposal of the leader; the leaders of more powerful countries will possess a stronger bargaining position than the leaders of less influential nations. As directly elected French President, Mitterrand had a strong element of personal and political legitimacy, as well as being at the head of an influential European nation. This fortuitous combination of circumstances gave Mitterrand more powerful resources than in those systems where power is more diffused and fragmented (Italy); where collegial government structures make decision-making a genuine collective enterprise (Switzerland, Austria); or where there are situations of permanent coalition (Belgium, Holland, Denmark).

However strong his institutional and political position, the evidence presented in the preceding chapters indicates that the imposing weight of economic and international constraints had a circumscribing effect upon the policy choices that could be enacted by Mitterrand as President. The political, economic, social and international constraints imposed on leaderships in all liberal democratic polities are imposing: in an increasingly globalised era, the autonomy of national political leaderships is limited, even when political discourse is highly voluntaristic, as is the case in France. Indeed, the traditionally 'heroic' French presidential leadership style, modelled by de Gaulle in the 1960s, appeared increasingly anachronistic in a Europe committed to closer political and economic integration, a development imposing less idiosyncratic forms of national political leadership.[17] Although Mitterrand inherited de Gaulle's presidential mantle, the *grandeur* associated with the French presidential office is itself in a process of redefinition, partly as a result of policy changes effected under Mitterrand.

From the brief appraisal in the preceding paragraphs, we might conclude that Mitterrand's personal characteristics, the resources at his disposal as President, and environmental constraints and opportunities interacted with each other in a continuous manner. Insofar as distinctions might be drawn between these three types of explanation, we would argue that the imposing weight of economic and international constraints had a circumscribing effect upon the policy choices that could be enacted by Mitterrand as President. Any other left-wing President would probably have been compelled to face similar choices as Mitterrand.

Chapter 12

Mitterrand's political legacy

MITTERRAND'S FINAL YEARS, 1993–96

Physically weakened by a prostate cancer, politically immobilised after the Socialists' electoral defeat in the National Assembly elections of March 1993, and morally subdued by new revelations of his wartime record, the incumbent President was little more than an observer throughout the second period of *cohabitation* (1993–95). During the twilight years of his presidency, Mitterrand's personal and political resources appeared more fragile than at any other period, including during the first *cohabitation* of 1986–88. This was partly because he was an obvious non-contender for a third presidential term; partly because the Socialists' electoral humiliation of March 1993 had removed any real illusions of *grandeur*.

It was also increasingly obvious that Mitterrand was seriously ill. This became publicly apparent during the President's televised interview of 13 September 1994, which rested in the memory as much for the obvious physical suffering of an old man, as for his justification of the wartime activity of a young man. However personally courageous Mitterrand's decision to respond to the allegations contained in Pierre Péan's *Une Jeunesse française*, the portrait the President painted of the Vichy regime as one of brave resistants serving alongside extreme-right opportunists was an interpretation contested by many. Although he denied any knowledge of the anti-semitic policies of the Vichy regime, Mitterrand admitted exercising a minor function in the Vichy regime longer than had originally been thought.[1] While neutral observers could comprehend his wartime ambiguities, the fact that Mitterrand had maintained friendly relations with Réné Bousquet – a leading police chief of the Vichy state – for decades after the war was for many simply unpardonable.[2] The Bousquet episode might be seen to illustrate the dangers of Mitterrand's political style. Mitterrand's nurturing of a range of clienteles formed part of his political *modus vivandi*, inspired by a strong dose of seduction as a political, as well as a personal, weapon. Loyalty to friends and to clients formed part of this style, even if they had doubtful pasts. The President's televised self-defence in relation to Bousquet lacked conviction.[3]

Mitterrand's prestige never really recovered from these allegations, which revealed a nation still at pains to come to terms with its Vichy past. Other personal incidents, such as evidence of phone-tapping of journalists, or the suicide of a former trusted friend and adviser within the Elysée Palace (de Grossouvre in May 1994), cast further doubts upon Mitterrand's integrity and that of his advisers.

In such circumstances, politics appeared as a secondary concern. Mitterrand had little visible input during the second period of *cohabitation*. In domestic policy Mitterrand attempted to reinvent the role of the arbiter-President that had served him so well during the first *cohabitation*, but to much less effect. In contrast with 1986–88, Mitterrand did not insist upon availing himself of the remaining constitutional weapons available to him. Mitterrand accepted most of the appointments made by Prime Minister Balladur after the 1993 elections, limiting his intervention to a number of specific cases. Nor did he refuse to sign any government decrees, as he had in 1986.

Mitterrand's policy input was limited to the traditional 'presidential sector' of foreign policy, defence and Europe. In an interview with *Le Figaro* in September 1994, Mitterrand accepted that 'the constitution confers important responsibilities on the Prime Minister in the sphere of foreign policy', and explained that 'there is no fundamental disagreement between us on foreign policy issues. Both of us are concerned to preserve French interests'.[4] This did not prevent Mitterrand criticising premier Balladur for intervening too frequently in foreign policy issues, for not informing the President, or for adopting stances with which the President did not agree, as in Algeria. In fact there were serious foreign policy divisions between Mitterrand and Balladur, most notably on NATO. The Balladur government adopted a far more participatory stance towards NATO than under Mitterrand's governments, to the extent of preparing the ground rules for future French participation in a Europeanised NATO structure (a process accelerated under President Chirac after May 1995). This was not to Mitterrand's taste.

Residual presidential influence continued to manifest itself in relation to foreign policy and defence, most notably with regard to Mitterrand's refusal to agree to renewed nuclear testing in the South Pacific, and in his continuing attachment to certain symbols of Gaullist nuclear policy (such as the Albion Platform) that even RPR military advisers considered outdated. A stalemate on these issues meant that Mitterrand preserved a de facto right of veto. Moreover, Mitterrand reputedly inspired the French humanitarian intervention in Rwanda (*Opération Turquoise*) in spite of certain misgivings on behalf of premier Balladur and Foreign Affairs Minister Léotard.[5]

As in foreign policy, official French executive discourse towards Europe was one of harmony. The main political actors had supported the Maastricht treaty in the September 1992 referendum: notably Balladur and Chirac (but not Interior Minister Pasqua). Both President and Prime Minister were anxious to minimise the divisive impact of European integration amongst the ranks of RPR deputies (two-thirds of whom had opposed ratification of the Maastricht treaty), and to prepare France to participate in a future European currency. Certain divisions within the executive did emerge, notably in relation to further enlargement (with Mitterrand hostile and Balladur more favourable), and with respect to Balladur's explicit endorsement of a Europe of concentric circles. As in foreign policy, decision-making during the second *cohabitation* depended upon preserving a maximum consensus in order to protect French interests in Europe. The French presidency of the European Union from January to June 1995 was notable for the absence of French initiatives in a period running up to the presidential election in France.

During the final months of his presidency, Mitterrand was concerned symbolically to defend the Maastricht agreement, to consolidate his image as a great European statesman, and to reaffirm cultural affinities between the French and German peoples. The final Mitterrand years were visibly those of the growing impact of Europeanisation upon domestic French politics. This was manifested in the independence of the Bank of France in 1995, which was a major step on the path towards future monetary union and, to some extent, the consecration of Mitterrand's European mission.[6]

Mitterrand's diminishing political resources were demonstrated by his absence from the 1995 presidential election campaign. The incumbent President exercised no real influence over the selection of the PS candidate, Lionel Jospin. The fact that Jospin was the candidate at all was surprising. The PS disposed of at least two more obvious presidential contenders, Michel Rocard and Jacques Delors. Former premier Rocard had captured control of the PS from Fabius in March 1993, with the presidency in mind, but was in turn ousted by Henri Emmanuelli in an internal party coup in July 1994, after the Socialists' dismal performance in the 1994 European election (14.49 per cent). This poor performance fatally compromised the presidential chances of Mitterrand's eternal rival Rocard. From July to December 1994, the Socialist presidential campaign was paralysed by the party awaiting the decision of Jacques Delors, former President of the European Commission, whether or not to stand as a presidential candidate. Mitterrand made it clear that Delors was his personal choice. With the polls suggesting that a Delors candidacy would triumph, the Socialists were forced to encourage their assumed champion. Delors' refusal to stand in December 1994 left the Socialists in a desperate position. With no candidate, and the prospect of failing to reach the second ballot once one had been selected, the Socialist Party leadership agreed on the procedure of internal party primaries. After various abortive candidacies (Jack Lang, Bernard Kouchner), the Socialist Party primary pitted First Secretary Emmanuelli against Jospin, a former party leader (1981–88) and education minister (1988–92). Rejecting the advice of key figures in the Socialist hierarchy, party activists overwhelmingly backed Jospin, against the advice of most avowed *mitterrandistes* within the party, notably Fabius.

Jospin's narrow defeat on the second ballot against Jacques Chirac (47.37 per cent to 52.63 per cent), and the latter's election as President closed the Mitterrand era within the country at large. Upon leaving the Elysée palace for the last time, Mitterrand paid a final visit to Socialist Party headquarters at the Rue de Solferino, where the President was greeted by tearful party activists nostalgic for the memory of 10 May 1981.

As in life, controversy surrounded Mitterrand in death. His death on 8 January 1996 occurred shortly before his eightieth birthday. The fixation with leaving his name in history had become increasingly obsessive. The curious alchemy of courage and duplicity coexisted within Mitterrand until his final hours. The belief that Mitterrand stage-managed his death (by voluntarily ceasing his treatment against cancer) provided the final political curtain. Evidence emerging shortly after his death that the former President had suffered from prostate cancer since late 1981[7] produced mixed emotions: admiration for the embattled fighter; and anger over Mitterrand's duplicity in hiding evidence of his cancer from public opinion, in spite of the publication of six-monthly health bulletins. The manner of his death thus confirmed the pervasive image that Mitterrand was 'the Prince of the equivocal'.

MITTERRAND'S LEADERSHIP: AN INTERPRETATION

Notwithstanding the melancholic decline of the *fin de règne*, François Mitterrand will be remembered by any standards as one of the key statesmen of his century. His principal achievement was to have survived at the helm for longer than any other French political leader in the twentieth century. As outlined in Chapter 11, when assessing the individual legacy of any political leader, attention will be drawn to features such as political style, beliefs, attitudes, goals and policy achievements. While none of these is satisfactory on its own, their consideration facilitates a fuller appreciation of the multi-faceted aspects of an individual political persona. A broader understanding of political leadership also requires a comprehension of the interactive quality of the relationship between the individual leader and the cultural and contextual environment within which this leadership is exercised.

As we saw in Chapter 4, the prevailing journalistic image of Mitterrand was as a tough political operator and a survivor, rather than a man of high principle. Biographers frequently depicted Mitterrand as a political animal adept at cunning, deviousness and with an unerring survival-like instinct. Mitterrand as a sly fox, or as a toad able to look both ways perfectly embodied this tendency. Most biographers converged to discern in Mitterrand a Machiavellian Prince.

The portrayal of Mitterrand as the Machiavellian Prince is probably necessary, but certainly insufficient. It might be objected that the consistency with which Mitterrand held to his strategic objectives after 1958, throughout difficult political circumstances, contrasted strongly with the portrait some-times painted of him as a political dilettante. However rich in political manoeuvres and manipulations, there was a definite sense to Mitterrand's political activity at each of the major stages of his career. Mitterrand's long career was permeated by a relatively small number of guiding themes, which slowly changed as circumstances evolved, but which gave a sense to his political activity: these related to Africa and colonial reform in the 1950s, republican opposition to de Gaulle in the 1960s, the union of the left in the 1970s, and the building of Europe for most of the 1980s and 1990s.

Within Mitterrand's political persona, there was a curious combination of pragmatic and idealistic political traits. Throughout his presidency, there was ample evidence of principled political activity, notably in relation to Euro-pean integration, which became a crucial mission from the mid-1980s onwards. But it is clear that Mitterrand's beliefs were neither rigid, nor impermeable. Mitterrand's political persona recalled the classical traditions of radical republicanism of the Third Republic, transposed to the political conditions of the Fifth. The apparent paradoxes and contradictions of Mitterrand's beliefs were themselves typical of a particular type of republican tradition. In accordance with the Radical tradition, there were two faces to Mitterrand. A firm belief in values such as the Republic, the state, the nation, social justice or the rule of law coexisted alongside a highly developed sense of politics as an autonomous activity (or game), with its own rules and rites which occasionally conflicted with the former.

Mitterrand will be remembered not only as one of the key statesmen of his century, but also as a gritty and determined political survivor. His ability to survive repeated political and personal setbacks had been well established before his election as President, as in 1958, 1968 and 1978. Finally elected President in 1981, Mitterrand remained in office for fouteen years, longer than any other French political leader in the twentieth century. His status as a survivor is highlighted by most biographers. Survival testified in part to his political skill and determination; in part to fortuitous circumstances; in part to the strategic mastery over the resources available to him, especially as French President after 1981.

In most respects Mitterrand's key achievements as President were in those spheres where his action had been least expected. He promoted European integration beyond the limits agreed by former French presidents; he contributed under pressure towards the modernisation of French industry and financial capitalism; he de-ideologised the left and reconciled it to the market economy. Certain reforms were transient; the effects of others only became slowly apparent. The decentralisation reforms of 1982–3 proved a case in point. The transfer of major policy responsiblities to the 96 de-partmental councils, and the direct election of the 22 regional assemblies had a major long-term impact whose effects were only becoming clearer one decade later. Other measures had unintended consequences, notably in the sphere of industrial policy and economic management. Mitterrand was elected in 1981 on the basis of Keynesian reflationist policies, wide-scale nationalisations, and support for traditional industrial sectors. By 1984, a complete reversal had taken place, under the combined pressures of the international environment and domestic political constraints.

The roles Mitterrand was called upon to perform varied in accordance with political and policy circumstances, as well as with the changing opportunity structures existing at various stages of his career. As the republican opponent to Gaullism in the 1960s, and later as leader of the Socialist Party in the 1970s, Mitterrand appeared as a catalyst for the expression of various social and political movements. As President of the Republic, Mitterrand appeared first as the personification of *le changement*; later on as an imperfect legitimator of new policy directions, notably after the economic U-turn of March 1983. To some extent this legitimising role was predetermined, given the extent of the policy shifts that were imposed upon Mitterrand's governments. Moreover, the legitimising function was imperfectly performed; Mitterrand's secretive style arguably prevented a full and free discussion of the economic policy choices facing the country. Nonetheless, by his consistent and determined support as President for policies he had previously eschewed, or underplayed, Mitterrand helped to legitimise new policy directions. This role was especially important in relation to economic policy, to European integration, and in his acceptance of key aspects of the *gaullien* legacy in foreign policy. Mitterrand's leadership was most effective as a legitimator of new directions, rather than in a directive sense. Mitterrand also appeared as an imperfect consensus builder, notably over European integration and foreign policy, and as a reluctant moderniser of capitalism.

Mitterrand was responsible – at least symbolically – for the democratic maturation of the Fifth Republic. The political institutions of the Fifth Republic experienced a double evolution during the 1980s under Mitterrand's aegis: the first alternation in power between right and left in 1981; the first *cohabitation* between left and right in 1986. The transfer of power from right to left in 1981 legitimised the Fifth Republic in two key senses. It proved that the regime could withstand the democratic alternation in power, the key measurement of any liberal democracy; it represented the final rallying of the left to the presidential institutions created by de Gaulle. The advent of *cohabitation* in 1986 was equally significant, since the regime did not collapse under the pressure of competing political forces controlling the presidency and the National Assembly. Instead, for the first time, the 1958 constitution was actually applied as it was written: the President presided, but the government governed. Mitterrand facilitated these developments, notably by playing the game of *cohabitation* in accordance with the constitutional rules.

Taking the period 1981–95 as a whole, Mitterrand practised a more arbitral conception of the presidency than that of his two predecessors. As personally representative of *le changement* in 1981, Mitterrand symbolised the arrival of a new political order, and was involved in many of the important policy decisions of the early period in office. Presidential interventionism was particularly marked during the early reformist years of the Mauroy premiership in 1981–84, but gradually Mitterrand intervened less frequently in matters of domestic politics. Mitterrand's most critical policy arbitration occurred in March 1983, when the French President opted for France to remain within the European monetary system, at the expense of abandoning the Socialist government's Keynesian attempt to reflate the French economy.

However constrained the policy-making environment, there was a Mitterrand style which was recognisably different from that of other French presidents and European political leaders. Certain facets of this style were encouraged by the presidential office itself, notably the aloofness and monarchical posture of the French head of state. Mitterrand adopted this traditional posture far more ostentatiously than his successor Chirac, the citizen President. Other features of Mitterrand's style revealed an individual manner of operating within the political arena. As observed in Chapter 7, the prevalent features of Mitterrand's individual style involved patient reflection and a refusal to be rushed into decision-taking; the cultivation of plural sources of information and rival policy advisers; a taste for secrecy; an antipathy towards collective forms of decision-making; a sharp awareness of the balance of power in any given situation; and a proclivity for the counter-attack. These positional and personal attributes translated into a political leadership style which combined adaptability to changed circumstances with the pursuit of a limited number of precise policy objectives.

Mitterrand's style of reactive, adaptable leadership had its positive and its negative facets. At best, his flexible style of political leadership gave a degree of credibility to a series of difficult policy choices and necessary reversals, as in the spheres of economic policy, industrial policy and foreign affairs. In many areas of policy, as in the sphere of economic policy, major changes in direction were imposed upon Mitterrand by complex forces outside his control. Mitterrand usually accompanied unforeseen policy changes, occasionally resisting, but more often facilitating developments, as in the sphere of European integration. The secret of Mitterrand's leadership lay in his ability to accommodate constraints, and transform them into opportunities. Thus, the reluctant acceptance of limited sovereignty in domestic economic policy provided the opportunity for Mitterrand to perform a more expansive role in relation to European integration. The pursuit of limited but precise objectives was the counterpart to a generally facilitating style. This was illustrated in the sphere of European integration from the mid-1980s onwards, especially in relation to economic and monetary union, an issue that Mitterrand pursued with determination from 1988 onwards.

Flexibility was a practical virtue of Mitterrand's political leadership, almost a price for survival, as with other social-democratic leaderships elsewhere, forced to come to terms with the constraints represented by existing society, and by the external economic and international environment. Mitterrand's style of adaptable leadership might be contrasted with a more innovative and voluntaristic brand of affirmative leadership, of the type associated with Margaret Thatcher and – possibly – Jacques Chirac.[8] While occasionally imparting the impression of reacting to events and of drift, Mitterrand's leadership style enabled policy reversals to be undertaken with a degree of credibility. This style of adaptable political leadership might be contrasted with that of former British premier Thatcher, who appeared unable to assume the consequences of unpalatable decisions which could not be avoided, notably the Single European Act of 1986.

It appears irrefutable that Mitterrand's personal characteristics had an impact upon his manner of operating within the political system, especially via his cultivation of leader–follower ties, his distrust of party and his building of personal networks upon which to base his authority. Most observers discerned powerful negative features of Mitterrand's leadership style. These included cynicism, a weakness of long-term perspectives, and an excessive taste for personal *règlements de comptes*. The proliferation of corruption scandals throughout the course of the second presidential term led to a pervasive mistrust of Mitterrand's *entourage*. The belief was widespread that the President was too bound by ties of personal loyalty to apprehend the corrupt practices of those around him. This rebounded against the President, as did his attempts to mitigate the gravity of corrupt practices.

The Machiavellian manoeuvrer was only one face of Mitterrand but it would be futile to deny that it formed a powerful part of the public's impression of him. Widespread cyncism in relation to politics was aggravated by Mitterrand's rather cynical political style, notably his obvious divide and rule tactics which appeared to many to lie beneath the dignity of a statesman. On occasion, this was unfortunate for Mitterrand himself, since it fuelled suspicions that the President was engaged in base political manoeuvres even when his motives were noble. As a political leader even of the PS in opposition, Mitterrand favoured a system based on the cultivation of personal networks in all walks of life, and amongst all types of politician. This might have been appropriate – inevitable – for a presidential system, but it ultimately rebounded against him, leaving him an isolated, and lonely figure at the end of his presidency. The manner in which Mitterrand set leading PS tenors (Fabius and Jospin) against each other proved highly damaging to the Socialist Party, the vehicle for his conquest of power in 1981. The manner in which the President undermined his own prime ministers (especially Rocard, 1988–91) ultimately weakened his own political powerbase. Towards the end of his presidency, the appearance of the Mitterrand as a manoeuvrer came more starkly to the forefront, since his ideological and policy achievements lay in the past.

THE MITTERRAND LEGACY

Whether Mitterrand left a legacy, and, if so, how best this should be understood is a matter of some contention. Mitterrand's legacy can be understood on at least three levels: his personal legacy, his party legacy and his policy/political legacy.

The personal legacy   As appraised above, any judgement of Mitterrand's political leadership must be mitigated in its conclusions. An astute comprehension of the changed rules of political competition of the Fifth Republic, of the importance of presidentialism as a political and organisational principle, and of the need to embrace the Communists made Mitterrand a shrewd leader for the conquest of power preceding 1981. Mitterrand's political style was carried over into the exercise of power after 1981. His personal system of governing ultimately inspired mistrust, including amongst traditional supporters.

The party legacy   The question of Mitterrand's political inheritance is one that deeply divides the French left, not just predictably Socialists and Communists, but also within the Socialist movement itself. The ambivalent status of the Mitterrand legacy might best be illustrated with respect to the French Socialist Party. The renovation of the PS in the 1970s crystallised itself around the personality of Mitterrand. However important the underlying structural and social forces explaining the rise of the PS, it was attributed in part by the actors involved to Mitterrand's own personality. Mitterrand displayed great political skill in transforming the old Socialist Party (SFIO) into a new presidential-style rally in the 1970s, helping to break the hold of the PCF on the left, making the non-Communist left fit for government, and building up the PS as the natural alternative governing party to the parties of the right. While the resurrection of the French PS in the 1970s depended ultimately on fundamental changes in the nature of French society, Mitterrand's astute political leadership contributed to its success.

   The first-term presidential mandate (1981–88) had witnessed an unsteady, if generally loyal, subordination of party to president and a stout defence of presidential policy during the 1981–88 period. This mechanism has been explored in Chapter 5. By the end of his second term, references to the personality of Mitterrand had become potentially embarrassing. By any standards, this was a measure of personal failure on Mitterrand's behalf. After its crushing defeat of 1993, the Socialist Party purged itself of its *mitterrandiste* identity, even while Mitterrand remained at the Elysée. The controversy over Mitterrand's Vichy past occasioned by the publication of Pierre Péan's *Une Jeunesse française* in September 1994 helped accelerate the movement. This greatly facilitated the post-Mitterrand period; overt *mitterrandistes* became rarer after 1993.

Lionel Jospin symbolised this transition. Jospin had been introduced to the PS by Mitterrand in 1973. He had been one of a handful of young pro-Mitterrand PS cadres in the 1970s, before taking over as First Secretary of the party from 1981 to 1988. As party leader, Jospin had already begun marking his distances from Mitterrand in the mid-1980s, as the tensions between the presidential and party logics became apparent. Jospin won the Socialist Party's 1995 presidential nomination against most traditional *mitterrandistes* in the party (notably arch-rival Fabius). With a certain ambiguity, moreover, Jospin reserved the right to judge the legacy of the Mitterrand years on a case-by-case basis, a clever tactical decision to attempt to distance himself as far as decently possible from Mitterrand's heritage. As candidate, Jospin stoutly resisted moves from Mitterrand loyalists to enrol the incumbent President's assistance in the campaign.

The 1980s and 1990s suggested that there are natural limits to the type of party renovation undertaken by Mitterrand, strongly personalist in character. The exercise of power in the 1980s and early 1990s shattered the optimism upon which the PS had built its revival in the 1970s. It also revealed the fragility of a party based on factional identities, and which reproduced presidential rivalries within its midst. The PS was racked by instability throughout Mitterrand's second presidential term in office; four party leaders succeeded each other in brief succession in five years. The new PS leader Jospin – himself invested with presidential stature after his narrow defeat in 1995 – maintained his distance with Mitterrand's legacy, in spite of being initially a product of Mitterrand's patronage.

Mitterrand's most enduring party legacy was nonetheless to erect the Socialist Party as the cornerstone of the French left. The PS appears as a permanent feature of the French political landscape, as a natural alternative to the parties of the mainstream right. Had Mitterrand not existed, it would have been necessary to invent someone to fulfil the task of modernizing the Socialist Party, and of reconciling it to the institutions of the Fifth Republic.

As a party of government from 1981–93, the Socialists were victims of their idealistic but unrealistic pre-1981 discourse, and of their early reformist programme of 1981–82. From a party viewpoint, the real achievements of economic management after 1983 were overshadowed by the fact that the economy tended to exclude any other social or political perspectives. The post-Mitterrand Socialist Party accepted the Mitterrand policy heritage, but appeared critical in relation to the limited manoeuvre this implied. Hence, the party attempted to reconstruct an identity at the margins which went beyond the obligation to recall its management capacities, and to proclaim itself as cleansed after the corruption scandals of the later Mitterrand years.

Until 1981, the French Socialist Party lacked a solid social-democratic tradition upon which to base claims of managerial competence. Social-democracy was a dirty word in the cultural context of the French left, and remains so despite the government experience. Under the influence of Marxism and of political competition from the PCF, the PS had traditionally adopted a radical discourse. Such a discourse is henceforth excluded on account of changed political and policy circumstances, as a result of the experience of the Mitterrand *septennat* itself. It is uncertain what can replace this discourse.

Mitterrand's principal achievements were difficult to reconcile with a traditional social-democratic political agenda. Moreover, they were couched in a political discourse borrowed from traditional adversaries of the left (constraints, rigour – the language of Barre during the 1970s). In European policy, for instance, the Single European Act and the Maastricht treaty were major achievements for which Mitterrand could claim some credit. But however fine Mitterrand's discourse evoking a 'social Europe', the Maastricht treaty imposed a monetarist vision of an ever closer union, a logic which had little in common with Keynesian reflation, anti-unemployment policies, and traditional social-democracy. The defence of a strong franc, and the crusading anti-inflation policy were likewise references borrowed from traditional adversaries. These new references cannot be abandoned, for they form the real Mitterrand legacy, with which the Socialist Party leadership remains indelibly associated.

Political scientists will observe with interest the limitations of the personalist type of political movement produced by the Fifth Republic. As Gaullism could not really survive without de Gaulle, neither could Mitterrandism without Mitterrand. Despite renovating the PS on the basis of being a presidential rally, Mitterrand distrusted political parties. In time, the Socialist Party learned to distrust Mitterrand. The former President's long-term influence over the French Socialist Party was manifestly an important one: notably in terms of the pursuit of power, the adaptation to the presidential system, and the conversion to governmental realism. But ultimately it is difficult to point to a specifically *mitterrandiste* heritage that is reserved for the PS, except arguably for a historic memory of shared victories and a particular type of party organisation.

The policy and political legacy   It is a genuine paradox that political change often comes from the least expected source. A Socialist President Mitterrand helped to reconcile the French with the market economy; since 1995 the Gaullist President Chirac has helped partially to ease France back into NATO. This is in part inherent in the nature of the policy process. In an increasingly interdependent and global age, governments have limited margins of manoeuvre. Difficult political decisions impose themselves on governments of left and right; ideological justifications follow. Whatever their political hue, governments are anxious to demonstrate legitimacy by governing in the interests of the whole nation, at least symbolically. In practical terms, this explained why Mitterrand's governments appeared most competent when carrying out conservative policies; and why only a Gaullist President could begin to supersede the Gaullist foreign policy legacy.

As explored above, the policy record of the Mitterrand presidency was one of unintended achievements. In important respects the legacy of Mitterrand involved the weakening of the 'French exception', both domestically and on the international stage. In most respects France was a country rather less different from its European neighbours in 1995 than in 1981. The modification of French exceptionalism is associated with Mitterrand in part because of the policy record of the 1981–95 governments, in part because Mitterrand was President at a period of major socio-economic and political change. It can be measured in relation to several spheres: the reshaping of the state as a result of powerful domestic and international pressures; the dilution of left–right cleavages; a weakening of traditional 'anti-system' movements (albeit tempered by the advent of new ones); a new policy of convergence amongst French elites, and the growing impact of European integration on domestic French politics. The French model – based on centralism, state intervention in economic management, high inflation, and growth – has been modified by a German model, with its insistence on low inflation, high productivity, central bank independence and a strong currency. Under Mitterrand's guidance, French economic policy was driven after 1983 by a determined effort to match Germany in terms of economic performance, a precondition for preserving French rank as a pre-eminent European power. The policy legacy of the Mitterrand presidency was far too imposing to be ignored by any serious party, either of the left or of the right. This was notably the case in relation to European policy, where the fundamental policy choices undertaken by Mitterrand – notably in relation to the Single European Act and economic and monetary union – have in all probability bound themselves upon his successors.

Mitterrand's principal political legacy has been a blurring of the identity of left and right. The bipolar, partisan political culture of the 1970s, and the mobilising references to socialism, or the defence of freedom it induced, appeared archaic in the mid-1990s as France moved towards the twenty-first century. Put simply, the left–right cleavage was of less significance in French politics in the mid-1990s than it was in the mid-1970s. The general ideological climate had changed, both in France and elsewhere, as had perceptions of the possibilities of governmental action. Until 1981, left and right were able to mobilise by referring to distinctive sets of values. Whichever side one was on, the sense of identity and of belonging to one camp or another was strong. Since the Socialist experience in office (1981–86, 1988–93), the ideological bearings of left and right have become far more confused. Each side has borrowed themes hitherto voiced by others in order to justify its policies. This is a legacy that the French left cannot willingly ignore, however hard it attempts to rediscover its identity.

In practice, it is difficult to distinguish a personal Mitterrand legacy from the more general lessons of more than a decade of French history. For all the popular enthusiasm sparked by his presidential victory on 10 May 1981, the Mitterrand legacy is not a specifically left-wing one. The salient characteristic of the Mitterrand legacy revolves around a necessary but painful abandoning of traditional left-wing mythology. Its impact was most obvious on the left. Indeed, in order to avoid engaging in an incrementalist type of public policy, a future Socialist government would have to call into question the crucial choices determined during the Mitterrand presidency, notably the particular type of European integration project launched in the 1980s. This is unlikely. The core of the 1981 policy agenda – nationalisations, reflation, welfare expansion, wealth redistribution, the priority of anti-unemployment – is off the policy agenda for the foreseeable future. The *mitterrandiste* heritage – one of European integration, governmental realism and economic rigour – has to be considered as part of a more general one imposing itself on left and right alike. For this reason, it is far from certain that Mitterrand will be treated with the same reverence on the Socialist left as Léon Blum or Jean Jaurès, despite being markedly more successful than either.

Notes

1 THE ORIGINS OF A POLITICAL LEADER, 1916–58

1 Among the numerous biographies covering Mitterrand's early life, the following ought to be signalled for attention: P. Péan, *Une Jeunesse française*, Paris, Fayard, 1994; C. Moulin, *Mitterrand Intime*, Paris, Hachette, 1982; T. Desjardins, *François Mitterrand: un socialiste gaullien*, Paris, Hachette, 1978; F-O. Giesbert, *François Mitterrand ou la tentation de l'Histoire*, Paris, Seuil, 1977; C. Nay, *Le Noir et le Rouge*, Paris, Grasset, 1984; J-M. Borleix, *Mitterrand lui-même*, Paris, Grasset, 1973; J-P. Liegois, *Le Feu et l'eau*, Paris, Grasset, 1990.
2 Interview with Jean Daniel.
3 Cited in J. Daniel, *Les Religions d'un Président*, Paris, Grasset, 1988, p. 167.
4 Nay, op. cit., p.63.
5 The *Cagoule* allegations are made in the dossier 'Mitterrand et la Cagoule', *Le Choc du Mois*, no. 42–43, August 1991, pp. 7–21. Péan rejects these, op. cit., pp. 34–35, 113–14.
6 Giesbert, op. cit, p. 29.
7 F. Mitterrand, *Ma part de verité*, Paris, Fayard, 1969, pp. 19–20.
8 F. Mitterrand and E. Weisel, *Mémoires à deux voix*, Paris, Odile Jacob, 1995.
9 This interpretation was favoured by Hubert Védrine (son of Jean Védrine, one of Mitterrand's resistance companions) in an interview with the author.
10 F. Mitterrand, *Mémoires interrompus*, Paris, Jacob, 1996. Péan insists repeatedly on this point, but it is not convincingly demonstrated by the evidence provided.
11 This thesis, with which I agree, was defended by Eric Duhamel, 'François Mitterrand entre Vichy et Résistance', Association for the Study of Modern and Contemporary France Conference, Royal Holloway College, London, 12–14 September 1996.
12 According to Péan, this contact took the form of links with a member of Pétain's *cabinet*, who provided various forms of covert assistance to the POW movement. Mitterrand did not deny this.
13 Mitterrand met Pétain briefly in 1943. He had family ties with General Giraud, former head of the resistance within the French army, who fought with de Gaulle for supremacy amongst the external resistance, until de Gaulle emerged victorious in late 1943.
14 Moulin, op. cit., p. 54.
15 Mitterrand's name was forwarded by a notable collaborator of the Vichy regime, Gabriel Jeantet, and by the journalist Simon Arbellot, a pro-Pétainiste.
16 *Ma part de verité*, pp. 21–22. Mitterrand gives a more sympathetic account of this meeting in a later collection *La Paille et le grain*, Paris, Flammarion, 1975, pp. 10–11.
17 This point was stressed in an interview with Jean Daniel.

18 Desjardins, op. cit., p.80.
19 Ibid., p. 97.
20 As minister for DOM-TOM, Mitterrand's authority covered essentially Black sub-Saharan Africa. Algeria came directly under the Interior ministry; Tunisia and Morocco (being protectorates) came under the Foreign Affairs ministry; French Asian territories under still another minister.
21 Desjardins, op. cit., pp. 100–22.
22 Mendès combined the posts of President of the Council (PM) and Foreign Affairs Minister, leaving Interior as the next most prestigious. That Mitterrand actually wanted Interior, the first policeman in France, was a matter of criticism for certain Mendès supporters, especially the intellectual circles surrounding *L'Express*. Interview with Jean Daniel.
23 *Année Politique*, 1955, p. 192.
24 Cited in Moulin, op. cit., p. 120.
25 F. Mitterrand, *Politique 11*, Paris, Fayard, 1981, p.9.
26 In its founding charter, the UDSR recognised the existence of different tendencies within the resistance, but proclaimed that 'Diversity is not division'. Cited in 'Un Manifeste de l'Union démocratique et socialiste de la résistance', *Combat*, 7 July 1945.
27 R. Cayrol, *François Mitterrand, 1945–67*, Paris, CEVIPOF, 1967, pp. 16–17.
28 P. Williams, *Crisis and Compromise*, London, Longmans, 1964, pp. 174–76.
29 Cayrol, op. cit., p. 17.
30 L'Union démocratique et socialiste de la résistance, *L'UDSR: le Parti qui grandit*, UDSR, Paris, 1952, p. 1.
31 *Le Monde*, 15 October 1958.

2 FROM REPUBLICAN OPPONENT TO PRESIDENT, 1958–81

1 F. Mitterrand, *Politique*, Paris, Fayard, 1977, p. 197.
2 'A Republican regime cannot be based on the omnipotence of a single man.' Ibid., p. 195.
3 This appreciation was offered by Jean Daniel in an interview with the author.
4 'I cannot forget that General de Gaulle, the candidate for Prime minister, was carried to power by an undisciplined army.' Mitterrand's speech to National Assembly, 1 June 1958. Cited in Mitterrand, *Politique*, p. 201.
5 F. Mitterrand, *Le Coup d'état permanent*, Paris, Plon, 1964.
6 L. Megne, *François Mitterrand dans la Nièvre*, unpublished DEA thesis, University of Paris 1, 1988, p. 40. Mitterrand lost a three-cornered fight against UNR and SFIO candidates.
7 Ibid, p.45.
8 J. Mossuz, *Les Clubs et la politique en France*, Paris, Armand Colin, 1970.
9 See D. Loschak, *La Convention des Institutions Républicaines: François Mitterrand et le socialisme*, Paris, Armand Colin, 1970.
10 J. Lacouture, *Pierre Mendès-France*, Paris, Seuil, 1981.
11 See R. Rémond, 'L'Election présidentielle et la candidature Defferre', *Revue Française de Science Politique*, vol, 14, no. 3, June 1964, pp. 513–526.
12 J. Mossuz, 'Les fédérés et leurs problèmes', *Revue Française de Science Politique*, vol. 16, no. 7, October 1966, pp. 960–974.
13 'Deux leaders?', *Réforme*, 7 May 1966.
14 The integral text of the FGDS–PCF agreement is reprinted in *Le Monde*, 25–26 February 1968. On the impact of the second-ballot electoral system in enticing Socialists and Communists to form electoral pacts after 1962, see A. Cole and P. Campbell, *French Electoral Systems and Elections since 1789*, Aldershot, Gower, 1989, Chapter 6.

15 Cited in *Le Monde*, 29 May 1968.
16 To a lesser extent, the Unified Socialist Party (PSU), led by Rocard, enjoyed a measure of support among the students.
17 The text of Mitterrand's press conference is reprinted in *Le Monde*, 29 May 1968.
18 C. Hurtig, *De la SFIO au Nouveau Parti Socialiste*, Paris, Armand Colin, 1970.
19 R. Schwarzenberg, 'Le cas Mitterrand dans la guerre de succession', *Le Monde*, 12–13 October 1969.
20 Notably, those based around Alain Savary (the UCRG), who became party leader. Jean Poperen's UGCS group of clubs joined the party in July 1969 at the Congress of Issy-les-Moulineaux.
21 The results obtained by the competing motions at Epinay were as follows: Mollet-Savary, 34 per cent; Mauroy-Defferre, 30 per cent; Mermaz-Pontillon, 15 per cent; Poperen, 12 per cent; CERES, 8.5 per cent; *Le Monde*, 15 June 1971.
22 On the development of the Socialist Party from 1971–81, cf., *inter alia*, D.S. Bell and B. Criddle, *The French Socialist Party: the Emergence of a Party of Government*, Oxford, Clarendon, 1988; R.W. Johnson, *The Long March of the French Left* London, Macmillan, 1981; N. Nugent and D. Lowe, *The Left in France*, London, Macmillan, 1982.
23 See, *inter alia*, D.C. Beller and D. Belloni, *Faction Politics*, Washington, Clio Press, 1978; D. Hine 'Factionalism in the West European Party System: a Framework for Analysis, *West European Politics*, vol.5., no.1, January 1982, pp.39–52.
24 Cited in F-O. Giesbert, *François Mitterrand ou la tentation de l'histoire*, Paris, Seuil, 1977, p. 267.
25 H. Sevin, *La Coalition majoritaire du Parti socialiste, 1971–1975*, unpublished *doctorat d'état* thesis, Institute of Political Studies Paris, 1983, p. 503.

3 MITTERRAND AND THE LEFT IN POWER, 1981–93

1 According to one observer, for Mitterrand, Rocard was condemned to be an eternal 'Under Secretary of State for the Budget', with a message that was incomprehensible to the public. Interview with Jean Daniel.
2 See, *inter alia*, A. Gélédan, *Le Bilan économique des années Mitterrand*, Paris, Le Monde editions, 1993; P. Favier, and M. Martin-Roland, *La Décennie Mitterrand. 1. Les ruptures 2. Les épreuves*, Paris, Seuil, 1990 and 1991; S. Mazey, and M. Newman, *Mitterrand's France*, London, Croom Helm, 1987; G.Ross, S. Hoffmann, and S.Malzacher, *The Mitterrand Experiment*, Oxford, Polity Press, 1987; H. Machin and V. Wright (eds), *Economic Policy and Policy-Making under the Mitterrand Presidency: 1981–84*, London, Pinter, 1985.
3 Gélédan, op. cit. pp. 48–49. The state thus obtained a majority shareholding in the following major industrial sectors: energy, mining, steel, chemicals, artificial fibres, arms, aerospace, telecommunications, electronics.
4 Ibid.
5 See, *inter alia*, B. Soulage, 'Un épisode du colbertisme', *Projet*, no. 203, February 1987, pp.83–92; M. Blin, 'Nationalisations: la fin d'une idéologie?', *Politique Industrielle*, no. 3, Spring 1986, pp. 65–78; E. Cohen, 'Nationalisations: une bonne leçon de capitalisme', *Politique Economique*, no. 1, April 1986, pp. 10–14; C. Stoffaës, 'The nationalizations, 1981–84', in Machin and Wright, op. cit., pp. 144–169.
6 J. Daniel, *Les Religions d'un président*, Paris, Grasset, 1988, p. 149–154.
7 But the armaments group Matra figured as an exception, since the state obtained only 51 per cent. The aerospace firm Dassault was the subject of a special compromise which guaranteed the state 66 per cent of voting rights with only 46 per cent of the shares.

8 See B. Belassa, 'Five years of Socialist economic policy in France: a balance sheet', *The Tocqueville Review*, vol. 11, no. 7, 1986, pp. 269–283.

9 See, *inter alia*, S. July, *Les années Mitterrand*, Paris, Grasset, 1986, pp. 77–101; P. Bauchard, *La Guerre des deux roses*, Paris, Grasset, 1986, pp. 139–154.

10 The economic balance-sheet of the first Socialist administration was mitigated for the following reasons:

- By 1986 *inflation* had declined to under 5 per cent from its 1982 peak of over 20 per cent (14 per cent in 1981), although it remained above that of its main trading partners.
- The *trade deficit* had been all but eliminated.
- The *budget deficit* remained elevated, at over 3 per cent of GDP (3.3 per cent in 1985).
- The economy was beginning to expand modestly, although growth of French GDP (average 1.2 per cent, 1981–85) underperformed that of the US, Japan, Germany and the UK throughout the 1981–85 period.
- The record on *unemployment*, the key economic policy in the 1981 manifestos, was the most disappointing: notwithstanding attempts to camouflage the figures, the French rate of unemployment (11 per cent) exceeeded that of the FRG, the US and Japan, while slightly below that of the UK. All figures from Balassa, op. cit.

11 Bauchard, op. cit. p. 145.

12 C. Nay, *Les Sept Mitterrand*, Paris, Grasset, 1988, pp. 115–159.

13 P. Favier and M. Martin-Roland, *Les épreuves*, pp. 44–54. Mitterrand had made the commitment to industrial modernisation in a televised address in December 1983.

14 For details of the Savary bill, see A. Prost, 'The Educational Maelstrom', in Ross, op. cit., pp. 229–236; for the overwhelmingly negative public reaction, see 'Les libertés et la querelle scolaire', in *Opinion Publique – SOFRES*, Paris, Gallimard, 1985, pp. 31–45.

15 See J. Gaffney, *France and Modernisation* Aldershot, Gower, 1989; V. Lauber, 'Reinventing French socialism: economic policy, ideology, political strategy', *Parliamentary Affairs*, vol. 38, no. 2, September 1985, pp. 150–162; G. Ross and T. Daley, 'The wilting of the rose: the French socialist experiment', *Socialist Review*, vol. 16, no. 3–4, August 1986, pp. 7–40.

16 Favier and Roland, *Les Epreuves*, op. cit., pp. 184–190. Of great symbolic importance, in 1985, the state refused to bale out the worker's cooperative ManuFrance. In June 1984, the state refused to save Creusot-Loire, the mechanical engineering giant employing 22,000 workers. On the reform of the Paris Bourse, see P. Pons, 'A la bourse, de la fin du monde à la fin d'un monde', *La Croix*, 5–6 May 1991.

17 A. Bizaguet, 'L'évolution récente du secteur publique français', *La Revue du Trésor*, June 1987, pp.355–388. Cohen, op. cit., p.13.

18 From August 1982 to March 1983, J-P. Chevènement, leader of the CERES faction, had been a highly interventionist industry minister, much to the chagrin of the leadership teams appointed to run these industries. It was indicative that it was Chevènement who was forced out in March 1983, rather than the heads of the state firms; this symbolised a turning point. Under the next industry ministers, Fabius and Cresson, the profit motive prevailed.

19 Cited in L. Rapp, 'Le secteur public français entre nationalisations et privatisations', *Droit Administratif*, 20 May 1987, pp. 303–308.

20 The precedent was not strictly speaking repeated in 1993, not least because the RPR leader Chirac did not want the premiership. The nomination of Balladur corresponded in many respects to this model, however, since Balladur had 'emerged' as the RPR's contender for premier.

21 For a detailed assessment of the 1988 presidential election, see J. Gaffney (ed.), *The French Presidential Election of 1988: Ideology and Leadership in Contemporary France*, Aldershot, Dartmouth, 1989.

22 The surprising factor was that Mitterrand called upon voters not to elect a large Socialist majority, in order to encourage non-Socialists to rally to support the government. This infuriated his old party, the PS, but failed to convince the centrists.

23 The best known of the so-called *Ministres de l'Ouverture* were J-M. Rausch, J-P. Soisson and L. Stoléru, the latter two both ministers in the centre-right governments of Raymond Barre. Neither was initially present in the Bérégovoy administration, although Soisson returned later on. Several non-Socialists were present in Bérégovoy's team, of whom Bernard Kouchner, the secretary of state for humanitarian action (and habitual escort of Danielle Mitterrand) was the most effective.

24 In November 1990, and in June 1992, the government survived votes of no confidence supported by all groups except the PS, *including* the PCF. The repeated use that Rocard and his successors had made of article 49, clause 3 (which allows a government to stake its future on the successful vote of a government bill) was one factor helping to accentuate the divergence between a discourse based on consensus and a political practice – necessarily – based on executive manipulation.

25 A. Duhamel, 'Le triennat de Michel Rocard', *SOFRES – l'Etat de l'opinion*, Paris, Gallimard, 1992, pp. 89–107.

26 For detailed analysis, see *La Lettre de Matignon*, no. 232, 6 September 1988; no. 245, 23 January 1989; no. 286, 23 January 1990; no. 297, 17 April 1990. Rocard himself liked to cite the reform of the PTT as a major achievement: in 1990, the huge *Postes et Telecommunications* was broken up into two separate, more market-oriented, organisations.

27 For a partisan assessment, see J-P. Worms, 'The Rocard government and reforming French society', *French Politics and Society*, vol. 9, no. 2, Spring 1991, pp. 1–8.

28 This disillusioned certain of his traditional supporters, who accused Rocard of having abandoned the legacy of the second left, notably the duty to 'speak the truth'. Interview with J-P. Worms.

29 Witness Mitterrand's comments of mid-1990: 'We must take account of the needs of workers, without forgetting the constraints imposed by the economy'; or, in relation to the protesting schoolchildren: 'We must satisfy the demands of schoolchildren without upsetting their teachers'. As always, Mitterrand attempted to occupy the position of the *juste milieu*. Cited in J-L. Andreani 'Rocard a besoin de temps', *Le Monde*, 18–19 November 1990.

30 See E. Dupin, 'Les Hauts et les bas de la décennie Mitterrand', *SOFRES: L'Etat de l'opinion*, Paris, Gallimard, 1992, pp. 73–85; A. Duhamel, 'Le Triennat de Michel Rocard', *SOFRES: L'Etat de l'opinion*, Paris, Gallimard, 1992, pp. 89–107.

31 Gélédan, op. cit., pp. 209–215. By 1993, inflation had stabilised at under 3 per cent, compared with over 14 per cent in 1981. France obtained a rare trade surplus in 1992. Under the impact of the economic downturn after 1990, the budget deficit had deteriorated from 1.4 per cent of GNP in 1989 to an estimated 3 per cent in 1993, but this compared favourably with most of France's partners, and remained within the Maastricht guidelines. The main public policy failure was in relation to unemployment (from 8 per cent in 1981 to over 10 per cent in 1992), well above the OECD average (8 per cent). Economic growth oscillated from 5 per cent in the exceptional year of 1988, to 1 per cent in 1991, when the effects of the downturn made themselves felt.

32 The 1989 budget stands out as the best example of this: Rocard managed to negotiate the abstention of the UDC group on the 1989 budget, thereby facilitating

its passage through the Assembly without having to resort to article 49, clause 3.

33 In the words of one analyst, 'François Mitterrand does not seem to be in a hurry to descend into the domestic arena'. C. Fauvet-Mycia, 'Rocard et Mitterrand se repassent l'élan', *Libération*, 3 April 1991.
34 Interview with an anonyomous PS deputy.
35 Interview with J-P. Worms, PS deputy.
36 Figures derived from 'Dix mois de solitude', *Le Monde*, 3 April 1992; O. Duhamel and J. Jaffré, 'Edith Cresson à Matignon, ou la confection d'une impopularité', *SOFRES: l'état de l'opinion*, Paris, Gallimard, 1992, pp.109–123; and J. Jaffré, 'Socialistes et l'opinion: le divorce', *Le Monde*, 23 January 1992.
37 On the latter aspect, see J. Shields, 'Race: France's new political agenda', unpublished paper presented to the Political Studies Association conference, Belfast, 7–9 April 1992, p. 9.
38 *Lettre de Matignon*, no. 370, 14 March 1992.
39 This was confirmed in various interviews.
40 Gélédan, op. cit., pp. 155–58.
41 Interviews with PS deputies.

4 THE ENIGMA OF FRANÇOIS MITTERRAND

1 See in particular P. Favier and M. Martin-Roland, *La Décennie Mitterrand*, Paris, Seuil, 1990 and 1991; F-O. Giesbert, *Le Président*, Paris, Seuil, 1990; C. Nay, *Les Sept Mitterrand*, Paris, Grasset, 1988. The two volume set by Favré and Roland can claim to be the most informative, deriving its material from access to the Elysée archives, although it contains the usual pitfalls of the journalistic genre. The penetrating work by Serge July, *Les Années Mitterrand*, Paris, Grasset, 1986, comes closer than any other to capturing the essence of François Mitterrand. Little of sustained biographical interest has appeared in English.
2 The image has arisen in numerous conversations with David Goldey of Lincoln College, Oxford; the expression was conveniently used in an editorial in *The Independent*, 3 September 1992.
3 These themes were forwarded in several interviews with close Mitterrand aides.
4 The expression *énarque* is that commonly attributed to graduates of the *Ecole Nationale d'Administration*, the highly prestigious school for administration which trains France's politico-administrative elite.
5 See P. Yana, 'Sur l'homme d'état écrivain', *Lignes*, no. 5, February 1989, pp. 97–108; C. Imbert, 'Un personnage de roman', *Le Débat*, no. 20, May 1982, pp. 4–13.
6 J. Daniel, *Les Religions d'un Président*, Paris, Grasset, 1988, p.63.
7 These themes are all apparent in F. Mitterrand, *Ma part de vérité*, Paris, Fayard, 1969. See pp. 24–25 in particular.
8 *Ma part de vérité*, p. 8.
9 In Mitterrand's own account: 'My parents detested hierarchies based on the privileges of money. For them, money was the enemy, the corrupter with which one should not compromise. Their Christian faith strengthened this belief.' *Ma part de vérité*, p. 17.
10 In his journal entry for 16 March 1978, Mitterrand bewails: 'Money, always money. Money, Money everywhere', François Mitterrand, *Politique* II, Paris, Fayard, 1981, p. 201.
11 R. Cayrol, *François Mitterrand, 1945–67*, Paris, CEVIPOF, 1967, pp. 25–26. The *loi Barangé* of 1951 introduced an element of state support for private (i.e. church) schools.
12 Mitterrand's distrust of the Catholic hierarchy was repeated in various interviews.

13 Interview with Jacques Attali.
14 Cited in *Influences*, no. 1, January 1988.
15 Mitterrand, *Ma part de vérité*, pp. 19–20.
16 Interview with Jean Daniel.
17 Cited in *Combat*, 7 July 1945.
18 See J. Lacouture, *Pierre Mendès-France*, Paris, Seuil, 1983, pp. 229–230. The attraction exercised by Mendès-France on Mitterrand at this stage was repeatedly stressed by Jean Daniel in an interview with the author.
19 Mitterrand, *Politique II*, p. 167.
20 Daniel, op. cit., p. 311.
21 'Le Contrat socialiste', in D. Loschak, *François Mitterrand et la Convention des institutions républicaines*, Paris, PUF, 1971, pp. 48–55; Parti socialiste, *Changer la Vie*, Paris, Flammarion, 1972; PS, PCF, and MRG, *Le Program Commun*, Paris, Flammarion, 1972.
22 H. Hamon and P. Rotman, *La Deuxième gauche*, Paris, Seuil, 1986.
23 'La rencontre socialiste de Grenoble', *Le Monde*, 3 May 1966.
24 Interview with Mitterrand in *Témoignage chrétien*, 26 February 1979.
25 This thesis was supported in the author's interview with Jean Daniel.
26 Interview with *Témoignage chrétien*, 26 February 1979.
27 Rocard's speech is reprinted in the *Nouvelle Revue Socialiste*, no. 27, 1977, pp. 69–76.
28 Interview with *Témoignage chrétien*, 26 February 1979.
29 On this aspect, see Michel Rocard, *Qu'est-ce que la social-démocratie*, Paris, Stock, 1977.
30 Mitterrand, *Politique* II, p. 172.
31 See G. Groux and R. Mouriaux, 'François Mitterrand et les ouvriers', *French Politics and Society*, vol. 9, no. 3–4, summer/fall 1991, pp. 43–62.
32 Mitterrand, *Politique* II, pp. 219.
33 Interview with Serge July in *Libération*, 10 May 1984.
34 Ibid.
35 John Gaffney, 'Mitterrand as President', unpublished paper presented to the PSA conference, Queen's University of Belfast, 7–9 April 1992, p.30.
36 See H. Portelli. 'Le républicanisme de François Mitterrand', *La Vie française*, 17 February 1985.
37 This assessment is provoked by Gaffney's stimulating article, 'Mitterrand as President', op. cit.
38 This was repeatedly affirmed in interviews with people close to Mitterrand, perhaps rather over-anxious to rehabilitate their man?

5 THE PARTY LEADER

1 According to Louis Mexandeau, Mitterrand prevented the CIR from transforming itself into a small party, because 'he was too big for a small party'. Interview, 22 September 1987.
2 Mitterrand was a member of the praesidium and a deputy. He was President only from December 1970 to May 1971. D. Loschak, *La Convention des Institutions Républicaines: François Mitterrand et le socialisme*, Paris, Armand Colin, 1970, p. 76.
3 Louis Mermaz, 'La quatrième session de la Convention de Lyon', unpublished circular dated 12–13 March 1966. Also Loschak, op. cit., p.74.
4 For instance: Roland Dumas in Corrèze; Charles Hernu in Indre; Jacques Maugein in Gironde; Louis Mermaz in Isère; Georges Vinson in Rhône; Guy Penne in Vaucluse, et cetera.

5 Jean-Claude Vajou, 'M. Maroselli quitte la Convention', *Combat*, 1 March 1968. Maroselli claimed that Mitterrand personally had nominated the Convention's representatives to the executive committee of the Federation, without consulting the CIR's Standing Committee.
6 Loschak, op. cit. p. 77.
7 See A. Cole and P. Campbell, *French Electoral Systems and Elections since 1789*, Aldershot, Gower, 1989, pp. 116–120, 124–131 for further explanation.
8 It was not the only party which aspired to represent these groups; it faced fierce competition from the centre–right, most especially Giscard d'Estaing's UDF. On the evolution of the *cadres* in postwar France, see H. Mendras and A. Cole, *Social Change in Modern France*, Cambridge, Cambridge University Press, 1991, Chapter 2.
9 See in particular Jacques Capdeveille *et al.*, *France de gauche, vote à droite*, Paris, Presses de la FNSP, 1981; E. Schweisguth, 'Les couches moyennes salariées sont-elles socialistes?', *Intervention*, no. 5–6, August-October 1983, pp. 58–66.
10 See, *inter alia*, P. Hardouin, 'Les caracteristiques sociologiques du parti socialiste', *Revue française de science politique*, April 1978, pp. 220–256; P. Hardouin,' Le PS: un parti d'intellectuels', *Intervention*, no. 5–6, August-September 1983, pp.66–76; H. Rey and F. Subileau, 'Les militants socialistes en 1985', *Projet*, no. 198, April 1986, pp.19–34.
11 Hardouin, 'Le PS: un parti d'intellectuels?', p. 68. This was in spite of the fact that the new party created workplace sections (*sections d'entreprise*), and loudly proclaimed its attachment to the working class.
12 Ibid. The parties of the Right, by contrast, were largely dominated by a business and professional elite.
13 S. Padgett, 'The Godesburg model: the transformation of the German Social-Democratic Party', pp. 27. Unpublished paper presented to the 1992 PSA conference, Belfast, 7–9 April 1992.
14 The expression is from R. Cayrol, 'La direction du Parti socialiste: organisation et fonctionnement', *Revue Française de Science Politique*, vol. 28, no. 2, April 1978, pp. 202–220.
15 On this concept, see A. Cole, 'The Presidential Party and the Fifth Republic', *West European Politics*, vol. 16, no. 2, April 1993, pp. 44–66.
16 Cited in J. Charlot, 'Le Président et le parti majoritaire', *Revue politique et parlementaire*, no. 905, August 1983, p. 28.
17 H. Portelli, 'Le Parti socialiste à l'épreuve du pouvoir', unpublished paper presented to the AFSP conference 1985, p.7. See also H. Portelli, *Le Parti socialiste*, Paris, Montchrestien, 1992.
18 D. Chagnollaud, 'La nomination des hauts fonctionnaires ou les arcanes de la politisation', unpublished paper presented to the AFSP National Congress, 5–8 October 1988, pp. 34.
19 *Le Monde*, 31 October 1983.
20 Document consulted in PS archives, Lille.
21 M. Schifres and M. Sarazin, *L'Elysée de Mitterrand*, Paris, Alain Moreau, 1985, pp. 278–80. This was confirmed in several interviews held by the author in Paris in February and March 1993.
22 See J-M. Colombani, 'Le Président et le parti', *Le Monde*, 17 March 1990.
23 Thus, at the party's Directing Committee of 26–27 March 1983, Jospin admitted that the measures adopted in the Delors plan 'do not correspond to what we wanted'. Cited in *Le Poing et la rose, spécial responsables*, no. 158, 26 March 1983.
24 *Libération*, 31 October 1983.
25 The negative effect of these amendments was stressed in an interview with PS deputy J-P. Worms in February 1993.

26 It was suggested to the author in an anonymous interview with a leading Socialist deputy that Mauroy's victory was actually engineered by Mitterrand in order to chasten a disloyal Fabius. Even this machiavellian interpretation would not diminish the importance of the divisions produced among former *mitterrandistes*.

27 According to J-P. Worms, divisions within the Socialist group occurred not only in relation to official *courants*, but also in relation to geographical location (with deputies from neighbouring areas often forming common cause) and attitudes adopted to specific policies.

28 R. Elgie, *The Influence of the French Prime Minister in the Policy-Making Process, 1981–1991*, unpublished PhD thesis, London School of Economics, 1992, pp. 130–135.

29 This was affirmed by J-M. Belorgey, PS deputy, President of the Social Affairs Commission of the National Assembly, in an interview in March 1993.

30 See P. Jarreau, 'Le fait accompli', *Le Monde*, 8 January 1992; J-M. Colombani, 'Changer, jusqu'au où?, *Le Monde*, 10 January 1992.

31 This impression was confirmed in several interviews.

32 1988 figure from Cole and Campbell, op cit., pp. 160–173. Figures for 1993 from *Le Figaro*, 23 March 1993, *Le Monde*, 30 March 1993.

33 This point was stressed by J-P. Worms. Mitterrand forced through an amnesty for the rebellious general in the French Algerian army involved in the attempted 1961 coup against the Gaullist regime.

34 It was suggested in interviews that this occurred notably in relation to the 1982 nationalisation programme, and to early pro-Third World foreign policy initiatives.

35 In February 1993, *Le Canard enchaîné* revealed that Bérégovoy had obtained an interest-free loan of 1,000,000 francs from Patrice Pélat, a close Mitterrand aide hopelessly compromised over the Pechiney scandal. While not illegal, this increased public cynicism with regard to the ruling Socialists.

6   THE PRESIDENT

1 F. Mitterrand, *Le coup d'état permanent*, Paris, Plon, 1964.

2 Cited in R. Hadas-Lebel, 'François Mitterrand et la fonction présidentielle', *French Politics and Society*, vol. 9, nos 3–4, Summer–Fall 1991, p.2.

3 V. Wright, 'President and Prime Minister during the Fifth Republic', in J. Hayward (ed.), *De Gaulle to Mitterrand: Presidential Power in France*, London, Hurst, 1994, pp. 101–119.

4 Cited in Hadas-Lebel, op. cit., p.1.

5 See, *inter alia*, S. Rails, *Le Premier ministre*, Paris, PUF, 1985; F. de Bacque, *Qui gouverne la France*, Paris, PUF, 1976; J. Massot, *Le chef du gouvernement en France*, Paris, Documentation française, 1979; J. Massot, *L'Arbitre et le capitaine*, Paris, Flammarion, 1987.

6 See R. Elgie, *The French Prime Minister*, London, Macmillan, 1993, Chapters 1 and 2, for a coherent explanation of alternative policy-making models. Also R. Elgie and H. Machin, 'France: the limits to prime ministerial government in a semi-presidential system', *West European Politics*, vol. 14, no. 2, pp. 62–78.

7 J-L. Thiebault, 'Jalons pour une analyse des conflits gouvernementaux sous la Vème République', *Les Cahiers du CRAPS*, no. 7, 1989, pp. 20–48.

8 See, for instance, Hadas-Lebel, op. cit. This impression was confirmed in interviews with leading members of Mitterrand's entourage.

9 F. Mitterrand, 'Sur les institutions', *Pouvoirs*, no. 45, 1988, pp. 132–139.

10 Thiebault, op. cit. ,pp. 42–44.

11 Massot, *L'Arbitre et le Capitaine*, pp. 133–135.

12 Interviews with Jacques Attali, and Hubert Védrine.

13 A. Duhamel, 'Les sept ans de F. Mitterrand: le Président-phénix', pp. 11–29, *SOFRES: L'Etat de l'Opinion*, Paris, Gallimard, 1988.

14 In an anonymous interview, one member of Savary's *cabinet* stressed the animosity reigning between members of the said *cabinet*, and the presidential entourage in relation to the 1984 bill.

15 P. Favier and M. Martin-Roland, *La Décennie Mitterrand: 2. Les Epreuves*, Paris, Seuil, 1991, p. 177.

16 Ibid., pp. 175–176. On the Mauroy premiership, see T. Pfister, *A Matignon au temps de l'Union de la Gauche*, Paris, Hachette, 1985, pp. 7–63.

17 See J-M Colombani, 'Les habits neufs de François Mitterrand', *Le Monde*, 20 March 1991. According to one advisor, in his frequent meetings with Rocard, Mitterrand would offer his opinion on government policy, which varied between expressions of neutrality and polite preferences.

18 'Dix mois de solitude', *Le Monde*, 3 April 1992; see also O. Duhamel and J. Jaffré, 'Edith Cresson à Matignon, ou la confection d'une impopularité', *SOFRES: l'état de l'opinion*, Paris, Gallimard, 1992, pp. 109–123.

19 See Elgie, *The French Prime Minister in the Policy-Making Process*, Chapters 1 and 2 for a detailed and skilful dissection of the various models governing presidential–prime ministerial relations in France.

20 O. Duhamel 'Cinq innovations de l'alternance', *Le Monde*, 26 March 1986; H. Portelli, 'Les conquêtes tranquilles du Premier ministre', *Projet*, no. 202, December 1986, pp. 49–59. No such attempt was made in 1993, with the President greatly weakened by electoral defeat.

21 On Mitterrand's cultural and media policy see M. Harrison, 'The President, cultural projects and the mass media', in Hayward, op. cit., pp. 190–218.

22 Notably, from Laurent Fabius, President of the National Assembly; and from Henri Emmanuelli and Jean Auroux, successive presidents of the Socialist group.

23 J. Fournier, *Le Travail gouvernemental*, Paris, Presses de la FNSP, 1987; R. Py, *Le Secrétariat Général du Gouvernement*, Paris, Documentation Française, 1985; B. Chenot *et al.*, *Le Secrétariat Général du Gouvernement*, Paris, Economica, 1986; M. Long, 'L'organisation du travail du gouvernement', *Revue des Sciences Morales et Politiques*, 1982, pp. 91–107.

24 See, *inter alia*, M-C. Kessler, 'Le cabinet du premier ministre et le secrétaire général du gouvernement', pp. 69–103 in F. de Baecque et J-L. Quermonne, *Administration et politique sous la cinquième république*, Paris, Presses de la FNSP, 1982.

25 See J-P. Huchon, *Jours tranquilles à Matignon*, Paris, Grasset, 1993, for an insider view.

26 Anne Stevens, 'The President and his staff', in Hayward, op. cit., pp. 76–100. For a general evaluation of the presidential staff in the Fifth Republic, see the various works by Samy Cohen, notably 'Le Secrétariat général de la présidence de la République' in de Baecque and Quermonne, op. cit., pp. 104–127.

27 Stevens, op. cit., p. 76–83. These figures do not include part-timers and unofficial advisers.

28 For a comparison of the Elysée with the White House, see S. Cohen, 'Les conseillers de l'Elysée face aux hommes de la maison blanche: spécificité du cas français', in J-L. Seurin *et al.*, *La Présidence de la République en France et aux Etats-Unis*, Paris, Economica, 1986, pp. 206–217.

29 Interview with H. Védrine.

30 Figures from Stevens, op. cit., pp. 76–83.

31 P. Simmonnot, 'Régis Debray: le prêcheur de respect' *L'Express*, 15 October 1982. Debray, an ex-freedom fighter with Che Guevara, acted as the 'third world conscience' within the Mitterrand entourage.

32 C. Fauvet-Mycia, 'L'Elysée: maison des fidèles, puis machine présidentielle', *Libération*, 6 May 1991. Of 60 advisers serving in the presidential staff from 1981–91, Fauvet-Mycia calculates that:

- 5 became Ministers or Secretaries of State;
- 5 were elected as deputies;
- 4 were named *Directeurs du cabinet* in government departments;
- 17 acceded to *grands corps* (7 Conseil d'état, 2 Cours des comptes, 3 Inspection générale; 5 Prefects);
- 18 to top civil service, or to management posts in nationalised industries;
- with the remainder occupying lesser posts within the civil service; international postings, or, very exceptionally, positions in private industry.

33 For instance, Michèle Gendreau-Massalou, who failed in her attempt to be elected as a PS deputy in 1988.

34 F. Lazare, 'Le mystère Lauvergeon', *Le Monde*, 12 April 1991.

35 E. Guigou, Secretary of state for European Affairs, 1992–93; S. Royal, Minister of the Environment, 1992–93.

36 This point was stressed in an interview with Jean Daniel.

37 E. Izraélewicz and P. Jarreau, 'Une génération aux commandes', *Le Monde*, 11 May 1991.

38 A. Rollat, 'Les vigies de l'Elysée', *Le Monde*, 29 July 1992. They were H. Védrine (General Secretary), P. Dreyfus, F. de Grossouvre, P. Dayan, L. Soudet and P. Decraene. We should note that Védrine, de Grossouvre, and Dreyfus had not served continually since 1981.

39 G.Ottenheimer, 'Les nouveau hommes de Mitterrand', *Quotidien de Paris*, 9 May 1989, and Fauvet-Mycia, op. cit. maintain the interventionist thesis; Massot, in *L'Arbitre et le capitaine* doubts this, arguing that it would have been 'materially impossible for the 18 or so presidential advisers to attend several meetings daily', p. 135.

40 The contention was from Fauvet-Mycia, op. cit. Interviews with members of Mitterrand's staff contradicted this precise information, but agreed that presidential advisers performed a more restrained role after 1982.

41 Ibid. Fauvet-Mycia points to the clashes between Alain Boulbil, Mitterrand's industrial adviser, and Jean Pierre Chevenement, Industry Minister.

42 'Colé-Pilhan, 'Vénération Mitterrand', in *La Famille tonton*, Paris, Les Dossiers du canard, 1991, pp. 24–26.

43 G. Bresson, 'L'Elysée en cure de demi-sommeil', *Libération*, 28 April 1986.

44 They were B. Pecheur, H. Védrine (who replaced Bianco as General Secretary in May 1991), E. Guigou (to become European affairs minister in 1992), J. Audouze, and Attali's replacement as special adviser, A. Lauvergeon.

45 Interview with H. Védrine.

46 See A.M. Le Bos-Le Pourhiet, 'Les emplois à la discrétion', *Pouvoirs*, no. 40, 1987, pp. 121–133; A. Passerron, 'Comment ils ont placé leurs amis', *Pouvoirs*, no. 40, 1987, pp. 25–30.

47 Figures vary somewhat according to source. Figures cited are from D. Lochak, 'Les hauts fonctionnaires et l'alternance', unpublished paper presented to the AFSP colloquium on *Le Modèle Français d'Administration: Est-il en crise?*, 7–8 February 1993, pp. 1–17.

48 Figures from D. Chagnollaud, 'La nomination des hauts fonctionnaires ou les arcanes de la politisation', unpublished paper presented to the 3rd National Congress of the French Political Science Association, 5–8 October 1988, Bordeaux. p. 34.

49 'Les rocardiens et l'état', *Le Monde*, 30 November 1990.

50 Cited in Le Monde, *Bilan du septennat*, 1988, p.37.

51 F. Mitterrand, 'Lettre a tous les Français', *Libération*, 7 April 1988.
52 Especially article 49, clause 3 of the 1958 constitution, which allows a government to stake its future on the passage of a bill through the National Assembly. This device was used repeatedly by the Rocard, Cresson and Bérégovoy governments.

7 MITTERRAND'S GOVERNING STYLE

1 On the accuracy of the comparison, see O. Duhamel, 'Sur la monarchie présidentielle', *Le Débat*, no. 55, August 1989, pp. 23–27.
2 S. July, *Les années Mitterrand*, Paris, Grasset, 1986, pp. 77–101; P. Bauchard, *La Guerre des deux roses*, Paris, Grasset, 1986, pp. 139–154.
3 Bauchard, op. cit., p.145.
4 The best account is M. Schifres and M. Sarazin, *L'Elysée de Mitterrand*, Paris, Albin Moreau, 1985, pp. 109–124.
5 Ibid., pp. 109–110.
6 C. Fauvet-Mycia, 'Elysée: maison des fidèles, puis machine présidentielle', *Libération*, 6 May 1991.
7 Mitterrand proposed to change the 1958 constitution to enable more frequent referendums, and to hold a referendum to this effect. The proposal was killed off by the Senate, but served its immediate purpose of distracting attention.
8 S. Hayward, 'French politicians and political communication, in A. Cole, *French Political Parties in Transition*, Aldershot, Dartmouth, 1990, p. 28.
9 See Raymond Kuhn, *The Media in France*, London, Routledge, 1995, for an overview of media reforms during the Mitterrand presidency. Also M. Harrison, 'The politics of media reform', in P. Hall *et al.*, *Developments in French Politics*, London, Macmillan, 1990, pp. 237–252.
10 Mitterrand once maintained that 'my wife is far more left-wing than I am'. Cited in D. Frémy, *Quid des présidents de la République*, Paris, Laffont, 1987, p. 552.
11 D. de Montvalon and B. Mazières, 'L'Enigme Danielle Mitterrand', *L'Express*, 3 November 1989.
12 According to one observer: 'The Franco-Mexican declaration of 28th August 1981 in support of the Sandanista regime [was] vetoed by the Foreign ministry, revived and awarded the presidential imprimatur through a cabal involving the Socialist Party international affairs bureau, the inclinations of Elysée expert Régis Debray, and the influence of the president's wife'. Cited in Michael M. Harrison 'Mitterrand's France in the Atlantic System: a foreign policy of accommodation', *Political Science Quarterly*, vol. 99, no. 2, Summer 1984, p. 222.
13 F-O. Giesbert, *Le Président*, Paris, Seuil, 1990, p. 357.
14 Interview with J-P. Cot, 30 March. Cot had criticised French policy towards Africa, and decried the influence of Guy Penne, Mitterrand's African adviser. Cot's departure represented the 'normalisation of Socialist policy towards Africa'.
15 Under *cohabitation*, there was a concerted, partially successful effort to capture control of African policy for Chirac's conservative government; an African cell was established at Matignon to this effect under the control of de Gaulle's key adviser Jacques Foccart. And yet, the President's African adviser remained a key figure.
16 'Famille: touche pas à mon népote', in *La Famille Tonton*, Paris, Les dossiers du Canard, 1991, pp. 32–34.
17 The following information is based on S. Smith and A. Glaser, 'Les réseaux africains de Jean-Christophe Mitterrand', *Libération*, 6 July 1990; and 'Les tribulations du fils de Tonton', *L'Evénement du jeudi*, 7 June 1990.
18 M-P. Subtil, 'M. Bruno Délaye remplace M. Jean-Christophe Mitterrand', *Le Monde*, 7 July 1992.

19 It is alleged by P. Favier and M. Martin-Roland, in *La Decennie Mitterrand: 2. Les Epreuves*, Paris, Seuil, 1991, p. 566n, that Mitterrand intervened personally in relation to Pasqua, Chirac's Interior Minister, in order to safeguard Gilbert Mitterrand's Gironde constituency from excessive gerrymandering in the 1986 boundary revision. This did not help Gilbert in 1993, when the President's son narrowly lost his seat.

20 M. Peltier, 'La Dynastie des Mitterrand', *Le Quotidien de Paris*, 2 December 1982.

21 M. Peltier, 'La Dynastie des Mitterrand', *Le Quotidien de Paris*, 8 November 1982.

22 Ibid., 9 November 1982.

23 M-T. Guichard, 'La cour', *Le Point*, 21 November 1988.

24 Giesbert, op. cit., pp. 357–358.

25 Guichard, op. cit.

26 See 'La chambre d'amis', in *La Famille Tonton*, op. cit. pp. 105–106.

27 Giesbert, op. cit., p. 357.

28 Frémy, op. cit. p. 515.

29 Guichard, op. cit.; Peltier, *Le Quotidien de Paris*, 18–19 December 1982. In the case of Frédéric, there was no evidence that Mitterrand had explicitly intervened; rather, that it was considered an astute move to promote a relative of the President.

30 See D. Mohlo, 'Elysée an III: les choses de la vie', *Le Point*, 7 May 1984; 'Merci Tonton Noël', in *La Famille Tonton*, op. cit., pp. 103–104; Fauvet-Mycia, op. cit. The tragic suicide of François de Grossouvre in his office within the Elysée Palace in 1994 cast a shadow over the final year of Mitterrand's presidency, leading to the darkest, if unsubstantiated, rumours.

31 Dayan was named as General Secretary of the *Conseil supérieur de la magistrature* in December 1992, a key post in the judicial hierarchy. *Le Monde*, 26 December 1992.

32 This was stressed notably in interviews with Jean Daniel and Jacques Attali.

33 Guichard, op. cit; 'Merci Tonton Noël', op. cit. Thus, the *légion d'honneur* was bestowed upon: Gerard Dépardieu, Barbara, Jeanne Moreau, and Jacques Seguela for services rendered to Mitterrand.

34 'Claude Gubler: un personnage ausculte', in *La Famille Tonton*, op. cit., pp. 10–11. Gubler was named to serve in the *Inspection générale de la securité sociale*. Gubler caused serious controversy immediately after Mitterrand's death, when he revealed that the former President had been suffering from cancer since 1981. The Mitterrand family cried foul, and obtained an injunction against the distribution of Gubler's book, *Le Grand Secret*.

35 Pierre Joxe, president of the PS group in the National Assembly, 1981–84, Minister of the Interior, 1984–86, 1988–91, Minister of Defence 1991–93. Claude Estier, ex-Socialist deputy. Charles Hernu, Defence minister 1981–85, until forced to resign over the Greenpeace scandal. Edith Cresson, prime minister May 1991–April 1992. Georges Fillioud, former Minister for Communications (1981-86).

36 H. Tincq, 'Les trois générations de mitterrandistes', *Le Matin*, 23 September 1982. This article designates only three generations.

37 See B. Abescat, and C. Lhaik, 'Les patrons du patron', *Le Point*, 16–22 May 1988. Also 'Bernard Tapie: le repreneur récupéré', in *La Famille Tonton*, op cit., pp. 81–85.

8 THE EUROPEAN STATESMAN

1 R. Dulith, 'Au congrès de l'UDSR', *Le Monde*, 20 October 1952.

2 Cited in R. Barrillon, 'Après le congrès d'Aix-les-Bains', *Le Monde*, 2 November 1954.

3 F. Mitterrand, *Réflexions sur la Politique Extérieure de la France*, Paris, Fayard, 1986, pp. 66–67.

4 Cited in T. Desjardins, *François Mitterrand: un socialiste gaullien*, Paris, Hachette, 1978, p. 116.

5 From 1965–66, de Gaulle refused to attend the Council of Ministers, in protest against proposals to extend the powers of the European parliament, and to introduce majority voting within EC institutions. In 1966, the 'Luxembourg compromise' was reached, according to which countries could veto matters of 'vital national interest'.

6 'History will condemn de Gaulle for having blocked the construction of Europe'. Interview with *L'Express*, 11–17 September 1967.

7 F. Mitterrand, *Un Socialisme du possible*, Paris, Le Seuil, 1970, p. 97.

8 These themes are developed in greater detail in G. Lemaire-Prosche, *Le P.S. et l'Europe*, Paris, Editions universitaires, 1990; and G. Lemaire-Prosche, 'L'Identité européenne du Parti socialiste français', *Revue du Marché commun*, no. 343, January 91, pp. 49–56.

9 Motion reprinted in *Le Poing et la rose*, supplement to no. 73, August 1978.

10 The expression is used in H. Drake, 'François Mitterrand, France and European Integration', in G. Raymond, *France during the Socialist Years*, Aldershot, Dartmouth, 1994, pp. 32–65.

11 'The hopes and the holes in Mitterrand's plan', *The Economist*, 17 October 1981; see F. de la Serre, 'La Politique européenne de la France: new look, or new deal'? *Politique Etrangère*, no. 1, 1982, pp. 125–137, for an early appreciation of Mitterrand's European policy.

12 P. Meutey, 'La France va-t-elle sortir du Marché commun?', *Le Figaro-Magazine*, 29 January 1983.

13 'M.Mitterrand semble résolu à faire des questions européennes une affaire personnelle', *Le Monde*, 9 January 1984.

14 P. Moreau-Défarges, 'J'ai fait une rêve...Le président Mitterrand, artisan de l'union européenne', *Politique Etrangère*, no. 2, 1985, pp. 359–375.

15 Mitterrand, *Réflexions sur la politique extérieure de la France*, pp. 183–208.

16 Ibid., speech at the Hague, February 1984, pp. 267–279.

17 J-J. Kourliandsky, 'Europe: le grand chantier du Président', *Cosmopolitiques*, no. 5, December 1987, pp. 33–46; *The Economist*, 11 February 1984, 'Mitterrand looks to the stars'.

18 See S.J. Wells, 'Les Politiques étrangères de Mitterrand', *Commentaire*, no. 11, Autumn 1988, pp. 655–666.

19 The expression is Helen Drake's, op cit.

20 The Genscher–Colombo reform proposals aimed to strengthen EC institutions and to extend their competence to foreign affairs, security and cultural affairs.

21 The Spinelli initiative was so named after the Italian MEP Altiero Spinelli, who chaired a committee established by the European Parliament in July 1981, with the objective of producing a draft treaty for a new European Union.

22 See Lemaire-Prosche, *Le P.S. et l'Europe*, pp. 77–133 for an overview of Socialist European policy from 1981–86. Also E.Z. Haywood, The French socialists and institutional reform', *Journal of European Integration*, vol. 12, no. 2–3, 1989, pp. 121–150.

23 Mitterrand, *Réflexions sur la Politique Etrangère*, pp. 280–297.

24 This could be inferred from Mitterrand's Strasbourg speech of May 1984: 'Certain people have evoked a several speed Europe, or a Europe of "variable geometry". This approach, which translates a reality, is inevitable. We must make sure that it is complementary to the Community, and not in competition with it'. Ibid., p. 296.

25 A. Grosser, 'Raymond Barre, François Mitterrand et l'Europe', *Le Monde* 24 December 1985.

26 Cited in L. Chauvin, *L'Idée d'Europe chez François Mitterrand*, unpublished thesis, Institute of Political Studies, Paris, 1989, pp. 108–9.

27 See S. Cohen, 'François le gaullien et Mitterrand l'Européen', *Histoire*, no. 143, April

1991, pp. 30–36; and S. Cohen, 'La politique étrangère entre l'Elysée et Matignon', *Politique Etrangère*, no. 3, 1989, pp. 487–503, for a more detailed account.

28 J. Howorth, 'The President's special role in foreign policy and defence'. Paper presented to the conference on the French Presidency from de Gaulle to Mitterrand, Maison française, Oxford, June 1991. Howorth claims: 'the one area where Jacques Chirac failed markedly to exercise any real influence was in defence and foreign policy'.

29 One of Mitterrand's key foreign policy advisers, in an anonymous interview with the author, dismissed the Right's attempt to deprive Mitterrand of information as a 'trivial game', which did not prevent the President from receiving all relevant information. We should note that, prior to the 1993 elections, Mitterrand ensured that the Elysée was linked by computer to the Quai d'Orsay so that the presidency would receive all documentation.

30 Opinion poll cited by Chauvin, op. cit., p. 111.

31 Drake, op. cit., p. 55.

9 THE WORLD LEADER

1 See F. Heisbourg, 'Défense et sécurité extérieure: le changement dans la continuité', *Politique Etrangère*, no. 2, 1985, pp.377–395.

2 F. Mitterrand, *Ici et Maintenant*, Paris, Fayard, 1980, pp. 241–42.

3 These general themes are developed in detail in J. Howorth, 'The President's special role in foreign policy and defence'. Paper presented to the conference on the *French Presidency from de Gaulle to Mitterrand*, Maison française, Oxford, June 1991.

4 The most comprehensive and informed judgement is that of S. Cohen, *La Monarchie nucléaire*, Paris, Hachette, 1986.

5 Article 15 of the 1958 constitution stipulates that the President of the Republic chairs meetings of the Defence Council (involving heads of the armed forces), and is Commander-in-Chief of the Armed Forces. Article 21 asserts that the prime minister is in charge of National defence.

6 This analysis is based on an interview with Hubert Védrine.

7 Howorth, op. cit. Mitterrand's appointment of Charles Hernu to the defence portfolio occurred mainly in order to reassure the military. The Defence ministry certainly exercised more influence under Hernu's tutelage than under that of any previous incumbent. After the Greenpeace affair Mitterrand was determined to reassert presidential control over defence policy. Once Hernu had been forced out by the *Rainbow Warrior* affair, Mitterrand named three less prestigious Defence ministers: Paul Quilès (September 1985–March 1986), André Giraud (March 1986–May 1988) and Chevènement (May 1988–January 1991). In March 1991, Chevènement was replaced by Pierre Joxe. During his second mandate, Mitterrand was in complete and undisputed control over defence issues.

8 In an interview, Védrine evoked the convening of a weekly *conseil restreint* on Yugoslavia from late 1992.

9 This title is inspired by the article by S. Hoffmann, 'Mitterrand's foreign policy, or Gaullism by any other name', in G. Ross *et al.*, *The Mitterrand Experiment*, Oxford, Polity Press, 1987, pp. 294–305.

10 W.J. Feld, 'Franco-German military cooperation and European unification', *The Journal of European Integration*, vol. 12, no. 2–3, 1989, pp. 151–164.

11 '110 Propositions', in F. Mitterrand, *Politique 11*, Paris, Fayard, 1981, p. 314.

12 F. Mitterrand, *Réflexions sur la Politique extérieure de la France*, Paris, Fayard, 1986, pp. 183–208.

13   See A. Fontaine, 'Diplomatie Française: un Modèle Gaullien?' *Politique Internationale*, Summer 1991, pp. 57–67.

14   The Conference for Security and Cooperation in Europe was initially composed of 35 nations, including US, Canada and all European nations save Albania. Mitterrand could legitimately claim some credit for the permanent creation of this organisation from the 1975 Helsinki Declaration.

15   On Mitterrand's Soviet policy by comparison with that of his predecessors, see E. Kulesza, 'Les rélations Paris–Moscou de Yalta à la péréstroïka', *Regards sur l'Actualité*, no. 147, January 1989, pp. 3–12.

16   P. Favier and M. Martin-Roland, *La Décennie Mitterrand: 2. Les Epreuves*, Paris, Seuil, 1991, pp. 225–228. The expulsion of 47 Soviet diplomats in 1983 for reasons of industrial espionage gave another indication of Mitterrand's firm approach to the USSR.

17   In a press conference on the first evening of the coup, Mitterrand appeared willing to negotiate with the coup leaders. The French President had great difficulty in dispelling the unfavourable impression created by this intervention, once the coup had failed. Earlier, Mitterrand had refused to receive Yeltsin at the Elysée.

18   Mitterrand, *Politique 11*, p. 318.

19   M.M. Harrison, 'Mitterrand's France in the Atlantic System: a foreign policy of accommodation', *Political Science Quarterly*, vol. 99, no. 2, Summer 1984, pp. 219–246.

20   P. Simmonnot, 'Régis Debray, le prêcheur de respect', *L'Express*, 15 October 1982.

21   See J-P. Maulny, 'Les Relations Nord-Sud', *Cosmopolitiques*, December 1987, pp. 18–32; also S. Hessel, 'Socialist France and Developing Countries', *French Politics and Society*, vol. 9, nos 3/4, summer/fall 1991, pp. 130–139.

22   Fontaine, 'La diplomatie française', p. 61. Also A. Grosser, 'Le Rôle et le rang', *Commentaire*, no 58, summer 1992, pp. 361–365.

23   *Le Nouvel Observateur*, 21 June 1967.

24   See D. Beauchamp, 'La fin d'une illusion: la politique arabe de la France', *Commentaire*, no. 58, summer 1992, pp. 367–371.

25   See S. Cohen, 'Les conseillers de l'Elysée face aux hommes de la maison blanche: spécificité du cas français', in J-L. Seurin *et al.*, *La Présidence de la République en France et aux Etats-Unis*, Paris, Economica, 1986, p. 210–11.

26   C. Batsch, 'L'Afrique noire plus proche que jamais', *Cosmopolitiques*, December 1987, pp. 67–78.

27   Hessel, op. cit., p. 133.

28   J-F. Bayart, *La Politique Africaine de François Mitterrand*, Paris, Kathala, 1984; J-F Bayart, 'France-Afrique: La fin du pacte colonial', *Politique Africaine*, no. 39, September 1990, pp. 47–53. A. Chenal, 'La Politique française au Maghreb et au Proche-Orient', *Cosmopolitiques*, December 1987, pp. 79–87.

29   E. Kolodziej, 'Socialist France faces the world', *Contemporary French Civilisation*, vol. 8, no. 1–2, Winter 1984, pp. 158–180.

30   J-F. Bayart, 'La problématique de la démocratie en Afrique noir', *Politique Africaine*, no. 43, October 1991, pp. 5–20.

31   Interview with Hubert Védrine.

32   See J. Jenson, 'How the French Left learned to love the bomb', *New Left Review*, no. 146, August 1984, pp. 5–36.

33   Flexible response stipulated that tactical nuclear weapons would be used in the first resort to deter an attack, conventional or otherwise, on a NATO member. A strategic nuclear riposte would occur only after one, or a series of, tactical nuclear warning shots.

34   Cohen, *La Monarchie Nucléaire*, p. 15; J. Howorth, 'Foreign and Defence Policy:

from Independence to Interdependence', in P. Hall, J. Hayward and H. Machin, *Developments in French Politics*, London, Macmillan, 1990, pp. 201–218.
35 See D. Yost, 'Mitterrand and Defence and Security Policy', *French Politics and Society*, vol. 9, no. 3–4, summer/fall 1991, pp. 141–158.
36 M. M. Harrison, op. cit., p. 223.
37 H. Stark, 'Dissonances franco-allemandes sur fond de guerre serbo-croate', *Politique Etrangère*, vol. 57, no. 2, summer 1992, pp. 339–346.
38 See S. Cohen, 'Le Président, chef des armées', *Pouvoirs*, 58, 1991, pp. 33–40. Also J-M. Colombani, 'L'exercice solitaire de la décision', *Le Monde*, 22 January 1991. Premier Rocard maintained a discreet public silence. Defence minister Chevènement was forced to resign in January 1991 for contradicting presidential policy. A daily *Conseil restreint* met at the Elysée to provide Mitterrand with advice, but decision-making was taken by the President alone, in conjunction with France's allies.

10 MITTERRAND AND THE NEW EUROPE

1 A. Fontaine, 'L'Europe et le rang', *Le Monde*, 25 May 1989.
2 For an intelligent attempt to expound these themes, see D.S. Yost, 'France in the new Europe', *Foreign Affairs*, vol. 69, no. 5, Winter 1990–91, pp. 107–128. Also E. Weisenfeld, 'Les craintes françaises à l'égard de l'Allemagne', *Le Trimestre du Monde*, 1st Trimester, 1990, pp. 67–70.
3 G. Valence, *France–Allemagne. Le retour de Bismarck*, Paris, Flammarion, 1990.
4 The expression is that of the French ambassador to the Federal Republic in late 1989. J. Morizet, 'Le problème allemand vu de France', *Défense Nationale*, vol. 46, February 1990, pp. 11–23.
5 Cited in C. Tréan, 'La France et le nouvel ordre européen', *Politique Etrangère*, no.1, Winter 1991, p. 82. In his posthumous memoirs, Mitterand firmly denies any hesitation over the subject of German unification: F. Mitterrand, *De l'Allemagne, de la France*, Paris, Odile Jacob, 1996. This appears rather difficult to reconcile with interviews and televised speeches of the time.
6 Ibid.
7 See R. Morgan, 'French perspectives on the new Germany', *Government and Opposition*, Winter 1991, vol. 26, no. 1, pp. 108–114.
8 C. Fauvet-Mycia, 'M. Mitterrand veut une Europe élargie à l'Est', *Libération*, 1 January 1990. Mitterrand periodically called thereafter for the creation of a European confederation, for example, at the *Les tribous ou l'Europe* colloquium on 29 February 1992.
9 *La Tribune de l'Expansion*, 31 May 1991. In May 1991, the Germans declared themselves unwilling to consider a confederation which did not include the US: their preferred option was for cooperation to take the form of the CSCE, linking the Americans with the Europeans. The CSCE established its permanent head-quarters in Prague in June 1991: the CSCE linked all European states except Albania, along with the US and Canada, including Yugoslavia. It appeared still-born, given its total incapacity to respond to events in Yugoslavia.
10 Cited in P. Haski, 'Pour le meilleur et pour le pire', *Libération*, 30 March 1990.
11 The *Länder* of East Germany were incorporated into the Federal Republic by means of article 23 of the Basic Law, which provides for the accession of new states into the German federation. The historic process of unification was accomplished with considerable informality; there was no accession treaty. The method of unification itself gave the impression of a western takeover of former East Germany.
12 See F. Cornut-Gentille and S. Rozes, 'La réunification vue de l'Hexagone: les

Français engourdis', in O. Duhamel and J. Jaffré (eds), *SOFRES: l'Etat de l'opinion 1991*, Paris, Gallimard, 1991, pp. 75–91.

13　A pertinent commentary of the treaty is provided by A. Padoa-Schioppa, 'Sur les institutions politiques de l'Europe nouvelle', *Commentaire*, no. 58, Summer 1992, pp. 283–292.

14　See M. Duverger, 'L'Héritage européen', *Le Monde*, 26 April 1991.

15　The European parliament was to be invested with the power of co-decision in four policy spheres: research, the environment, consumer affairs and the single market. The parliament would retain its right of veto over the accession of new members and the signing of association agreements, as well as a new right of veto over international agreements and changes in its electoral procedure. The parliament was to be given the right to invest the Commission, in addition to its ultimate right of no confidence in the Commission. Much to the chagrin of Jacques Delors, the Commission did not emerge greatly strengthened, although its legitimacy was reinforced, insofar as it was henceforth to be invested by the European parliament.

16　The decision to move towards a single currency would in principle be taken either by a qualified majority vote within the Council in 1996; or, failing sufficient economic convergence, by a minority of countries determined to go ahead with a single currency by 1 January 1999. The CFSP provisions kept foreign policy firmly in the hands of national governments; decisions relating to EC competence to intervene in foreign policy affairs would require first a unanimous vote within the Council; qualified majority voting would apply to details of implementation thereafter. The Commission was to be excluded from involvement in either sphere.

17　Quotation taken from W. Hutton, 'Maastricht's mistakes', *The Guardian*, 10 February 1992.

18　K. Dyson and K. Featherstone, 'France, EMU and construction européenne: empowering the executive, transforming the state', *Politiques et Management Public* conference, Paris, 20–21 June 1996.

19　W.J. Feld, 'Franco-German military cooperation and European unification', *The Journal of European Integration*, vol. 12, no. 2–3, 1989, pp. 128–151.

20　P. Haski, 'Europe: Les douze comme fer de lance', *Libération*, 12 September 1991.

21　*Le Monde*, 17 October 1991, 18 October 1991.

22　In the words of one German diplomat, 'the simple fact is that we have to have a way of allowing the French to save face. A Europeanisation of NATO cannot be the answer for Paris – these proposals offer a solution'. Cited in *The Independent*, 17 October 1991.

23　Notably, the NATO decision to set up a British-led Rapid Reaction Force (RRF) in May 1991. The French government considered that the creation of a NATO European corps would deepen US authority over European defence, and exclude the French from influence over West European defence arrangements. This attitude was not shared by the Germans, who envisaged EC and NATO forces as complementary. The Germans were the second largest component within the RRF.

24　A political declaration accompanying the Maastricht summit asserted that 'the WEU will be developed as a defence component of the European union, and as the means of strengthening the European pillar of the Atlantic alliance'.

25　H. Stark, 'Dissonances franco-allemandes sur fond de guerre serbo-croate', *Politique Etrangère*, vol. 57, no. 2, summer 1992, pp. 339–346.

26　PS leader Fabius barely concealed his discomfort; while ex-First Secretary Jospin was more forthright in his criticism. The referendum campaign divided the Socialist Party into pro- and anti-Maastricht factions, preliminary to a formal split, with eurosceptic J-P. Chevènement transforming his *Mouvement des Citoyens* into a separate party to contest the 1993 legislative elections.

27 The disparity between 89 per cent parliamentary support, and 51 per cent in the referendum revealed the division separating the mainstream politicians of all parties from powerful sections of the electorate on this issue. The same conclusion had imposed itself after the Danish referendum.

28 The No campaign was unofficially led by a triumvirate consisting of P. Séguin (RPR), C. Pasqua (RPR) and P. de Villiers (UDF). J-P. Chevenèment was the leading Socialist opponent, but was isolated in a small minority of the party.

29 See O. Duhamel and G. Grunberg, 'Référendum: les dix France', *SOFRES: L'Etat de l'Opinion – 1993*, Paris, Seuil, 1993, pp. 79–85.

30 For a critical approach, see J-F. Roche, 'La politique étrangère de François Mitterrand', *Politiques*, no. 3, summer 1992, pp. 47–58.

31 Interview in *Le Monde*, 9 February 1993.

32 The importance of the Franco-German partnership for Mitterrand was repeatedly stressed in interviews with the author.

11 MITTERRAND'S POLITICAL LEADERSHIP

1 R. Skidlesky, 'Only Connect: biography and truth', in E. Homberger and J. Charmley (eds), *The Troubled Face of Biography*, London, Macmillan, 1988, p. 2.

2 J. March and J. Olsen 'The New Institutionalism: organisational factors in political life', *American Political Science Review*, vol. 78, 1984, pp. 734–739.

3 J. Blondel, *Political Leadership*, London, Sage, 1987.

4 L.J. Edinger, 'Approaches to the comparative analysis of political leadership', *Review of Politics*, 52, 4, autumn 1990, pp. 509–523.

5 On core executives, see R.W. Rhodes and P. Dunleavy (eds), *Prime Minister, Cabinet and the Core Executive*, London, Macmillan, 1995. See also R. Elgie *The Role of the Prime Minister in France, 1981–1991*, London, Macmillan, 1993; and his *Political Leadership in Liberal Democracies*, London, Macmillan, 1995. On local political leadership, see C. Stone, 'Political leadership in urban politics', in D. Judge, *et al.*, *Urban Politics and Theory: An Introduction*, London, Sage, 1995.

6 See R. Rose and E. Suleiman, *Presidents and Prime Ministers*, Washington, AEI, 1980 for a wide-ranging and comparative overview.

7 Blondel, *Political Leadership*, p. 13.

8 R. Van Dooren, 'The problem of charismatic leadership and the psychobiography method'. Unpublished paper presented at the joint sessions of the ECPR, Bochum, West Germany, 2–7 April 1990.

9 See H. Berrington, 'The fiery chariot: British Prime Ministers and the search for love', *British Journal of Political Science*, vol. 4, no. 3, July 1974, pp. 345–369. The central theme of Berrington's review is to enquire why 'eminence in politics should be distinctively, perhaps peculiarly, linked with personal maladjustment', p. 363. The common feature of the British Prime ministers reviewed by Berrington was their unsatisfactory private lives.

10 G. Little, *Strong Leadership: Thatcher, Reagan and an Emminent Person*, Melbourne, Oxford University Press, 1988. Little contends (p. 258) that: 'our three leaders (all of them the younger of two children) establish a special relationship with the opposite-sex parent, and at the same time, make an enemy of the other. With what results? A spur to ambition, because they achieve favour and believe themselves something special. A twist towards aggressiveness, wariness, competitive individualism, because their gain in the politics of the family was at others' expense'.

11 J. Blondel, *Political Leadership*, pp. 80–96. At one stage, Blondel suggests that

leaders have one overriding goal, whereas later on he concedes that goals must have a time dimension and be subject to change.

12 See 'Leadership and performance of group functions: introduction', in D. Cartwright and A. Zander, *Group Dynamics: Research and Theory*, London, Tavistock, 1968, pp. 301–317.

13 See G. Jones (ed.), *Heads of Government in Western Europe*, London, Frank Cass, 1992.

14 The expression 'chief executive' is, of course, juridically incorrect to describe the French President, on account of the hybrid nature of the French executive. It corresponds more accurately than any other to the position occupied by the French President throughout most of the Fifth Republic.

15 Notably, article 49, clause 3 of the constitution, allowing governments to stake their future on the passage of a bill.

16 For further development of this argument, see A. Cole, 'Studying political leadership: the case of François Mitterrand', *Political Studies*, vol. 42, no. 3, September 1994, pp. 453–468.

17 I am grateful to Robert Ladrech for this point.

12 MITTERRAND'S POLITICAL LEGACY

1 J-M. Colombani, 'Le viel homme et la France', *Le Monde*, 14 September 1994.

2 This was the most damaging accusation contained in P. Péan, *Une Jeunesse française*, Paris, Fayard, 1994.

3 Mitterrand's defence rested upon the fact that the former Vichy chief of police had been acquitted by the High Court of Justice at the Liberation, and gravitated around the political elite. Mitterrand admitted that he continued to see Bousquet 'occasionally' until 1986.

4 Interview with *Le Figaro*, 12 September 1994.

5 Ibid.

6 In the Maastricht negotiations, Mitterrand had initially been reluctant to agree to central bank independence without political counterparts, but this had been imposed as a precondition of a single curency by German negotiators. Insofar as an independent central bank formed a preliminary to introduction of a single currency, its implementation formed part of Mitterrand's European legacy. See K. Dyson and K. Featherstone, 'France, EMU and Construction Européenne: Empowering the Executive, Transforming the State', *Politiques et Management Public* conference, Paris, 20–21 June 1996.

7 These allegations were made in Claude Gubler's banned book, *Le Grand Secret*.

8 On Thatcher's leadership, see especially J. Moon, 'Innovatory leadership and policy change: lessons from Thatcher', *Governance*, vol. 8, no. 1, 1995, pp. 2–25.

Bibliography

Adler, L., *L'Année des adieux*, Paris, Flammarion, 1995.

Année Politique, 1946–62.

Attali, J., *Verbatim 1, 1981–86, Verbatim 11, 1986–88, Verbatim 111, 1988–91*, Paris, Fayard, 1994, 1995.

Batsch, C., 'L'Afrique noire plus prôche que jamais', *Cosmopolitiques*, December 1987, pp. 67–78.

Bauchard, P., 'Mitterrand sait-il compter', in *Influences*, no. 1, January 1988.

Bauchard, P., *La Guerre des deux roses*, Paris, Grasset, 1986.

Bayart, J.-F., *La Politique Africaine de François Mitterrand*, Paris, Kathala, 1984.

Bayart, J.-F., 'France–Afrique: la fin du pacte colonial', *Politique Africaine*, no. 39, September 1990, pp. 47–53.

Bayart, J.-F., 'La problématique de la démocratie en Afrique noire', *Politique Africaine*, no. 43, October 1991, pp. 5–20.

Beauchamp, D., 'La fin d'une illusion: la politique arabe de la France', *Commentaire*, no. 58, summer 1992, pp. 367–71.

Belassa, B., 'Five years of Socialist economic policy in France: a balance sheet', *The Tocqueville Review*, vol. 11, no. 7, 1986, pp.269–83.

Bell, D.S. and Criddle, B., *The French Socialist Party: the Emergence of a Party of Government*, Oxford, Clarendon, 1988.

Beller, D.C. and Belloni, D., *Faction Politics*, Washington, Clio Press, 1978.

Bergonioux, A. and Grunberg, G., *Le Long Remords du Pouvoir*, Paris, Fayard, 1992.

Bizaguet, A., 'L'évolution récente du secteur publique français', *La Revue du Trésor*, June 1987, pp. 355–88.

Blin, M., 'Nationalisations: la fin d'une idéologie?', *Politique Industrielle*, no. 3, spring 1986, pp. 65–78.

Blondel, J., *Political Leadership*, London, Sage, 1987.

Borleix, J.-M., *Mitterrand lui-même*, Paris, Grasset, 1973.

Bourdieu, P., 'L'Illusion biographique', *Actes de la Recherche en Sciences Sociales*, no. 62–3, June 1986, pp. 69–72.

Braud, P., 'La Biographie politique invente ses héros', *Libération*, 9 April 1991.

Capdeveille, J. et al., *France de gauche, vote a droite*, Paris, Presses de la FNSP, 1981.

Carver, T., 'Methodological issues in writing a political biography', *The Journal of Political Science (Clemson)*, vol. 20, April 1992, pp. 3–13.

Cayrol, R., *François Mitterrand, 1945–1967*, Paris, CEVIPOF, 1967.

Cayrol, R., 'La direction du Parti Socialiste: organisation et fonctionnement', *Revue Française de Science Politique*, vol. 28, no. 2, April 1978, pp. 202–20.

Cerny, P. and Schain, M., *Socialism, the State and Public Policy in France*, London, Pinter, 1985.

Chagnollaud, D., 'La nomination des hauts fonctionnaires ou les arcanes de la politisation', unpublished paper presented to the AFSP National Congress, 5–8 October 1988.

Charlot, J., 'Le Président et le parti majoritaire', *Revue politique et parlementaire*, August 1983, pp. 27–40.

Chauvin, L., 'L'idée d'Europe chez François Mitterrand', unpublished DEA thesis, Institute of Political Studies, Paris, 1989.

Chenal, A., 'La Politique française au Maghreb et au Proche-Orient', *Cosmopolitiques*, December 1987, pp. 79–87.

Cohen, E., 'Nationalisations: une bonne leçon de capitalisme', *Politique Economique*, no. 1, April 1986, pp. 10–14.

Cohen, S., 'Les conseillers de l'Elysée face aux hommes de la maison blanche: spécificité du cas français', in J.-L. Seurin *et al.*, *La Présidence de la République en France et aux Etats-Unis*, Paris, Economica, 1986, pp. 206–17.

Cohen, S., *La Monarchie nucleaire*, Paris, Hachette, 1986.

Cohen, S., 'La politique étrangère entre l'Elysée et Matignon', *Politique Etrangère*, no. 3, 1989, pp. 487–503.

Cohen, S., 'François le gaullien et Mitterrand l'Européen', *Histoire*, no. 143, April 1991, pp. 30–3.

Cohen, S., 'Le Président chef des armées', *Pouvoirs*, no. 58, 1991, pp. 33–40.

Cohendet, A.-M., *La Cohabitation*, Paris, PUF, 1993.

Cole, A., 'Factionalism in the French Socialist Party, 1971–81', unpublished DPhil thesis, Oxford, 1985.

Cole, A., 'Factionalism, the French Socialist Party and the Fifth Republic', *European Journal of Political Research*, vol. 17, no.1, January 1989, pp. 77–94.

Cole, A. 'The Presidential Party and the Fifth Republic', *West European Politics*, vol. 16, no. 2, April 1993, pp. 49–66.

Cole, A., 'Studying political leadership: the case of François Mitterrand', *Political Studies*, vol. 42, no.3, September 1994, pp. 454–68.

Cole, A., and Campbell, P., *French Electoral Systems and Elections since 1789*, Aldershot, Gower, 1989.

Colombani, J.-M., *Portrait d'un Président*, Paris, Gallimard, 1985.

Colombani, J.-M. and Portelli, H., *Le Double Septennat de François Mitterrand*, Paris, Grasset, 1995.

Cornut-Gentille, F. and Rozes, S., 'La réunification vue de l'Hexagone: les français engourdis', in O. Duhamel and J. Jaffré (eds), *SOFRES: l'Etat de l'opinion 1991*, Paris, Gallimard, 1991, pp. 75–91.

Dagnaud, M. and Mehl, D., 'L'Elite rose confirmée', *Pouvoirs*, no. 50, 1989, pp. 141–50.

Daniel, J., *Les Religions d'un président*, Paris, Grasset, 1988.

de la Serre, F., 'La Politique européenne de la France: new look, or new deal?', *Politique Etrangère*, no. 1, 1982, pp. 125–37.

Desjardins, T., *François Mitterrand: un socialiste gaullien*, Paris, Hachette, 1978.

Drake, H. 'François Mitterrand, France and European Integration', in G. Raymond, *France during the Socialist Years*, Aldershot, Dartmouth, 1994, pp. 32–63.

Duhamel, A., 'Les sept ans de F. Mitterrand: le Président-phénix', *SOFRES: L'Etat de l'Opinion*, Paris, Gallimard, 1988, pp. 11–29.

Duhamel, A., *De Gaulle–Mitterrand: la marque et la trace*, Paris, Grasset, 1990.

Duhamel, A., 'Le triennat de Michel Rocard', *SOFRES: l'Etat de l'Opinion*, Paris, Gallimard, 1992, pp. 89–107.

Duhamel, E. 'François Mitterrand entre Vichy et Résistance', *Association for the Study of Modern and Contemporary France Conference*, Royal Holloway, London, 12–14 September 1996.

Duhamel, O., 'Sur la monarchie présidentielle', *Le Débat*, no. 55, August 1989, pp. 23–7.

Duhamel, O. and Jaffré, J., 'Edith Cresson à Matignon, ou la confection d'une impopularité', *SOFRES: l'Etat de l'Opinion*, Paris, Gallimard, 1992, pp. 109–23.

Dupin, E., *L'Après-Mitterrand: le Parti Socialiste à la dérive*, Paris, Calmann-Levy, 1991.

Dyson, K. and Featherstone, K., 'France, EMU and Construction Européenne: empowering the executive, transforming the state', *Politiques et Management Public conference*, Paris, 20–1 June 1996.

Edinger, L.J., 'Approaches to the comparative analysis of political leadership', *Review of Politics*, vol. 52, no. 4, Autumn 1990, pp. 509–23.

Elgie, R., *The French Prime Minister*, London, Macmillan, 1993.

Elgie, R., *Political Leadership in Liberal Democracies*, London, Macmillan, 1995.

Elgie, R. and Machin, H., 'France: the limits to prime ministerial government in a semi-presidential system', *West European Politics*, vol. 14, no. 2, April 1991, pp. 62–78.

Faux, E., Legrand, T. and Perez, G., *La Main droite de Dieu*, Paris, Seuil, 1994.

Favier, P. and Martin-Roland, M., *La Decennie Mitterrand. 1. Les ruptures 2. Les épreuves*, Paris, Seuil, 1990 and 1991.

Fontaine, A., 'Diplomatie Française: un Modèle Gaullien?', *Politique Internationale*, summer 1991, pp. 57–67.

Frémy, D., *Quid des présidents de la République*, Paris, Laffont, 1987.

French Politics and Society, 'A symposium on Mitterrand's past', vol. 13, no.1, winter 1995, pp. 4–35.

Friedman, M., 'Mitterrrand: portrait d'un conquistador', *Jeune Afrique*, no. 1340, 17 June 1987, pp. 6–12.

Friend, J.-W., *Seven Years in France: François Mitterrand and the Unintended Revolution*, Boulder, Colorado, Westview Press, 1989.

Gaffney, J. (ed.), *Political Parties in the European Union*, London, Routledge, 1996.

Gaffney, J. (ed.), *The French Presidential Election of 1988: Ideology and Leadership in Contemporary France*, Aldershot, Dartmouth, 1989.

Gélédan, A., *Le Bilan économique des années Mitterrand*, Paris, Le Monde Editions, 1993.

Giesbert, F.-O., *François Mitterrand ou la tentation de l'histoire*, Paris, Seuil, 1977.

Giesbert, F.-O., 'Du terroir à l'histoire', *Influences*, no. 1, January 1988.

Giesbert, F.-O., *Le Président*, Paris, Seuil, 1990.

Giesbert, F.-O., *La Fin d'une époque*, Paris, Fayard, 1993.

Grosser, A., 'Le Rôle et le rang', *Commentaire*, no. 58, summer 1992, pp. 361–5.

Groux, G. and Mouriaux, R., 'François Mitterrand et les ouvriers', *French Politics and Society*, vol. 9, nos 3–4, summer/fall 1991, pp. 43–62.

Hadas-Lebel, R., 'François Mitterrand et la fonction présidentielle', *French Politics and Society*, vol. 9, nos 3–4, summer/fall 1991, pp. 1–17.

Hall, P., *Governing the Economy: the Politics of State Intervention in Britain and France*, Oxford, Oxford University Press, 1986.

Hall, P., Hayward, J. and Machin, H., *Developments in French Politics*, London, Macmillan, 1990 and 1994.

Hamon, H. and Rotman, P., *La Deuxième gauche*, Paris, Seuil, 1986.

Hardouin, P., 'Les caracteristiques sociologiques du parti socialiste', *Revue française de science politique*, vol. 28, no. 2, April 1978, pp. 220–56.

Hardouin, P., 'Le PS: un parti d'intellectuels', *Intervention*, nos 5–6, August–September 1983, pp. 66–76.

Harrison, M.M., 'Mitterrand's France in the Atlantic System: a foreign policy of accommodation', *Political Science Quarterly*, vol. 99, no. 2, summer 1984, pp. 219–46.

Harrison, M., 'The President, cultural projects and the mass media', in Hayward, *De Gaulle to Mitterrand*, pp. 190–218.

Hayward, J. (ed.), *De Gaulle to Mitterrand; Presidential Power in France*, London, Hurst, 1994.

Haywood, E.Z., 'The French socialists and institutional reform', *Journal of European Integration*, vol. 12, nos 2–3, 1989, pp. 70–90.

Heisbourg, F., 'Défense et sécurité extérieure: le changement dans la continuité', *Politique Etrangère*, no. 2, 1985, pp. 377–95.

Hessel, S., 'Socialist France and developing countries', *French Politics and Society*, vol. 9, nos 3–4, summer/fall 1991, pp. 130–9.

Hine, D., 'Factionalism in the West European party system: a framework for analysis', *West European Politics*, vol. 5, no. 1, January 1982, pp. 39–52.

Hoffman, S., 'Mitterrand's foreign policy, or Gaullism by any other name', in Ross, *The Mitterrand Experiment*, pp. 294–305.

Howorth, J., 'Foreign and defence policy: from independence to interdependence', in Hall, *Developments in French Politics*, pp. 201–17.

Howorth, J., 'The President's special role in foreign policy and defence', in Hayward, *De Gaulle to Mitterrand*, pp. 150–89.

Huchon, J.-P., *Jours tranquilles à Matignon*, Paris, Grasset, 1993.

Hurtig, C., *De la SFIO au Nouveau Parti Socialiste*, Paris, Armand Colin, 1970.

Imbert, C., 'Un personnage de roman', *Le Débat*, no. 20, May 1982, pp. 4–13.

Jenson, J., 'How the French Left learned to love the bomb', *New Left Review*, no. 146, August 1984, pp. 5–36.

Johnson, R.W., *The Long March of the French Left*, London, Macmillan, 1981.

Jouve, P. and Magoudi, A., *Mitterrand: portrait total*, Paris, Carrère, 1986.

July, S., 'Le parrain converti', *Le Débat*, no. 20, May 1982, pp. 13–17.

July, S., *Les Années Mitterrand*, Paris, Grasset, 1986.

Ket de Vries, M., 'Leaders on the couch', *The Journal of Applied Behavioural Science*, vol. 26, no. 4, 1990, pp. 423–31.

Kourliandsky, J.-J., 'Europe: le grand chantier du Président', *Cosmopolitiques*, no. 5, December 1987, pp. 33–46.

Kramer, S., *Does France still Count?*, Washington, Washington Papers, 1994.

Kulesza, E., 'Les relations Paris-Moscou de Yalta à la perestroïka', *Regards sur l'Actualité*, no. 147, January 1989, pp. 3–12.

L'Union démocratique et socialiste de la résistance, *L'UDSR: le parti qui grandit*, Paris, UDSR, 1952.

La Famille tonton, Paris, Les Dossiers du Canard, 1991.

Lacouture, J., *Pierre Mendès-France*, Paris, Seuil, 1981.

Lauber, V., 'Reinventing French socialism: economic policy, ideology, political strategy', *Parliamentary Affairs*, vol. 38, no. 2, September 1985, pp. 150–62.

Laughland, J., *The Death of Politics: France under Mitterrand*, London, Joseph, 1994.

Le Bos-Le Pourhiet, A.-M., 'Les emplois à la discrétion', *Pouvoirs*, no. 40, 1987, pp. 121–33.

Le Monde, François Mitterrand: 14 ans de pouvoir, Le Monde: dossiers et documents, April 1995.

Lemaire-Prosche, G., *Le PS et l'Europe*, Paris, Editions Universitaires, 1990.

Lequesne, C., *Paris-Bruxelles*, Presses de la FNSP, Paris, 1993.

Liegois, J.-P., *Le Feu et l'eau*, Paris, Grasset, 1990.

Loschak, D., *La Convention des Institutions Républicaines: François Mitterrand et le socialisme*, Paris, Armand Colin, 1970.

Loschak, D., 'Les Hauts fonctionnaires et l'alternance', unpublished paper presented to the AFSP colloquium on *Le Modèle français d'administration: Est-il en crise?*, 7–8 February 1993, pp. 1–17.

McCarthy, P. (ed.) *The French Socialists in Power*, Westport, CT, Greenwood Press, 1987.

McCarthy, P. (ed.) *France–Germany, 1983–93: the Struggle to Cooperate*, London, Macmillan, 1993.

Machin, H. and Wright, V. (eds), *Economic Policy and Policy Making under the Mitterrand Presidency: 1981–84*, London, Pinter, 1985.

MacShane, D., *François Mitterrand: A Political Odyssey*, London, Quartet, 1982.

Martinet, G., 'Le crépescule du mitterrandisme', *Le Monde*, 10 September 1994.

Massot, J., *L'Arbitre et le capitaine*, Paris, Flammarion, 1987.

Maulny, J.-P., 'Les relations nord–sud', *Cosmopolitiques*, December 1987, pp. 18–32.

Mazey, S. and Newman, M., *Mitterrand's France*, London, Croom Helm, 1987.

Megne, L., *François Mitterrand dans la Nièvre*, unpublished DEA thesis, University of Paris 1, 1988.

Mitterrand, F., *Le coup d'etat permanent*, Paris, Plon, 1964.

Mitterrand, F., *Ma part de verité*, Paris, Fayard, 1969.

Mitterrand, F., *Un Socialisme du possible*, Paris, Seuil, 1970.

Mitterrand, F., *Politique 1*, Paris, Fayard, 1977.

Mitterrand, F., *Ici et maintenant*, Paris, Fayard, 1980.

Mitterrand, F., *Politique 11*, Paris, Fayard, 1981.

Mitterrand, F., *Réflexions sur la politique extérieure de la France*, Paris, Fayard, 1986.

Mitterrand, F., 'Sur les institutions', *Pouvoirs*, no. 45, 1988, pp. 132–9.

Mitterrand, F., *De l'Allemagne, de la France*, Paris, Odile Jacob, 1996.

Mitterrand, F., *Mémoires intérrompus*, Paris, Odile Jacob, 1996.

Mitterrand, F. and Weisel, E., *Mémoire à deux voix*, Paris, Odile Jacob, 1995.

Mitterrand, F., Beau, J.-F. and Ulmer, C. (eds), *Discours 1981–1995*, Paris, Europolis, 1995.

Montaldo, J., *Mitterrand et les quarante voleurs*, Paris, Grasset, 1994.

Moon, J., 'Innovatory leadership and policy change: lessons from Thatcher', *Governance*, vol. 8, no. 1, 1995, pp. 2–25.

Moreau-Defarges, P., 'J'ai fait une rêve . . . Le président Mitterrand, artisan de l'union européenne', *Politique Etrangère*, no. 2, 1985, pp. 359–75.

Morizet, J., 'Le problème allemand vu de France', *Défense Nationale*, vol. 46, February 1990, pp. 11–23.

Mossuz, J., 'Les fédérés et leurs problèmes', *Revue Française de Science Politique*, vol. 16, no. 7, October 1966, pp. 960–74.

Mossuz, J., *Les Clubs et la politique en France*, Paris, Armand Colin, 1970.

Moulin, C., *Mitterrand Intime*, Paris, Hachette, 1982.

Nay, C., *Le Noir et le rouge*, Paris, Grasset, 1984.

Nay, C., *Les Sept Mitterrand*, Paris, Grasset, 1988.

Northcutt, W., 'François Mitterrand and the political use of symbols: the construction of a centrist Republic', *French Historical Studies*, vol. 17, no. 1, Spring 1991, pp. 141–58.

Northcutt, W., *Mitterrand: a Political Biography*, New York, Holmes and Meier, 1992.

Nugent, N. and Lowe, D., *The Left in France*, London, Macmillan, 1982.

Padoa-Schioppa, A., 'Sur les institutions politiques de l'Europe nouvelle', *Commentaire*, no. 58, summer 1992, pp. 283–92.

Pasquino, G., 'Political leadership in Western Europe: research problems', *West European Politics*, vol. 13, no. 4, 1990, pp. 118–30.

Passerron, A., 'Comment ils ont placé leurs amis', *Pouvoirs*, no. 40, 1987, pp. 25–30.

Péan, P., *Une Jeunesse française*, Paris, Fayard, 1994.

Pfister, T., *La Vie quotidienne à Matignon au temps de l'union de la gauche*, Paris, Hachette, 1985.

Pimlott, B., 'The future of political biography', *Political Quarterly*, vol. 61, no. 2, April–June 1990, pp. 214–24.

Pinto Lyra, R., *La Gauche en France et la construction européenne*, Paris, LGDJ, 1978.

Plenel, E., *La Part d'Ombre*, Paris, Stock, 1993.

Portelli, H., *Le Parti Socialiste*, Paris, Montchrestien, 1992.

Py, R., *Le Secrétariat Général du Gouvernement*, Paris, Documentation Française, 1985.

Rapp, L., 'Le secteur public français entre nationalisations et privatisations', *Droit Administratif*, no. 20, May 1987, pp. 303–8.

Raymond, G., *France during the Socialist Years*, Aldershot, Dartmouth, 1994.

Rémond, R., 'L'Election présidentielle et la candidature Defferre', *Revue Française de Science Politique*, vol. 14, no. 3, June 1964, pp. 513–26.

Rey, H. and Subileau, F., 'Les militants socialistes en 1985', *Projet*, no. 198, April 1986, pp. 19–34.

Rondeau, D., *Mitterrand et nous*, Paris, Grasset, 1994.

Ross, G. and Daley, T., 'The wilting of the rose: the French socialist experiment', *Socialist Review*, vol. 16, nos 3–4, August 1986, pp. 7–40.

Ross, G., Hoffmann S. and Malzacher, S. (eds), *The Mitterrand Experiment*, Oxford, Polity Press, 1987.

Roussel, E., *Mitterrand ou la constance du funambule*, Paris, Lattès, 1991.

Schifres, M. and Sarazin, M., *L'Elysée de Mitterrand*, Paris, Alain Moreau, 1985.

Schmidt, V., *From State to Market*, Cambridge, Cambridge University Press, 1996.

Schneider, R., *Les dernières années*, Paris, Seuil, 1994.

Schweisguth, E., 'Les couches moyennes salariées sont-elles socialistes?', *Intervention*, nos 5–6, August–October 1983, pp. 58–66.

Sevin, H., 'La Coalition majoritaire du Parti socialiste, 1971–1975', unpublished doctoral thesis, Institute of Political Studies, Paris, 1983.

Singer, D., *Is Socialism Doomed? The Meaning of Mitterrand*, New York, Oxford University Press, 1988.

Skidelsky, R., 'Only Connect: Biography and Truth', in E. Homberger and J. Charmley (eds), *The Troubled Face of Biography*, London, Macmillan, 1988, pp. 1–15.

Soulage, B., 'Un épisode du colbertisme', *Projet*, no. 203, February 1987, pp. 83–92.

Stark, H., 'Dissonances franco-allemandes sur fond de guerre serbo-croate', *Politique Etrangère*, vol. 57, no. 2, summer 1992, pp. 339–46.

Stasse, F., *La Morale de l'histoire: Mitterrand–Mendès-France, 1943–1982*, Paris, Seuil, 1994.

Stevens, A., 'The President and his staff', in Hayward, *De Gaulle to Mitterrand*, pp. 76–100.

Thiebault, J.-L., 'Jalons pour une analyse des conflits gouvernementaux sous la Vème République', *Les Cahiers du CRAPS*, no. 7, 1989, pp. 20–48.

Tiersky, R., *France in the New Europe*, Boulder, Colorado, Westview Press, 1994.

Tiersky, R., 'Mitterrand's legacies', *Foreign Affairs*, vol. 74, no. 1, January–February 1995, pp. 112–21.

Tréan, C., 'La France et le nouvel ordre européen', *Politique Etrangère*, 1/91, winter 1991, pp. 81–90.

Webster, P., *Mitterrand: l'autre histoire*, Paris, Editions du Félin, 1995.

Weisenfeld, E., 'François Mitterrand: l'action extérieure', *Politique Etrangère*, vol. 51, no. 1, spring 1986, pp. 131–41.

Weisenfeld, E., 'Les craintes françaises à l'égard de l'Allemagne', *Le Trimestre du Monde*, 1st Trimester, 1990, pp. 67–70.

Wells, S.J., 'Les politiques étrangères de Mitterrand', *Commentaire*, no. 11, autumn 1988, pp. 655–66.

Williams, P., *Crisis and Compromise: Politics in the Fourth Republic*, London, Longman, 1964.

Worms, J.-P., 'The Rocard government and reforming French society', *French Politics and Society*, vol. 9, no. 2, spring 1991, pp. 1–8.

Wright, V., 'President and prime minister under the Fifth Republic', in Hayward, *De Gaulle to Mitterand*, pp. 101–19.

Yana, P., 'Sur l'homme d'état écrivain', *Lignes*, no. 5, February 1989, pp. 97–108.

Yost, D., 'Mitterrand and defence and security policy', *French Politics and Society*, vol. 9, nos 3–4, summer/fall 1991, pp. 141–58.

Index